gigs

An
American
Rock & Roll Odyssey

Peter K.K. Williams

Gene,
I hope you enjoy these
mad musical exploits.
Peter K.K. Williams

Table of Contents

gigs

An American Rock & Roll Odyssey

Introduction

For the millions of baby boomers that at one time played an instrument in a rock band, the flirtation with music was ephemeral. The years passed, the oft-touted real world intervened and the neglected guitar, drums, or bass were either sold or stored with all the other dusty artifacts of a misspent youth. "Enough foolishness," shouted an angry chorus of spouses, hungry children and obdurate mortgage lenders. But what of the exception? What became of the stalwart soul that pursued the chimera of music (for the next 50 years) with the single-minded determination of an army ant? What hilarious depths of depravity or astonishing heights of exaltation were achieved in the course of a thousand gigs played with a hundred bands?

I am that hardy survivor of such a slog through the musical trenches – a bass playing career that began at the dawn of time (surf music) and progressed to include the psychedelic 'sixties, the blues, Top-40, funk, country-rock, folk-rock, R&B, disco, western swing, stadium-rock, concertos for nuts and berries…and then, a billion notes later, the symphony orchestra as a jumping-off point for the most eclectic jazz to ever emerge from Vermont. (Yes, long before Phish conquered the world, the Green Mountains teemed with musicians, as it still does).

1

Gigs is a multi-media memoir comprised of forty chronological chapters, photographs and an archive of incredibly diverse music derived from recordings initially made on reel-to-reel tape, cassette and vinyl disc (music that has since been digitized.) These elements represent a unique socio-cultural journey, a musical odyssey that includes bands primarily from Vermont, but also from New Jersey, New Hampshire, Massachusetts, California and New Orleans. My motto continues to be: Never go anywhere without a bass, an amp, a journal, a camera and any number of sophisticated audio recording devices.

***

There was a time not long ago when the sight of a horse-drawn hay wagon rolling placidly along a dirt lane in Vermont was common. Times have changed. Nowadays, you are far more likely to see a Subaru loaded with drums cruising the interstate. For every dairyman hard at work milking cows at the crack of dawn, somewhere in Vermont there's a musician about to hit the hay after playing a late-night gig.

America swarms with guitar-toting battalions. Today's Guitar Army is filled with willing conscripts that strut onstage amidst the sizzle and glare – their Stratocasters glinting like futurist sculpture, their amplifiers cranked up to eleven. I watch from a safe distance and smile the wry smile of a Luna moth that understands all too well the flame's irresistible appeal.

No longer do the young leave their villages to undergo the rite of passage to adulthood by venturing onto the open savanna armed with a spear and the courage to kill a lion. Instead, rock 'n roll bands have replaced the village, the electric guitar has usurped the spear and a new CD is the preferred alternative to a lion's ear.

Question: Were you among the stoned throng that wallowed in the mud at Max Yazgar's farm at Woodstock? Did you listen to Janis and Big Brother at the Fillmore (East or West) and dance to the music of The Grateful Dead? If so, perhaps you were inspired to commit volunteer slavery by learning to play an instrument and joining a band. Perhaps your band attracted a devoted following and your albums sold well. None of the musicians died of drug overdoses; your manager did not abscond with the funds; nor did your record company saddle you with a larcenous contract. And finally, after all this, you've retained your sanity, your hearing and your hair…if so, congratulations! The bitch goddess Success has smiled all over you.

But what of the countless others for whom the golden sunshine of recognition and success lies perpetually hidden behind a cloud? What became of all the musicians that performed for the duration of one wink of the cosmic eye before vanishing forever into the bottomless quagmire of obscurity? If you came to your senses and renounced a life devoted to professional music before it took over completely, the chances are you now have a job, a family, a house and a vehicle built sometime during the current decade. But, if you were incapable of comprehending the depth of your obsession – like me – then here you are all these years later, still practicing your instrument, patiently awaiting the next gig.

I dedicate this rock 'n roll odyssey to all who survived their encounters with the lion (or provided it with a snack), to all who opted out of the music biz – for whatever reason – and to those eager to receive yet another jolt from Music's capricious electrode. In addition, I dedicate this collection of strange but true stories to all the listeners in the great pond of life – that vast shimmering ellipse where the sound of my bass still resounds in the primal darkness.

Hackensack

Amidst the flotsam and jetsam that wash ashore from the vast ocean of memory, certain events shine with an indelible, nacreous light. Like a precious stone polished in a tumbler, the constant friction between the miraculous and the mundane shaped my childhood. Then as now, I rarely knew which was which. Incidentally, I was raised by a maniac.

In 1957, I was eight years old, Eisenhower was king, Marilyn Monroe was queen, Henry Miller was Secretary of State and Mickey Mantle could do no wrong. I did not know it at the time, nor could I have imagined the consequences, but Leo Fender had begun to manufacture bass guitars – a fact that would shape my destiny.

1. Bogies at two o'clock

I remember walking home one afternoon after another successful day in the third grade. The birds sang and the sun warmed my knobby knees as I scuffed along the sidewalk in a pair of Keds, propelled by the knowledge that a glass of milk and a handful of chocolate-covered Mallows awaited me. I opened the front door and stepped into the living room in time to watch my father lambasting our piano with a fireman's ax. Insane with rage, Arnold drew back and swung the blade with all his might!

KAGRANG!

The piano emitted a terrifying peal of dissonance that shook the house with each shuddering impact. Again and again my father let fly, muttering curses as splintered wood flew about the room and felt-tipped hammers rained down upon the furniture and the rug. Speechless, I stared at the grizzly spectacle. "Hell's bloody bells," Arnold gasped as sweat flew from his brow. The vein in his forehead pulsed ominously as the assault continued. The doomed instrument shrieked each time the steel wedge bit deeper into its vitals – the chords were monstrous, the harmonies indescribable, the voicing impossible. Shattered keys spun through the air like shrapnel and strings snapped with a vicious twang.

Finally, after a barrage that seemed to last forever, the old Iver and Pond sank to its knees, keeled over and expired like a sacrificial cow pole-axed by fate itself. The ghostly hint of a diminished chord trembled in midair for a moment and vanished. The calm after the storm brought silence and a wheelbarrow. I watched as my father shoveled up the wreckage and carted it away. To this day I don't know why he murdered the piano. Was he venting an intolerable frustration at an instrument that refused to accept tuning? Was he fighting back against the general belligerence of inanimate objects? Or was he simply as mad as a March hare?

I suspect a combination of all three, but I'll never really know because Arnold took the secret with him to the grave. (This is not entirely accurate, because a decade later, under the bilious glow of a half moon, I scattered his ashes on a golf course.)

Did other children witness hot-blooded pianicide committed in their living rooms? Or was this simply the first of many lessons in my musical development? I'm certain that had my mother survived beyond my second year of life, if bone-marrow cancer had not claimed her at the age of 27, she would've intervened on the piano's behalf (as well as my own). In any event, I see no need to dwell upon the strict authoritarian mode my father felt compelled to employ in my upbringing, or the strappings I underwent, but I am grateful he refrained from using the axe on me. No doubt, my subsequent avoidance of the piano (in favor of the bass) stemmed from having witnessed the upright's evisceration that afternoon. I'd love to be able to tell Arnold that I've forgiven him for inflicting welts on my psyche – which didn't occur until I'd attained the age of fifty-two, the same age at which he was electrocuted – but I'll need a Ouija Board to convey the news. Till then, I prefer to remember my father immersed to the chin in a tub of steaming hot water, reading a copy of Fate Magazine and singing along to the finale of Die Fledermaus on the hi-fi, tears of joy welling up in his eyes. The magazine's cover featured an alleged photograph of a flying saucer silhouetted against the sky. One more example of the continual conflict between the miraculous and the mundane? No, just an old Pontiac hubcap flung into the air and snapped with an Instamatic.

The Surf Dogs

The feverish masturbatory years of junior high school still fester in my memory. A time when my grades weren't entirely rotten, the **B**s amidst the **D**s on my report card were written in blue ink, although my eighth grade music teacher saw fit to scribe an **F** in blatant crimson. (Einstein failed math, I remind myself). If my experience is any indication, all thirteen-year old males are completely insane: More than once I disrupted English class by diving headlong over a row of desks to fasten my claws around Allen Runfeldt's throat – unable to tolerate his half-witted taunts – to pummel the struggling miscreant while Mrs. Reynolds shrieked, "GET OUT, YOU SAVAGES!"

There's another compelling reason why the eighth grade stubbornly resists deletion from my memory…the night I first heard a live rock 'n roll band. It was a warm Friday evening in May. The air was charged with pollen and pheromones as I entered the Berkley Heights High School gymnasium, in itself a major evolutionary spurt above the dinghy cafeteria where all previous teenage soirees had taken place. The cavernous gym reverberated with excited chatter as two hundred nubile girls poised upon the very cusp of Womanhood frisked and pranced. For weeks I'd had my eye on Ann Donnelly, a dark-haired cutie still at that stage of life where the love of horses superceded all. Intent upon a prolonged grapple on the dance-floor, I ascertained her position amidst the herd and began my stealthy approach.

Suddenly the lights dimmed and an expectant hush fell over the crowd. The Fluorescents walked onto the stage. Each of the five musicians sported a gleaming pompadour, a great quiff of hair that projected forward in an immobile arch. Their iridescent burgundy suits flickered in the red and blue floodlights like chromatophores on amorous cuttlefish. The guitarists donned their instruments, snapped the standby switches on their Fender amps and shattered the silence with the instrumental hits "Sleepwalk," "Wild Weekend," and then a medley of Vitalis-slicked paeans from the Doo-Wop canon – songs of teenage love, lust and loneliness. Enthralled, I listened as the saxophone's golden-throated wail gave vent to every teenager's innermost longing. The drums commanded instant respect, while two candy-apple-red Stratocasters obliterated any lingering residue of my father's incessant Gilbert and Sullivan operettas. Nothing, however, could've prepared me for the glorious visceral impact of a Fender Dual Showman amplifier pumping out vision-blurring notes from the bass guitar! I staggered around the dance floor clutching Ann in a sweaty embrace, struck dumb with awe. I fell in love. No, not with my future wife, with something far more enduring – a Fender Precision bass!

After the dance I trudged home in a daze, convinced that all of life's problems could be solved if only I, too, could wield such an awesome instrument. To this day I'm convinced that the throbbing pulse of an electric bass awakened that most primordial core of my psyche – an alluvial zone where trilobites lurked – then stimulated it with energy as irresistible as evolution itself.

When not memorizing strange new words from the dictionary (like crepuscular) or reading Twilight Zone paperbacks, I pored over the Johnson-Smith Joke and Novelty Catalog. Often, I squandered my allowance on exploding cigarette loads, joy buzzers and stink bombs, but it wouldn't be very long before I discovered a catalog devoted to an infinitely more desirable commodity – Playboy Magazine – a publication whose prurient allure would soon pale all others to insignificance. Till that day, however, I also studied the Lafayette Electronics catalog, a cornucopia of electronic gadgetry and the precursor to today's Radio Shack.

2. A page from the Lafayette Catalog

Three items on page 70 beckoned hypnotically and have yet to fully relinquish their grasp. A Violin-Shaped Electric Bass, a 2-Pickup Solid-Body Electric Bass and a Deluxe 2-Pickup Hollow-Body Electric Bass. All three were Japanese, back when "Made in Japan" meant junk. I preferred the 2-pickup solid-body model because it most resembled a Fender. (The Fender bass' sculpted, polished contours remain, in my opinion, one of the most significant iconographic designs in the entire history of civilization.) Pickups, incidentally, are the mysterious metal appurtenances imbedded in the bodies of all electric guitars and basses. According to the Lafayette catalog, their output is controlled by an array of knobs and switches for "rhythm or solo work." How could a vibrating string and a few magnets surrounded by wire create such miraculous sound, I wondered? If the reason was ever divulged in science class, I must've been daydreaming about Hefner's Bunnies.

In 1961, a Fender Precision Bass cost three hundred bucks – an astronomical sum for a kid accustomed to receiving a weekly allowance doled out in quarters. Alas, the $49.95 needed to buy a Lafayette bass was also beyond my reach. I earned a few bucks shoveling snow in the winter and mowing lawns in the summer, but somehow the money slipped through my fingers, squandered on such instant gratifications as Hershey bars, crummy transistor radios, 45-rpm records and Playboy Magazine (which, of course, resulted in instant self-gratification).

I continued to pine and stew for a bass guitar, to crave as only a pubescent teenager can, re-reading the Lafayette catalog ad copy till I could repeat it verbatim like a mantra: "Long neck, slimline electric bass guitar of selected woods for excellent speed and response and easy fingering. Hand-rubbed, shaded, sunburst body finished in durable acrylic lacquer." The phrase "excellent speed and response" gnawed relentlessly at my vitals. What could be more insidious or alluring to an insecure adolescent male than the implicit promise of eventual mastery?

As my desire for a bass guitar grew more desperate I hatched various schemes; one involved waiting for a thunderstorm some dark night, then smashing the plate glass that stood between me and the Zimgar bass hanging in the window of the local music shop. I believed the thunder would mask the sound of shattering glass, and I'd have enough time to grab the bass, wrap it in a blanket and then speed away into the darkness on my bicycle. It was tempting, but my better judgment prevailed and the plan was abandoned.

My father loathed what he referred to as "Those bloody, long-haired, guitar-playing deadbeats," and I knew I could expect no encouragement from him. So, I hit upon the idea of building an electric bass from scratch. Why not, I reasoned? I'd been taking wood and metal shop classes in each of the numerous schools I attended (the result of frequent relocations), and I felt confident in my ability to carve wood, laminate plastic and knurl metal knobs.

Brian Etz was my best and only friend, another incipient delinquent who shared my obsession with acquiring an electric guitar. As freshmen in high school, we both faced the same penurious problem, arrived at the same conclusion and then colluded on a plan to build our own instruments, after first stealing a heavy oak plank from an wizened master woodworker named Ed. Old Ed conducted his business in an isolated barn situated alongside the railroad tracks in Summit, New Jersey, a structure stacked to the rafters with a magnificent assortment of oak, maple and mahogany. After casing the decrepit barn one Saturday afternoon, we selected and marked our target, determined to return late that night under the black lid of a moonless sky. As stealthy as rats, we carefully unscrewed and removed a window casing and slid the plank out. We replaced the window and carried off our prize as quietly as grave robbers in eighteenth century Edinburgh. Yes, brazenly and without the slightest pang of conscience, we burgled Ed's Shop, certain that he would never even notice the missing item. (May he forgive us and rest in peace.)

The purloined plank measured 12 feet long, a foot wide and 2 inches thick – enough raw material to build a dozen electric guitars and basses. We divided the spoils and I commenced sawing, routing, carving and sanding. Weeks later, after persistent questioning of Joe Blumeti, a luthier in Summit, I succeeded in building a playable bass. It resembled a Fender, but had no frets and no pickup and therefore, could not be plugged into an amp. It had strings and machine heads for tuning and a steel rod embedded in the neck, but the relentless pressure exerted by the strings caused the neck to gradually warp. The elevating string height made it increasingly difficult to play, but at least I had something to pluck.

In those days I was able to borrow a Japanese-made bass and amp from a high school friend, Ned Delaney, (items obtained via the Lafayette catalog – the same 2-pickup, solid-body bass I would eventually buy from Ned, and then destroy in a fit of rage, but that's another story).

As for the amplifier, the Lafayette catalog boasted "Impressive, 20-watt solid state peak music power, easy to reach controls and a bright-glow pilot light." Laughably pathetic by today's standards, the 20-watt amp was a technological miracle in my eyes. It had a woefully inadequate eight-inch speaker that produced little more than a gnash of distortion, especially when turned up. The Surf Dogs were formed when I teamed up with Rob Cross, who owned a Fender Jazzmaster guitar and an Ampeg Gemini II amplifier, and Bill Unwin on drums. Together we dipped our toes into the musical waters for hours at a stretch, hammering out furiously inept (but immensely satisfying) renditions of "Green Onions," "Walk, Don't Run," and the all-time surf classic, "Wipe Out." But, as ham-fisted neophytes, we had no thoughts of playing in public. Nor did we attempt to record a single note (for which I am grateful, although a photograph of my larval stage as a bass player would be amusing and sobering).

I continued to ride the curl of a hormonal tsunami – hanging ten on the nose of puberty, so to speak – at a time when the AM radio first entered my consciousness: Top-40 hits by day and Jean Shepherd's hilarious monologs on WOR at night, tuned in while huddled in my bed with a transistor radio under the pillow. My musical favorites included the guitar romp "Baja" by the Astronauts, the "Surfing" album by The Ventures and "Waikiki Run" by the Surfaris. When WABC DJ Big Dan Ingram played "The Lonely Surfer," the instrumental's reverb-drenched guitars and majestic French horns conjured up images of huge, thundering pipelines – immense tsunamis hurling blond demigods on Hobies towards the beaches of Waikiki.

The only pipelines I ever saw were those that belched effluent into the sky above the Jersey marshlands. Undaunted, I headed south on the Parkway with a borrowed surfboard, past the infernal refineries, on towards the shore, where, swaddled in a wetsuit, I paddled frantically to catch the piddling three-foot swells that advanced listlessly towards the shore. My hands and feet turned blue in the Atlantic's frigid water, but it didn't matter. I was surfing!

Surf music sounds incredibly archaic today – the musical equivalent of the Dead Sea scrolls – but in 1963 I correctly intuited it as the anthem for all sun-worshipping, job-eschewing Youth. It was, after all, only a short conceptual leap from indolent surfer to stoned hippie.

The Owsley Elevator

If you leave Manhattan and cross the Hudson River on the rusty skeleton of the Pulaski Skyway, and then head west on Route 22 – the most dangerous highway in America – you'll encounter a blighted zone that looks and smells like the aftermath of a nuclear war. Drive on; traverse a neon prairie congested with malls, White Manna Hamburger stands, Mafia bars, funeral parlors, Earl Shibe Auto Paint Emporiums, Dairy Queens, tuxedo rental shops, a Kiddieland amusement park, seedy motels, greasy-spoon diners and a furniture outlet built to resemble the Queen Mary. Make the correct turns and you'll arrive at the quiet suburban enclave known in colonial times as Turkeytown.

Renamed New Providence, this leaf-shrouded community nestles behind wooded hills named in honor of the long-dispossessed Watchung Indians. The brick ramparts of Bell Labs demarcated the town's eastern flank. Vast and aloof, the complex sprawled like a Forbidden City. Inside, slide-rule-toting scientists invented the transistor, composed the first-ever electronic music and captured echoes of the Big Bang. Nearby, relentlessly manicured lawns surrounded the homes of the rich, the respectable and the complacent. I hated every boring, tasteful inch.

I was born shortly after America's decisive victory in the game of nuclear mumblety-peg with Japan. As a baby boomer, my generation was the first to be raised with a steady diet of television. Suckled on the cathode ray tube, our upbringing passed from the capable hands of Doctor Spock to those of Mister Spock, with consultations from Soupy Sales, Jonathan Winters and Rod Serling along the way.

Another shared rite of passage took the form of a four-year sentence to high school, an interminable gauntlet that proved to be the most wretched years of my life. Burdened by ferocious teenage hormonal imbalance and the burgeoning conflict with my father – to say nothing of the bitter cynicism that resulted from the assassination of President Kennedy, Martin Luther King, and the escalation of the war in Viet Nam – I plodded through each day in a haze of confusion, banished to wood and metal shop, the outer academic darkness to which all hopeless, unmanageable or "disturbed" students were consigned.

"We know you have the aptitude, why won't you apply yourself?" asked Mr. Kenny, my beleaguered guidance counselor. The chisel-nosed Mr. Kenny also taught typing and it seemed ludicrous to me that anyone with so humble a vocation could offer guidance anywhere beyond the typewriter's so-called home row. Throughout those four dreadful years I got into trouble frequently, but never for the same reason twice; like the time I burst into the principal's office while an important meeting was underway. "Pardon me," I said, a moment before deftly tossing a half eaten ice cream bar across the room and into his oiled walnut wastepaper basket!

***

I don't know about the cliques formed by the females in high school, but we males were a mixed bag of acne-riddled specimens that sorted themselves into the categories of Serious Students, Surfers, Greasers, Mafia Hit-Men Trainees and Future Cops. Each contained subgroups: Greasers included individuals who played acoustic guitars equipped with De Armond pickups, plus an element that developed a taste for Robitussin AC and petty larceny. Often, the Surfers shared decent scholastic performance with the Serious Students, but indulged in beer binges on the weekends. Profound animosities formed between the various categories along natural fault lines. The Greasers hated the Surfers and vice versa, while lesser fauna – nerds, oddballs and misfits – scurried by, hoping to get to the next class without being set upon in the hall by some capricious Greaser.

An unwritten dress code varied accordingly: The Greasers favored shiny slacks made of imitation sharkskin, Banlon pullovers the color of Thunderbird wine and pointed black leather shoes known affectionately as "spic-kickers." Greasers invariably cultivated insolent hairstyles with a "DA" (duck's ass) around back, earning the appellation through the liberal application of the pomade that inspired the rallying cry for Vitalis, "Still using that greasy kid stuff?"

The Surfer dress code demanded off-white Levi's, paisley shirts and brown penny-loafers worn without socks. More often than not, a blue nylon windbreaker topped off this sartorial symphony, regardless of the prevailing gale or lack thereof. Some Surfers wore their hair "bushy" and even went so far as to bleach it blonde in order to achieve the image of a righteous, sun-worshipping Californian. In spite of our respective affiliations – be it catching the perfect wave or cruising for burgers in a '55 Chevy (with furry pom-poms dangling from the rear-view mirror) – the lock step of conformity echoed through the halls of NPHS, as resonant as a troop of jack-booted, brown shirt Fascists.

Every morning, under the baleful eyes of my homeroom teacher, Mr. Saledonez, who always looked like an exhausted Cosmonaut, I was obliged to salute the flag. The Cuban missile crisis was still a recent memory as I stood with right hand over my heart, pretending to parrot the pledge guaranteed to protect us all from the Commies. Already a godless anarchist, I murmured, "I pledge allegiance to the sky, under which I stand…"

Then, with our stomachs still weighted down with undigested breakfast, off we went to the gym for an hour of murder-ball, the best class of the day. There, the perennially crew-cut Mr. Botone split us into two teams, each with about forty players, before setting us loose on the shiny polyurethane floor with six volleyballs. The object was to grab a ball, pick a target, then rush to the gym's halfway line and hurl the cannonball with all your might. The action was fast and violent and I was a natural. What joy to race forward, wind up to unleash a devastating shot and then at the last instant fire in an unexpected direction, hitting some hapless runt! Sometimes Mr. Botone became distracted and the Future Cops crossed the line, deep into enemy territory, before firing at point blank range, carving up their victims like so much cheese. The Mafia Hit-Men trainees made good teammates. Endowed with the strength of mountain gorillas and brains the size of an avocado, they feared nothing. Stolid and implacable, they went about their task coolly and efficiently, as if to say, "Just business, you understand, nothing personal."

BAM!

You weren't supposed to aim at an opponent's head, but a really good shot would catch some pimpled weakling in midair and crumple him to the floor with a bloody nose. Disgraced, the sniveling casualty slunk away to the nurse's office to the sound of an approving chortle from both teams. Sometimes one side gathered up all six volleyballs and deployed a flying wedge, charging like bulls through the streets of Pamplona, before unleashing a withering crossfire. If the intended target was skillful and caught a ball, the person who threw it was "out" and had to watch from the sideline. Often I alone remained standing, pirouetting to the left or right, which enraged my murderous opponents, especially after repeated salvos whizzed past and slammed against the wall. Eventually they fired a pattern on either side and I too bit the polyurethane.

Once the murder-ball ended, all allegiances were null and void. The locker room then became the scene of other forms of cruelty, often instigated by a fire-plug shaped hominid named Frank, a classic Greaser Hit-Man Trainee who exuded brutality like one of Capone's triggermen. One day Frank grabbed me with his simian paw and punched me on the arm – whap! whap! whap! – three sharp jabs. I wrenched free and shouted, "Who the hell do you think you are?" He stopped dead in his tracks, the question resonating in the carved coconut he called a head. I'm convinced Frank experienced his first introspective thought ever, that day. Like the shaggy proto-human at the dawn of time in Kubrick's film "2001," I can still see him kneeling amidst the polished tapir bones on that windswept, antediluvian plain – poised, femur bone held high – smashing skulls and then hurling his new-found weapon aloft, an instant before making that astonishing leap into the Future.

***

In 1966, the San Francisco Sound hit my ears like a comet and suddenly my Ventures albums sounded ludicrously tame. California was not only the wellspring of all blonde surfer girls, it fostered unprecedented musical exploration by such groups as The Grateful Dead, The Doors,

Quicksilver Messenger Service, Big Brother, Country Joe and the Fish, Jefferson Airplane, Moby Grape and a dozen others. New Providence, in comparison, exhibited about as much vitality as the nails and hair that continue to grow on a fresh corpse. Speaking of which, hair length on males had become a barometer of hipness – the so-called freak-flag – and I wasn't even remotely in the running. Determined to nip my escalating rebelliousness in the bud, Arnold inflicted upon me one hideously vindictive haircut after another. Each scalping resulted in a wide circular swathe of naked skull around my ears, and to make matters worse, I was all too aware of the yawning chasm that separated my drably repressive cultural environment from the one that launched the Merry Pranksters in their LSD scorched bus.

One Friday evening a mysterious purple DeSoto rolled through the center of New Providence. I sat in the backseat while Lonnie, a fellow inmate from high school, drove. There were four other miscreants onboard, relative strangers united only by our desire to "cop" nickel bags of "grass" and forget, however briefly, our teenage blues. Suddenly Lonnie swerved to the right, drove up and over the curb, then accelerated – gouging deep ruts through half a dozen adjacent front lawns, crushing rosebushes and shattering birdbaths – all while narrating like a crazed TV sportscaster, "Yes folks, they're on the lawn and they're careening!" We laughed like idiots as the DeSoto veered back onto the road and sped away into the darkness.

From our first encounter with this nascent ambassador to Depravity, Lonnie influenced us much the way the Pied Piper charmed rats. He was spontaneous, funny and sardonic, and we knew of no one else capable of such brazen behavior, exhibited with apparent impunity. Lonnie, with his pocked, Saturnalian face, resembled Will Scarlet from Robin Hood's merry band. He dressed as neither a Greaser nor a Surfer, but instead wore black and white striped bell-bottoms, the loudest shirts we'd ever seen, an overdose of Jade East cologne and a pair of brown suede boots that made his feet look like those of an enormous chipmunk. A tiny globe-of-the-Earth earring dangled sarcastically from one earlobe. All in all, Lonnie was a thoroughly dissolute suburban pirate and lacked only a cutlass, a black eye-patch and a foul-mouthed parrot perched on one shoulder. We, on the other hand, were young and incredibly naïve, and had yet to learn that evil could appear in so entertaining a guise.

On that night, however, having recently acquired the ability to distinguish between marijuana and oregano, we sped east on Route 22, our destination Greenwich Village. We listened to the radio as WABC played "96 Tears," "Psychotic Reaction" and "Summer in the City." No longer under the collective thumbs of our parents – a condition that chafed our young necks like a choke chain on a Doberman eyeing the mailman – we emerged from the Holland Tunnel and entered Manhattan, that glittering hive where, unlike New Providence, life was lived to the fullest and absolutely everything was attainable.

Night was in full bloom as we approached Bleeker Street but I wore a pair of aviator sunglasses with lenses the size of saucers, perhaps to disguise my identity from myself. Although I bore the humiliating scars of my most recent scalping, I decided it was time to introduce myself to my soon-to-be accomplices in illegal euphoria. "My name's Peter," I said, "I play the bass."

The skinny guy with a Beatle haircut said, "I'm Rob and I play rhythm guitar."

The heavy-set guy riding shotgun turned and said, "Hi, I'm Doug, I play drums."

"Jerry here," said the person to my left. "I play lead guitar."

"My name is Dave," said the last to be identified. "I sing and play blues harp."

A moment of silence filled the DeSoto as the implications sank in.

"WE'RE A BAND!" we shouted in unison.

"I'll be your manager," said Lonnie.

"We'll call the band 'The Owsley Elevator,'" Rob decreed. "And our motto will be 'Blues with a Feeling'"

"Who's Owsley?" asked Doug.

"Augustus Stanley Owsley III is the chemist who brewed up a million hits of LSD and travels around with The Grateful Dead," said Rob. "We can practice at my house. There's plenty of space in the basement. My mother will say 'it's marvelous' and my father will think he's keeping an eye on us."

3. Jerry Williams in the Owsley Elevator

And so, The Owsley Elevator began its ascent, its occupants blissfully unaware of how quickly the cable would snap and plummet us to disaster.

We began to practice in Rob's basement and culled a repertoire from songs recorded by The Paul Butterfield Blues Band, The Blues Project, The Yardbirds and John Mayal's Bluesbreakers. Neither the high-school authorities nor the local police were happy about our choice of a name for the band, for they, too, had read the media accounts of drug-inspired musical experimentation taking place on the West Coast. What, in their eyes, could be more annoying than a bunch of punks naming their band after someone they viewed as a criminal mastermind?

There were other bands in town, but unlike Grizby's Clan, The Sandmen, The Penetrators or the ever-popular Decoys, The Owsley Elevator never once played a high school dance or enjoyed the subsequent adulation of mini-skirted teenyboppers. Instead, our gigs took place at private parties held in a local country club.

The first intimations of trouble appeared when Jerry's father forbade him to leave the house whenever we had a gig. We were prepared and played the dates with an alternate guitarist. Coviello was not only an excellent blues guitarist but also an entrepreneur who specialized in the distribution of hashish. Once, after an excursion to score some of Lebanon's finest, we were pulled over by the police. The officer ordered him out of the car and I watched as Coviello casually extracted a gram of hash from his pocket, unwrapped the foil and popped the little brown lump into his mouth as if it were a Tootsie Roll. Then, under the eyes of the cops, and still chewing, he crumpled the foil into a tiny ball and tossed it over his shoulder!

Not every encounter with the arraigners (Lonnie's term for the police) ended with so little consequence; like the time the Owsley Elevator played an apocalyptic dance held in a yacht club on the Jersey shore.

***

Lonnie's purple DeSoto (nicknamed "the drugmobile") looked like a pregnant hippo in full gallop as it lurched onto the Garden State Parkway for the trip south to Bay Head. All five members of the Owsley Elevator sat wedged tightly. The drums had been roped onto the roof and the open trunk bulged with amplifiers. Microphone stands bristled out the side windows like machine guns on a Huey. The first state trooper to catch a glimpse grew elated, convinced that his promotion had just been assured. Blue lights flashed as the cruiser drew up behind us. Lonnie cursed and pulled over. The trooper stepped out and approached. He wore a crisply ironed blue uniform, knee-high black leather boots, big iron on his hip and a flat-brimmed hat pulled low over his brow at the official no-nonsense angle. He looked in at me from behind mirrored lenses. I peered back from behind a pair of my own.

"I'm going to issue you a ticket," he informed Lonnie, after inspecting his license and registration. "Your vehicle is dangerously overloaded." The officer returned to his cruiser to write the citation.

"Are we touring yet?" I inquired.

We sat there and sweated as the July sun turned the DeSoto into a rolling pizza oven. After ten minutes Lonnie got out and sauntered over to the state police cruiser. Wearing wrap-around sunglasses that made him look like a giant mosquito, he leaned into the cruiser's open window and said, "Could you hurry it up, pal?"

I can only imagine what went through the officer's mind at hearing the word "pal," but five minutes later we were on our way once more. Lonnie crushed the ticket into a wad and tossed it out the window.

"What do you bet that cop radios every other cop all the way down the Parkway and alerts them to our approach?" I said. "We could get half a dozen more tickets."

"Naw," said Dave. "That's our one hassle for this gig."

Eighty miles later we exited the Parkway and made our way to the Bayhead Yacht Club, where it took less than an hour to assemble our gear onstage in the fine old ballroom.

"Let's get a 12-string guitar," Rob suggested. "I know someone who lives nearby who'll let me borrow one for the gig." We drove to an innocuous house on a quiet side street, but unbeknownst to us, it was the very house that had been under covert police surveillance for the last two weeks. Rob knocked on the door, entered and emerged a minute later with the guitar.

"We've got time to kill," said Dave. "Let's go down to the beach and smoke a bowl."

The sun's crimson Frisbee hovered above the western horizon as we sat facing the Atlantic's incoming waves. It was a tranquil summer evening and I felt unusually at peace with the world. Dave filled his stubby metal pipe with kiff – pollen derived from cannabis sativa, our favorite green vegetable. He was just about to strike a match when a phalanx of police officers sprinted across the sand from behind, and then surrounded us! Instead of dropping the pipe and stash onto the sand and burying them both with a quick sweep of the hand, Dave made a grievous mistake and jammed the incriminating evidence into his pocket.

"We're taking you down to headquarters," said one of the Bayhead cops, where they put us behind bars. I heard the Doors song, "Light My Fire" playing softly on the radio in the chief's office. The police interrogated us, one at a time, and found Dave's incriminating paraphernalia. When my turn came the police chief looked at me and said, "You seem like a decent kid. You say you had no idea your singer was on drugs?"

"No sir," I lied. "I've heard about that stuff. Who could imagine they would freak out in Kansas, I mean right here in New Jersey?"

Fortunately, I was sober, clear-eyed and polite, and my severe haircut must've convinced the chief of my innocence. Just then another cop entered the office, held up Dave's pipe and said, "This is what he used to sniff it." I didn't utter a word, although I wanted to say, "You don't 'sniff it,' you dolt, you inhale deeply and hold your breath."

When eight o'clock rolled around, we were still in jail. The police finally released us – all except Dave – and sped us to the yacht club, where their cruisers screeched to a halt in the parking lot filled with an expectant crowd. The siren abated as we emerged from captivity. The Owsley Elevator finally took the stage, but without our vocalist we were forced to ask, "Does anyone out there know the words to "Born in Chicago?" Yeah? Want to sing it? Great! How about "Key to the Highway?"

The band's forte consisted of feverish, thirty-minute renditions of "Mellow Down Easy," from the first Butterfield album, complete with Jim Morrison's infamous monolog…"Father! (Yes son?) I want to kill you!" But without Dave we were forced to play endless choruses of "Season of the Witch" by Donovan, "Seven and Seven Is" by Love and "Hey Joe" by The Byrds.

We made it through the gig but it was the beginning of the end for Dave. As time went on he grew ever more ensnared in New Jersey's legal system, to say nothing of his addiction to heroin. The Owsley Elevator never played another gig, we lost touch with Dave and to this day I don't even know if he's still alive.

Lonnie's little green spot faded from my radar screen too. Like a woolly mammoth trapped in a tar pit, he, too, sank deeper into the smothering quagmire of heroin. Who knows how many innocent young hippie-chicks he dragged to their doom with his oily insouciance and a hypodermic needle? Sadly, I know of two, but there must've been others. Recently, news reached me that Lonnie had survived the intervening decades, and lived near Philly. Not surprising, he'd become something of a derelict and had the habit of walking to a church mission once a day for free coffee and a doughnut. One morning he crossed the street without looking and was hit and killed by the truck that delivered the doughnuts.

Who said God doesn't have a sense of humor?

The Prince Valiant Strolling Electric Rock Band

"How many times have you taken LSD?" my father demanded early one morning, slapping me abruptly out of a sound sleep.

"Only once," I blurted, "but it was Sandoz, pharmaceutically pure!"

"You'll blow your mind," he warned.

"That's the idea."

Arnold strode away in disgust.

Not a typical Monday morning, but a memorable one as only five more days remained before the horror of high school ended, once and for all. After consuming a bowl of Cheerios I rode my rabbit (a Honda 50) to New Providence High School (home of the Pioneers). I sat in my homeroom and waited for the first period of the day to begin. Suddenly the intercom spat out an order: "Peter Williams, report to the principal's office immediately!"

"Not again," I groaned. With only a week to go before the class of '67 slid down the graduation chute, prior to joining the ubiquitous workforce, I thought I'd seen the last of Mr. McCarthy's grim visage.

"Now what?" I wondered as I trudged the lengthy halls. I entered the office and knocked on the door I knew so well.

"Come in, Peter. Sit down," said Mr. McCarthy as he scrutinized me through narrowed eyelids. After a moment of silence he picked up and leafed through a voluminous list of my transgressions. "Your academic career has been eventful, to say the least," he said. "You've been kicked out of class more often than any student I've ever known; you've been banned from the cafeteria; you've been suspended more than enough times to warrant

30

expulsion – how you managed to eliminate our written records is beyond me – and now I learn that you've recently acquired thirty days of detention. Is this true?"

I nodded. Yes, it was true but I saw no need to describe how easy it had been to infiltrate the main filing cabinet (as if on official school business), then deftly remove and destroy my file. And so what if I'd arrived for the first day of my senior year an hour late, riding a skateboard down the hall, barefoot, wearing shorts and a T-shirt?

"Tell me, Peter, to what do you attribute this spectacular disregard for authority?"

"Harpo Marx."

"Come again?"

"The single most influential person in my life has been Harpo Marx."

"I see," said Mr. McCarthy, who most certainly did not. "Well, after today there are only four more days remaining in your senior year. With that in mind I'd like you to report for detention every afternoon till the end of the week – a gesture of contrition. What do you say?"

"Not a chance."

"What about three days?"

"No."

"Two?"

"No!"

"Just one? One day of detention?"

I shook my head, as obdurate as stone. (If I'd had a bicycle horn and a pair of scissors under my overcoat, I would've emitted a loud derisive honk and snipped his tie in half.) Mr. McCarthy took a deep breath before proceeding. "I've also learned that you and you alone, of the entire student body, refused to have a photo taken for the yearbook."

"I want nothing to do with the yearbook."

"But why?"

"I can see it now," I said. "A ridiculous photo of me wearing a tie and a fraudulent smile, accompanied by an inane blurb written by some idiot I've never even met."

"But this is your only chance," said Mr. McCarthy, his face distorted with bewilderment. "What about the senior prom?"

"That's out, too."

"Surely you don't intend to skip graduation ceremonies as well?"

"Don't make me laugh," I replied. "The sooner I forget the very existence of this wretched institution, and New Providence, the better."

Mr. McCarthy heaved a sigh of infinite weariness. He turned and gazed out the window. "Go on," he said, after a minute of silence. "Get out."

***

I fled New Providence a week later, abandoning the little house I'd inhabited with my father on the banks of the turgid Passaic River. Arnold returned one afternoon to find my room empty. Too alienated and bitter to say goodbye or even leave a note, I simply vanished. Lured by the freedom or death explicitly guaranteed by all New Hampshire license plates, my destination was the village of Newmarket – a dying mill town where the last gasp of the Industrial Revolution still whistled through a set of clenched false teeth. I drove north in a borrowed '58 Oldsmobile, a ponderous red and white tank equipped with circular apertures along its fuselage. Although these so-called Cruiserline Ventiports served no purpose, the car was large enough to carry my bass, amplifier, clothes, stereo, albums, an Ampex 600 tape recorder, a number of indispensable books and my Honda 50, roped securely into the trunk.

I'd visited Newmarket the summer before and had friends there, but the main attraction was a rust-bitten railroad trestle that spanned the tea-colored waters of the Lamprey River. Surrounded by pine forest and cornfields, the river snaked circuitously to the Great Bay where a waterfall prevented the upstream invasion of the sea lamprey that gave the river its name. Tranquil, scenic and isolated, the trestle was an ideal place to hang out and swim. The river flowed between the bridge's two monumental granite bulwarks with the same quiet assurance enjoyed by all young men who believe themselves to be immortal.

In July the sun's golden disk reflected from the water's glassy surface. A rock dropped over the side produced expanding concentric ripples that coruscated with impossible colors. If in need of excitement, I had only to jump off the bridge and plummet twenty-five feet into the deep water below. In 1967, reality intruded only once a day, when a freight train thundered across the span and shook the webs slung by large gray trestle spiders. In the fall vast fleets of red and gold leaves glided majestically downstream.

One perfect blue-sky September day I drove south to Cambridge, Massachusetts, and wandered into a "head shop" near Harvard Square, where I spotted a handwritten note taped to the wall. "Bass player wanted, to live with band in country," it said. No kidding, that's how it was done in those days, just a scrap of paper and a phone number. I grabbed the note before some other child of Fender could beat me to it. The next day I called the number to introduce myself and made arrangements for an audition with a band in Northwood, New Hampshire, a tiny hamlet forty miles from Newmarket.

I set out on the appointed day and turned off Route 4 onto a dirt road that led me through dense forest and then into open fields festooned with twisted metal sculpture. When the road came to an end I faced a charming old farmhouse owned by Sylvana Cenci, the renowned artist (and anarchist) who had just rented the place to the band I was about to meet. Sylvana no longer lived in the farmhouse, but still kept a safe full of dynamite in the woods. She used the explosives to blast patterned indentations into large sheets of aluminum, her sculptural medium.

Sylvana had a beautiful young daughter, a tousle-haired nymph who wafted through the sun-drenched fields in a diaphanous white robe like some fairy child in a Donovan song. I fell in love instantly, but at 14, she was too young for me, and besides that, she was already keen on a local lout, an uncouth ruffian who, I was certain, did not deserve her. Between the dynamite and the daughter, who can say which was more dangerous?

I met the members of the band, recent émigrés from Boston eager to fulfill their musical aspirations in the as yet unspoiled wilds of New Hampshire. The drummer's name was Turkey Deptula, a gentle giant who beat the daylights out of a decrepit set of Slingerlands, drums so old they emitted a dull thud instead of a vibrant snap. Turkey wore a bowl-cut hairdo and looked like a medieval blacksmith hammering upon an anvil. An excellent drummer, he lived for the joy of forging exact duplicates of "Toad," Ginger Baker's revolutionary drum solo.

Rick was a red-haired, red-bearded, lead-guitar player, an extrovert who waltzed around in crimson clothes like a court jester. He was also an experienced actor, and had appeared in the Boston production of "Hair," but he knew almost nothing about the guitar. Being intelligent, however, he set about learning to play solos in a very scientific way. Using a turntable set at 16-RPM, instead of the usual 33, he copied the guitar solos from original recordings, learning each note as they crept by and then, once he had them all, playing the passage at a normal tempo, in the correct key.

Ron was the band's rhythm guitarist and an electronics technician – a useful skill in view of the fact that his Silvertone amplifier exploded after every hour of operation, an event marked by the formation of a miniature mushroom cloud that billowed toxic smoke into the air. Day after day, he sat upstairs in his room huddled over the amp's exposed chassis, soldering gun in hand, as he replaced melted resistors, inhaled solder smoke and shooed away a Siamese cat named Thwack. Ron was the first gay person I'd ever met, a fact not revealed till later, but one that found little chance of expression in the hinterlands of Northwood.

The band's key element was Judy, its lead singer and sponsor. A raven-haired beauty, she dreamt of becoming New Hampshire's version of Grace Slick. But as an untrained vocalist, she sang with a ferocity that invariably produced a sore throat after every rehearsal, forcing her into silence for days afterward. Judy's consort was an enigmatic presence known simply as The Poet. Tall, bearded, and with the longest, straightest black hair anyone in Northwood had ever seen on a male, The Poet never ventured forth without wearing sunglasses, day or night. "We're going to call the group 'The Prince Valiant Strolling Electric Rock Band,'" he said, "since everyone says I look exactly like the comic strip character."

I positioned my Fender Bassman amp next to Turkey's drums in a large, sunny room where pastoral views filled every window. We played some Beatles songs and then a couple by the Rolling Stones. The audition went well until they asked me to sing. I stared at a microphone connected to large metal horns atop tripods, a PA better suited for hollering out bingo numbers at the county fair. I had no choice but to squeak out a few feedback-raddled notes, but fortunately, they liked my playing and offered me the job. I vacated my apartment in Newmarket and moved into Sylvana's farmhouse on the last day of September.

The next morning found me seated at the kitchen table with Judy, The Poet and Turkey. Sylvana joined us for coffee and fresh-baked blueberry muffins and began to warn us about the old house's idiosyncrasies. "Whatever you do," she admonished, "Never walk between the planks in the attic. Because if you do..."

She never finished her sentence. The ceiling exploded. Ron hurtled down and hit the table with a terrific crash that shattered dishes and hurled hot coffee and muffin fragments in all directions! The oaf landed on his back, still gripping a soldering gun, and the table collapsed under the impact. Sylvana erupted into a blistering tirade of obscenity in fluent Italian. Her penchant for anarchy was well known; probably the only reason we weren't evicted on the spot.

That came later.

The Battle of the Bands drew nigh. After a solid month of daily rehearsals, The Prince Valiant Strolling Electric Rock Band was ready to conquer. Feverish excitement filled the Coe Brown Academy, in Northwood, the night we experienced our only fleeting moment of glory. The various competing ensembles had staked out corners of the gym, under the intense scrutiny of every kid for fifty miles around.

4. The Prince Valiant Strolling Electric Rock Band

I arrived in full battle regalia – bell-bottoms, Beatle boots, a navy blue shirt spattered with white polka dots, an air force officer's blazer and a pair of rose-colored granny glasses – the epitome of a counter-culture fop, lacking only a silver snuffbox filled with powdered LSD. The other members of the band went all out too. Rick's curls rioted in an unruly red nimbus;

Turkey swept in wearing a long black cape and looked like Oscar Wilde; Judy wore leopard-skin leotards, stiletto heels and brandished a dainty, leather bullwhip. The Poet hovered inscrutably in black. Ron looked like a Carnaby Street Mod in his silver, collar-less Beatle suit. All in all, we were a sight guaranteed to strike fear into the hearts of all decent, law-abiding citizens of New Hampshire.

The Battle of the Band judges took one look at us and fidgeted, no doubt wondering how such a collection of obviously deranged hippies could've slipped unnoticed into town to subvert the morals of their children. The judges were so rattled you'd think a clan of devil-worshipping cannibals had arrived to celebrate Christmas.

The battle began and a local band fired the first salvo, a spirited rendition of "Louie Louie." But after the thirty-seventh chorus I, too, fidgeted. The next act featured four grinning siblings in lederhosen (on roller skates) who played orange, sparkle-flake accordions! When our turn came we played – "She's a Woman," "Somebody to Love," "White Rabbit" and "Nowhere Man" – saving our knockout punch, "So You Want To Be A Rock 'n Roll Star," for last.

Our performance was polished, energetic and Judy's voice was at its peak. Ron's amplifier did not explode, Turkey's drums reverberated like the heartbeat of the universe, my Fender Precision bass boomed authoritatively and Rick's note-for-note guitar solos added authenticity. We sounded great and the kids loved us. The judges, however, did not. We gawked in disbelief when they awarded first-place to a Kingston Trio-style combo (in matching crew-cuts and sports coats!) The crowd hooted indignantly and the blatant injustice spawned a generation gap that nearly split the floorboards asunder.

Vanquished and forlorn, we loaded our amplifiers, drums and guitars into Ron's Ford Fairlane 500, the one with THE PRINCE VALIANT STROLLING ELECTRIC ROCK BAND painted boldly along its flanks, and then scuttled away into the night.

In losing the battle, we not only lost the 250-dollar prize money we sorely needed to buy food, but also our confidence. We had no clue as to how to go about hustling up real gigs. We were a sorry lot; the refrigerator was empty, I had about fifty bucks to my name, none of us had a job and Judy's limited supply of cash diminished with every passing day. We ate frugally, tightened our belts and bought groceries only after driving to Boston to sell our own blood for 35 bucks a pint!

Prince Valiant never played anywhere ever again.

As winter loomed, our predicament rocketed downhill faster than a sled on an icy slope. The plumbing in the farmhouse had never been intended to cater to the needs of six adults. We began to lose our tenuous grip on Utopia when the well ran dry. Forced to limit ourselves to one shower each a week, we became, quite literally, dirty hippies. The final blow – the straw that sent the camel to the chiropractor – struck when the septic tank overflowed and filled the bathtub with raw, stinking sewage.

The Tasker Brothers ran the local septic-tank-pumping business, so rather than alert Sylvana to our dire condition, we called them in. The brothers strolled around the yard and scratched their chins. "Can't seem to find the septic tank," said one brother.

"Most peculiar. Nothing we can do," said the other.

It was a rotten lie, but what better way to drive us out?

They must've called Sylvana, because she appeared early the next morning in high dudgeon and ordered us to leave. The citizens of Northwood heaved a collective sigh of relief the day we all drove away in different directions, never to darken their dance floor again.

***

In the six months since my departure from New Providence, I'd made no attempt to communicate with my father and it now seemed an appropriate time to let him know I was still alive. So, after getting a ride from New Hampshire to New Jersey with Rob (from the ill-fated Owsley Elevator), I walked unannounced into Arnold's living room one evening as he dozed in a reclining armchair, as a Gilbert and Sullivan operetta playing softly on the stereo.

"Hello," I said.

He opened his eyes, glared at me and said, "This had better be good."

The Quest for Immortality

My enduring fascination with audio recording technology began in 1955, when, at the age of six, my father brought home a wire recorder. The suitcase-sized machine weighed forty pounds and looked like a piece of Flash Gordon's luggage. Tape had yet to be invented. Instead, a strand of fine silver wire passed through a recording head as it rode up and down on a spindle, evenly distributing the metal filament on the take-up spool. A small red button activated the record mode. When pushed, a signal from the cast-metal microphone imbued the shiny strand with electromagnetic magic.

What child has not been shocked to hear his or her own voice for the first time played back on a recording, sounding as insignificant as a cricket?

When other kids wheedled and cajoled their parents for Daisy air rifles or cap-firing burp guns made by Mattel for Christmas, I lobbied (unsuccessfully) for a tape recorder. And so, during the interminable months that followed, I sold peanut brittle, seeds and greeting cards in a door-to-door quest to "win" battery-powered tape recorders – pathetic devices with three-inch reels, crystal microphones and atrocious fidelity. Once acquired, I held the disk-shaped plastic mike to my lips and mimicked the sounds of machine-gun fire and explosions, normal behavior for a male kid in America only a decade after the conclusion of World War II.

From the time of that first primitive wire recorder to the present, I've never known a minute's peace from the spiraling demands imposed by the quest for better fidelity – higher highs and lower lows. The subsequent march of technology delivered an ever-expanding assortment of recorders into my grasp, from four-track machines with ten-inch reels to sophisticated digital recorders with no reels at all.

In the early days of the 1960's all record players were monaural and the term hi-fi denoted the sine qua non of frequency response. The tone arm weighed a pound, a vinyl LP was almost an eighth of an inch thick and a Lafayette amplifier radiated heat from a cluster of glowing vacuum tubes. (In those days the pilot light came on when the amp was switched on – unlike today, where the standby light indicates the opposite.) When my father built a large wooden baffle for a 12-inch "tri-axial" speaker, installed it in a closet and then cut a circular hole in the wall to let the sound out, I knew the high-fidelity bug had bitten him too.

Music poured continuously through that hole in the wall: Gilbert and Sullivan operettas, Broadway show soundtracks, Burl Ives, classical symphonies and occasionally the bleating wail of the Scots Guards regimental bagpipes.

My father despised rock 'n roll, which forced me to hide my first LP, The Ventures' "Walk Don't Run." But every Friday when Arnold left for a night of poker with his cronies, I shook the house with the sound of twanging Mosrite electric guitars, instruments designed and marketed by The Ventures themselves.

5. The Ampex

A miracle transpired the day one of Arnold's tennis buddies presented me with a princely gift – an Ampex 600 – a half-track, monaural tape recorder light-years ahead of the contraptions I'd previously owned. My benefactor was Dr. Edward David, the director of Bell Labs in Murray Hill, as well as President Nixon's science advisor. Ampex tape machines were renowned for their dependability and superb fidelity, but it placed an immediate demand on my severely limited budget. I needed a better microphone, unaware that one mike would eventually lead to a dozen.

In the course of time I acquired additional mikes and a Shure 5-channel mixer. Thus equipped, I lugged the Ampex from coast to coast for the next twenty years and recorded every band I joined. It took a while, but after sufficient trial and error I learned to make good live recordings by utilizing sub-mixes and a line output from the PA, not so simple when one is required to monitor the input level on the recorder and play an instrument at the same time.

Since that first primitive wire recorder I've owned tape machines built by Invicta, Concord, Roberts, Tandberg, Sony, Wollensak, Uher, Dokorder, Pioneer, Fostex and a couple of Teaks, but none has ever surpassed my fondness for the old Ampex.

Thank you again, Dr. David.

Spike

After the overthrow of Prince Valiant I returned to the somnolent suburbs of New Jersey, as trapped as the tiny grub in a Mexican jumping bean whose writhing gives the bean its erratic impetus. I rented a room in a bachelor enclave in Berkeley Heights, not far from Bell Labs, and took a job working for the Amalgamated Soul-Crushing Corporation, also known as Azoplate. Jules, the hiring director, was a kindly old soul, who, being unaware of my extraordinary unsuitability, hired me. Thus began a season in hell. For months I endured the dreadful tedium of running a small printing press – a machine whose very name, AB Dick, still inspires revulsion. For eight hours a day, I printed vast reams of sheer gibberish in order to determine the point at which the image resolution broke down. Living death, in other words.

To counteract the drudgery, I invested in a block of hashish the size of a Chunky bar and devoted my evenings to self-medication. Night after night I bathed in the unholy radiance of a black light, practiced the bass and listened to albums by Iron Butterfly, Autosalvage and The Electric Flag.

In 1968 I ran off with the circus, or to be more precise, I bought a ticket to the Electric Circus in Manhattan and underwent a spectacularly effective form of brainwashing: Seated on the floor at Jerry Garcia's feet, I listened as The Grateful Dead unleashed a blistering, acid-scorched onslaught of musical energy – an overwhelming juggernaut that inspired hours of nonstop hysterical laughter. I resolved, then and there, to master my instrument and let nothing stand in the way of becoming a professional musician.

Owsley was there too, hovering behind the amps onstage. Yes, Augustus Stanley Owsley the Third, the inspiration behind my high school band The Owsley Elevator. I watched as he deposited a can of beer on top of each musician's amplifier, brews dosed with lysergic acid diethylamide. The Dead chugged their beers and about forty-five minutes later the band left planet Earth far behind and whisked us all into uncharted space aboard an auditory comet of unparallel brilliance. (People either love the music of the 'Dead or they hate it. One reason is the fact that not everyone wants to hear a group's songs played differently each time.) As for me, I loved it from the instant the sound of Lesh's bass first struck my tympanic membrane.

Meanwhile, back in the suburbs...

Although I now resided only a few miles from my father's house, I kept my distance. My emotional scars were still too tender. Vast reservoirs of anger still simmered within me like magma churning beneath a thin crust. I knew that time was my strongest ally, and if granted a sufficient amount, the devils that prodded me with pitchforks would be exorcised. Till then, however, there was nothing quite as effective for severing the link to one's troubled subconscious (and the conscious) as Lebanese hashish.

One day my father hit upon the idea of buying me a vehicle, perhaps as a way to bridge the apparently insurmountable gap between us. But instead of something practical, like a van, he selected an MG-TC, a classic English roadster – a black convertible with gull-wing fenders, wire-wheels, a windshield that folded flat and a steering wheel on the right. The TC had been built in 1949, the year I was born, and was in mint condition, having been stored in a sports-car museum.

6. The MG TC

"I'll buy this car for you if you'll promise to stop taking LSD," said Arnold.

I agreed on the spot. Arnold coughed up the cash and the rakish roadster became mine, but it wasn't long before I wrapped a white silk scarf around my neck, lowered a pair of goggles over my dilated eyes and rallied through the countryside under the blazing influence of Dr. Hoffman's infamous ergot fungus elixir.

"Hell's bloody bells!" as my father might've said…Talk about asking for bad karma!

After months of mind-numbing servitude I quit my job at Azoplate and gave the MG back to Arnold. I told him the roadster was unsuitable for daily use and instead, should be sheltered in a garage and taken for jaunts only on Sunday afternoons in the summer.

By that time Rob, the rhythm guitarist from the Owsley Elevator, had moved to Boston. He informed me that a room had become available in the house he inhabited, so I rented a U-Haul van, drove north and pulled up in front of a sinister old house on Mission Hill. I took one look and quailed. I should've driven away, but instead, I moved in.

The house had been built in 1787 by a ship's captain, but the intervening years had been as cruel as Ahab. Flanked by litter-strewn vacant lots, the old structure jutted from the ground like a rotten molar in a leprous jaw. It seemed to radiate a malevolent will of its own, stubbornly defying the demolition that had eliminated so many other dilapidated buildings nearby. The neighborhood was perilous. Muggings were routinely administered and car windows were shot out at night. Terrible things happened on Allegheny Street: Black cats died inexplicably on the doorstep; ghoulish junkies let themselves in at two in the morning to shoot heroin in our kitchen.

Curiosity got the better of us the day Rob and I descended into the basement to investigate a crypt-like cellar filled with a century's accumulation of moldering junk, a veritable midden heap from floor to ceiling. We shifted the detritus, cleared a path and then confronted an ancient door that had not been opened in a century. We pried it open and pointed our flashlights at a scene of horror. For in that noisome closet, rising from the primordial ooze, stood a spindly white plant as tall as a man – a living perversion with tendrils that seemed to reach out to grasp us. Faint daylight seeped in through a small circular hole in the ceiling, the drain from our shower. There was no pipe to carry off the wastewater, just a slimy malodorous pit at the core of the rotten old house. H.P. Lovecraft would've loved it, but we slammed the door shut and fled. Who knows how many countless gallons of warm water had splashed into that fetid cell over the decades? The only explanation for that skeletal plant involves a seed that washed down, germinated and somehow managed to grow without ever receiving a photon of sunlight.

Rob and I shared the first floor with Bill and Vance and their four flea-ridden dogs – a howling mutt named Bean and a pack of nervous Dobermans dubbed Blake, Rex and Sinjib. One afternoon all four of Vance's dogs got into my room and defecated repeatedly, and with great gusto, all over my bed, the pillow and in my shoes. I discovered the transgression and went berserk, hoisting mutt after struggling mutt over the porch railing and hurling them into the bushes below. It was my own fault for having wrenched my bedroom door off its hinges – never mind why – and then leaning it against the opening, leaving ample space for the brutes to get in.

After cleaning and disinfecting everything, I propped the door against the jam, turned and took two steps before it toppled and struck me squarely on the back of the head. Insane with rage, I grabbed my bass and bashed a huge hole in the wall. The next day I covered the gaping aperture with a Union Jack and then reattached the door. From then on, every time I approached the dogs skulked away with guilty expressions on their ugly muzzles.

No question about it, I was completely off my rocker – so unbalanced that bells rang as the pinball machine of my mind flashed a bright red TILT sign above my head.

7. The house on Allegheny Street

In 1968, the Young were at war with the Establishment. Boston seethed with anti-Viet Nam war marches, protests and riots, augmented by a police force determined to brutally suppress all such Communist-inspired subversion. The memory of President Kennedy's assassination remained fresh, as was the murder of Martin Luther King. The death of Bobby Kennedy only added to the conviction that the universe was completely insane. The Viet Nam war showed no signs of ending. Just the opposite, the conflict gained momentum every day and the palpable sense of jeopardy and anarchy my peers and I endured cannot be minimized. It looked to me as if the country was in the hands of deranged avatars, unscrupulous politicians and smiling Scientologists. I had friends that had been chewed and swallowed by the Southeast Asian jungle. Those who made it back alive were permanently damaged, both physically and emotionally. And as the body bags piled up on the TV news each night, I lived with the fear that the Army could draft me at any moment. Is it any wonder marijuana offered such an appealing escape?

Yet in spite of the war, the riots and the intoxicants, life on Allegheny Street settled into a routine: When I wasn't out prowling around the edge of the riots, or running headlong from baton-wielding thugs wearing police uniforms, or hawking copies of *The Old Mole* in Harvard Square, I was either practicing on my bass or chasing juicy, young hippie chicks. The Pill had arrived and Cambridge teemed with healthy young women endowed with healthy young appetites. The Sexual Revolution was going full blast and I hurled myself into the fray whenever possible. Which brings to mind the young goddess I met while in the waiting room of an outpatient VD clinic. (Fortunately, neither of us suffered from anything more serious than a urinary infection.) Andrea had luminous green eyes and long silken hair the color of honey that cascaded to her waist and swished provocatively against her shapely young buttocks. She wore purple tights beneath a turquoise mini-skirt and resembled a teenage Bridget Bardot.

In addition to beautiful women, Boston's other inexhaustible commodity consisted of guitar players – perhaps more per square foot than any other city on the planet. One afternoon I stood on a street corner waiting for the light to change. I clutched the black oblong case that held my Fender bass and scrutinized three longhaired, shifty-eyed scruffs waited on the other side. They, too, carried guitar cases. When the light turned green, we crossed and met halfway.

"You a bass player?" asked one.

"That's right," I replied, and bingo, another band materialized out of thin air. It didn't last long, nor the one after that, but with each fiasco I learned more about the essentials required for creating a viable band – things to look for or to avoid. Spike was another short-lived attempt and included Ron, the guitar player from The Prince Valiant Strolling Electric Rock Band. We tried but had little of the ego, the expertise or the equipment necessary to compete with Ultimate Spinach, Phluff or Earth Opera – to say nothing of The Fort Mudge Memorial Dump, a band in which Turkey Deptula pounded the same exhausted drums he played in Prince Valiant.

Listening

In those days Cambridge, Massachusetts, pulsed with vitality. There appeared to be less of the grim focus on business evident in Harvard Square today; instead, the street teemed with a boisterous and colorful vibrancy generated (in part) by the clash between the Establishment and the burgeoning counter-culture. On Sunday afternoons in the summer, the Cambridge Common hosted a gathering of self-proclaimed freaks where bands played and marijuana was smoked with impunity, unlike the Boston Common where mounted police conducted sweeps. Tension between the opposing factions was abundant. A rude, taunting outburst greeted John Wayne the day he rode the length of Mass Avenue atop an Army tank – Duke's way of giving the finger to the longhaired commie potheads gathered along the way to protest the war in Viet Nam.

Cambridge offered an exhilarating alternative to Boston's repression, but on the other side of the Charles River, I looked forward to ending my voluntary incarceration in the evil old house on Allegheny Street. The move to Cambridge became feasible after Doug, the drummer from The Owsley Elevator, and his girlfriend, Diane, rented an apartment on Brookline Street. The shotgun-style apartment had two extra rooms, one for me and one for Jerry, another veteran of the defunct Owsley Elevator. Once ensconced, we talked continuously about starting a new band but spent little time actually playing music. Instead, we drifted from one day to the next shrouded in a haze of Panama Red smoke as we listened to albums by Cream, The Beatles, Pink Floyd, Procol Harem and a dozen others. We never worked longer than was necessary to pay the rent or buy food, but our collective poverty didn't seem to matter. Weed cost fifteen bucks a "lid," and we wholeheartedly agreed with the maxim, "Weed will get you through times of no money better than money will get you through times of no weed."

I first met Marshal Goldberg the day he visited Northwood to record Prince Valiant's Strolling Delusional Rock Band in Sylvana's idyllic farmhouse. With his mop of curly black ringlets, Marshal resembled a portly, Jewish Tiny Tim, minus the ukulele. Marshal knew everyone in Boston involved in developing high-energy audio equipment and he introduced me to the owners of Intermedia Systems – a company started by multimedia artist Gerd Stern and George Litwin, the Harvard professor reputed to have given Timothy Leary his first dose of LSD. They hired me as a technician's assistant and my duties included the construction of electronic circuits, the installation of a monstrous light and sound system in the rock club originally known as The Ark (which later became the new Boston Tea Company). I used state-of-the-art tape recorders to make soundtracks for experimental films. It was a great job and they trusted me, as demonstrated by the weekly trips to the bank I made bearing a pouch with thirty grand in cash. But one day, without any warning, my supervisor took me aside – the same little weasel who sold me weed – and said, "Peter, we know you want to be a musician, so here's the deal: Either you stay and commit yourself to the company, or you leave."

I pondered the ultimatum for less than a minute, then handed him the keys and walked out the door. Not my most enlightened career decision, but what the hell, I was only 20 and determined to become a professional musician.

Marshal also introduced me to Listening, a jazz-rock band in search of a bass player. Michael Tchudin played a Hammond organ and led the band, with Peter Malick on guitar. They'd already released an album on the Vanguard label and appeared to be on their way. The musicians in Listening were five or six years older than me, possessed excellent musical educations and were far more accomplished on their instruments. At the time, I was a dotted half-wit, musically speaking; I knew nothing about music theory, had never read a jazz chart in my life and was completely ignorant of the edict that states "a dot increases a note's duration by half."

My audition lasted for three days. We improvised continuously and paused only for food, coffee and marijuana. I was in over my head, to be sure, but I possessed unlimited energy, an excellent sense of time and fast fingers on the electric bass. Yet in spite of these qualifications, they declined to hire me. Later, the organist admitted that the only time he liked my playing was immediately after smoking a joint!

***

In July of 1969, NASA prepared to catapult Neil Armstrong to the moon, a heroically optimistic event sorely needed to counteract the bitterness engendered by the ongoing war in Viet Nam. Suddenly, in spite of the war, everything seemed possible, but on Brookline Street our half-hearted efforts to form a band were not bringing us any closer to our goal. The deadlock broke when Howard Mangold, a fellow alumnus from New Providence High

School, called to announce his impending arrival and desire to conduct what he described as, "A very important meeting."

Howard had billowing curly hair, a full beard and a set of pointed teeth that made him resemble Lon Chaney, Jr.'s depiction of the wolf man. In truth, he was a gentle soul who shared our dream of creating a band.

8. Howard Mangold

Howard arrived at our apartment on Brookline Street as Doug's stereo played "Abbey Road" for the thousandth time. We gathered for that fateful meeting and Howard began by saying, "Every successful group has one thing in common: At one time or another, the musicians all lived under the same roof, in a house where they could practice every day. Where would The Band, the 'Dead or Moby Grape be if they had to worry about the neighbors calling the police every time they switched on their amps?"

"They'd be stuck in some shabby apartment in Cambridge," I replied.

"That's right," said Howard. "So, with that in mind, I suggest that we rent a house in Vermont, a place where we can put the band together, once and for all."

It sounded like a great idea, although the phrase "and if pigs could fly" should've leapt to mind, accompanied by a chorus of enthusiastic oinks. The debacle with Prince Valiant band, in Northwood, remained a painful memory, as was the collapse of The Owsley Elevator, but the "back to the land" movement had been gaining momentum – the hippie urban Diaspora – and Howard's idea offered a plausible way to escape the big city strife.

"Sounds groovy," said Doug. "But how do we pay for this wonderful house?"

"Don't worry about that," said Howard confidently. "I'll be the band's manager. I'll get a job and pay the rent."

(Oink! Oink! Oink!)

We agreed to pursue Howard's utopian plan and began to work towards its fulfillment by splitting up into teams, then driving to Vermont to scour the classified ads and talk to realtors. But, in those days, the folks in the Green Mountains were as apprehensive of the hippie invasion as their counterparts in the White Mountains of New Hampshire. Our youth and long hair placed us smack dab in the middle of the national media's accounts of jobless, Godless, dope smoking degenerates playing guitars all day and living in sin. As a result, not one Vermonter was willing to rent us so much as an empty corner of an unheated barn. Weeks turned to months. Frustration turned to anguish as Jerry and I drove past cabins, houses and ski chalets – each more appealing than the last and all beyond our grasp – countless dwellings tucked away in wooded hollows, nestled under effulgent maples or perched alongside tranquil ponds. We set out in search again and again, only to return empty-handed and depressed.

Then, after what seemed like an eternity of frustration, Doug and Diane came upon a 200-year old farmhouse for rent in the sleepy village of Ira, a town so small it lacked a country store, with Rutland – twenty miles away – as the nearest outpost of civilization. After pinning his flowing locks up inside a Red Sox cap, Doug introduced himself to the realtor. "Hello," he said with a smile, a hearty handshake and unwavering eye contact. "My name's Doug and this is my wife, Diane. We noticed a 'For Rent' sign on a charming old house on Route 133 in Ira. We're interested in finding just such a home where we can raise a family and start a business restoring and selling antiques."

The real-estate agent quickly sized them up and liked what he saw – two bright, young newlyweds eager to settle down, have children and become upstanding members of the community. The ploy worked. Doug signed a lease on the spot, and not a word was uttered about installing a rock band. The jubilant couple returned to Cambridge and informed us of their success. The next day we huddled around the tube as Neil Armstrong's boot indented the lunar surface. "One small step for Man," was about to be trumped by our own giant leap to Vermont.

***

A week before our long-awaited exodus from Cambridge, I answered a knock on the door. "Are you Peter Williams?" asked a policeman. I nodded and the officer handed me a slip of paper. "Call this number," he said. "There's been an accident."

A minute later I learned that my father was dead – electrocuted – fried to a smoldering crisp while gripping the controls of a buffing machine as he stood on a wet floor. "An accident caused by faulty wiring," I was told, "improper grounding." Numb with shock, I climbed to the roof of the apartment building and wept bitter tears for Arnold, and for myself. He was fifty-two; I was twenty. Although we had been at each other's throats for years and rarely spoke, all vestiges of a family were now gone forever, regardless of how incomplete or dysfunctional. Any hope of rapprochement had been eliminated, along with the chance to demonstrate that I was not, in fact, "A worthless little shit."

I gazed through tear-streaked eyes at the crimson and purple glory of a pollution-augmented sunset and knew it to be Arnold's epitaph.

The necessity of attending a funeral in New Jersey now loomed, as did a dreadful Greyhound bus ride, an interminable journey peering through green tinted windows as Connecticut slid past in the fog and rain – the ideal environment for morbid introspection. The demon sitting on my left shoulder whispered, "Serves him right, the brutal son of a bitch." The angel on my right countered with, "Poor bastard, swindled yet again."

Once more I became painfully aware of the rift between the actual and the possible, that apparently unbridgeable chasm between realism and idealism. I pondered the true meaning of cynicism – disillusioned idealism – not the glib, sardonic misinterpretation typically encountered. A decade before, Arnold had been briefly involved with an attractive, albeit married, woman named Dori. The affair had been problematic, but after an interval of years, and her divorce, she and Arnold reunited and began living together in a house in Watchung. The house now contained Arnold's furniture, clothes, records and books, the effluvia of a lifetime. Two cars sat in the driveway, an MGB and a Jaguar. A million details had to be confronted before I could get away and join Doug and Jerry in the house in Vermont. I remember little of Arnold's funeral except Dori's insistence that I kiss the coffin; a ridiculous gesture considering the tone of the relationship with my father, or more accurately, the lack thereof. His remains were soon cremated. Someone handed me a metal urn. "What the devil am I going to do with this?" I wondered. Dumping two pounds of ash into a garbage can seemed too disrespectful and placing it on the mantle-piece was out of the question. Instead, I crept onto a nearby golf course under the feeble light of a gibbous moon, then scattered the granules on a fairway where, previously, Arnold always shot under par.

The month dragged on as Dori and I sorted out Arnold's tangled affairs. Nothing is as depressing as going through a deceased parent's wardrobe before consigning it all – from sports jackets that don't fit to woefully outmoded ties – to the Salvation Army. Dori put the house on the market and it sold, but the proceeds barely equaled Arnold's debts, or so I was told. Although my father had cultivated the image of affluence by driving a Jag, playing lots of tennis and golf, there had never been an economic foundation to justify his lifestyle. We lived in one house of cards after another and the wind never ceased.

I consulted a lawyer in hopes of bringing a negligence suit against the gas company in Elizabeth where the electrocution had occurred, but the shyster wanted a large retainer up front. As broke then as I am now, no claim was ever filed.

And so, at the conclusion of the month-long ordeal in Watchung, I drove the MGB north to Vermont, determined to never again set foot within the accursed state of New Jersey. Dori kept the Jag and soon departed as well. The immensity of the world swallowed her and I lost all contact. Twenty-seven years later I made contact with an uncle, the sole survivor of five brothers, only to learn of his lingering suspicion that Arnold's death had not been an accident.

R.H.A. Williams

I know nothing about my father's life as a child or a young man, but clues abound in an old, tattered photo album and in an ancient scrapbook filled with yellow newspaper clippings. The photographs portray Arnold, his four brothers and my paternal grandparents – the venerable ancestors that comprise the ongoing tragicomedy of my line.

My favorite photo shows Arnold sitting in the open cockpit of a Spitfire. Dark goggles shield his eyes – but not his grin – in a photo taken upon his return from a round of golf. A true story; only an arrogant young RAF officer like Arnold could've borrowed a Spitfire, flown to a golf course and landed on a fairway, then played eighteen holes before flying back to base.

9. Arnold in a Spitfire

For many years I displayed no photos of my father where they could be viewed on a daily basis. Perhaps it was the Spitfire's reputation as the most lethal weapon of its day that finally allowed me to overcome the denial of his very existence. (After all the disciplinary beatings and ferocious psychological abuse I underwent as a child, is it any wonder I wanted no reminder?)

Another photo features my father in his prime, taken in mid-kick on a rugby pitch and surrounded by mud-spattered rugby players. Strong, agile and absolutely bursting with pugnacious aggression, Arnold was an alpha-male among his fellow rugby wolves. Rugger, as it is known in England, has never been a sport for the timid or the weak; every scrum practically guarantees bloody shins, a dislocated shoulder or a broken collarbone. For reasons more psychological than meteorological, the game is invariably played on the bleakest gray days in November, preferably amidst fog and drizzle, with a temperature that hovers at 37 degrees.

The genetic endowment that served my father so well on the rugby pitch also enabled him to excel in the Royal Air Force, first as a test pilot and then a fighter pilot. Adolph Hitler cared nothing for rugby and I'm certain that had the Second World War not intervened, Arnold's athletic fame would've spread beyond the northern English seaside city of South Shields.

10. Arnold in mid-kick

Fraught with deadly peril, the life expectancy for a fighter pilot was not much greater than that of a test pilot, yet Arnold survived both, although just barely. Once, while at 30,000 feet in a single-engine Hurricane, the fighter's prop blades detached and he suddenly found himself gliding like a brick. The crash-landing broke his neck.

Later, after the Luftwafta shot him down and he "pranged his kite," as the RAF pilots were wont to say with such jaunty insouciance, the rescue team carried him into hospital on a stretcher with a second broken neck. One of the nurses caught sight of him and said, "Christ, it's him again."

Arnold met Moira when she was a WAAF radio operator (and that, believe it or not, is the sum extent of my knowledge of her.) Did they speak to one another over the airwaves before meeting? Did she listen to his curses as

German machine gun bullets punctured his aircraft? I'll never know. After the war they immigrated to America, where they were married. I was conceived at Niagara Falls and nine months later, Dr. Johnson hoisted me aloft by my ankles and then smacked my glistening bottom to evoke an indignant, yet reassuring howl.

Two years later, Moira succumbed to bone-marrow cancer. Thus began a phase in my father's life devoted to the challenges of raising a small child while grappling with continual economic instability. The subsequent scramble for income included marketing do-it-yourself uranium prospecting kits, selling real estate and ultimately a job selling industrial cleaning chemicals; the latter directly responsible for the alleged accidental electrocution. Arnold came to the United States to pursue a career in aviation, but a commercial pilot's license required citizenship, which in turn required a seven-year residency. By the end of that period he was considered too old to enter the field. Why he didn't immediately return to England to enjoy a career as a commercial pilot is another question that must remain unanswered.

***

As a child I witnessed Arnold's growing interest in the occult, as well as his fondness for the irreverent. (Is it any wonder I developed a taste for the latter and applied it to the former?) Speaking of superstition, the Bible never intruded on my consciousness. Instead, Fate and Mad Magazine informed my childhood with mysterious and peculiar prognostications by the likes of Madame Blavatsky. Don Martin's cartoons in Mad Magazine always featured smiling maniacs swiveling around in gigantic shoes whose tips hinged straight up.

Nostradamus only knows how many séances our aged housekeeper, Mrs. Parmley, conducted in the attic. Perhaps Arnold's interest in the occult stemmed from a desire to contact Moira. Or, more likely, her loss dealt a blow to his equilibrium from which he never recovered. In any event, by the time I was five, he'd transferred his spiritual yen to Zen, a form of Buddhism in which, according to my Random House Dictionary, "the student gains enlightenment by the most direct means possible," whatever that means. For Arnold, it meant starting each day with a round of strenuous exercise followed by ten minutes in a full headstand. Every morning when I padded to the kitchen for a bowl of Cheerios, there he was – upside down in the middle of the living room, face crimson and moist with sweat.

My expulsion from nursery school formed an accurate prelude to my next twelve years of academic strife. Don't ask me why I was expelled, as it would require a deep hypnotic trance and questioning to dredge up the memory. One of the primary causes of my dismal academic performance stemmed from frequent relocation: Between fifth grade and high school I moved from Hackensack, to Garwood, to Nutley, to Maplewood, to Berkeley Heights and then to New Providence. No sooner had I begun to adjust to a new school than it was time to move again. And each time, I exhibited a diminished tendency to do my homework or stay awake in algebra class.

From the day in fourth grade when I was caught forging Arnold's signature on a bad report card, to the day I received a complimentary high school diploma, my grades descended to D minus and hovered there. By then, however, I'd perfected a freehand technique for duplicating his signature, avoiding the incriminating smudges left by my earlier reliance on carbon paper.

Arnold tried repeatedly to instruct me in algebra, especially during long drives. I dreaded the inevitable moment when polynomials raised their ugly heads. Too bad he never explained how it was possible to multiply letters. Accustomed to arithmetic with numbers, the thought of multiplying A and B was pure gibberish, and this, of course, convinced Arnold that I was a hopeless idiot. He invariably exploded with rage and used his quick hands to slap me silly as he drove; and as my resentment at such treatment increased, so too did the psychological distance between us, until eventually we achieved absolute polarization.

During my senior year of high school I brazenly signed each odious report card myself. If the school authorities were aware of my extracurricular penmanship, they didn't let on. Perhaps they thought I had enough problems already.

In any event, Arnold viewed me as the embodiment of his worst fears – a pot-smoking, guitar-playing deadbeat. Nothing could alter his conviction that I'd deliberately thwarted his efforts to inculcate the attributes of a "gentleman" – a word freighted with Empire and touted from my infancy to represent the very pinnacle of human behavior. Was I the only child under strict orders to address my father as "sir" and to carry a clean handkerchief in my pocket at all times? I strongly suspect that Arnold's idea of a model son resembled the salty tar onboard Gilbert and Sullivan's HMS Pinafore, who, when queried by the Monarch of the Sea, snaps smartly to attention, salutes and sings… "Quite well, and you sir?"

Roland Humphrey Arnold Williams died in August of 1969 and as I mentioned, accidental electrocution was recorded as the cause of death, but was it really an accident, or did Dori, his alleged wife, deliberately tip over a bucket of water while he operated a floor-buffing machine? Had she really taken out a huge life insurance policy on him only a month before, as my uncle asserted? Once again, I'll never know the truth – a condition I've come to expect in regard to all matters of any importance. Arnold never once spoke to me about his financial affairs or the way the economic world operates. In fact, the only good advice he ever imparted, other than on the tennis court, concerned the need for great care and attention when indulging in foreplay with a woman!

All such ambiguity aside, if asked to identify the positive traits I derived from my father, I'd demonstrate my superb vocabulary and then my excellent form on the tennis court. Although the origin of my exemplary sense of ethics remains a mystery, I suspect here, too, Arnold is somehow to blame. It's been 40 years since his death. Now, however, whenever I look at his photograph, either sitting in a Spitfire, or on the rugby pitch, I feel a glimmer of pride and affection. How poignant to consider that I was able to forgive him only upon attaining the same age at which he died.

Although the details of Arnold's childhood will remain obscure forever, I've tried to fill in one or two of the largest gaps by visiting the house in England where he and his four brothers were raised. A photograph taken of me standing at the gate at 15 Vespasian Street reveals little change in the building from one taken on the same spot in 1922. The current occupant emerged as I stood there pondering the mystery of continuity and loss. I introduced myself and explained why I'd traveled so far to loiter outside his door. He was a decent chap and invited me in for a quick look round. The interior resonated with the faint echoes of history; the only incongruous detail was the bong on a shelf in the kitchen.

Historians agree that Britain owes its existence to the Royal Air Force, to those doughty pilots that thwarted Hitler's invasion plans. And so, in hopes of forging yet another vicarious connection to a deceased parent, I rode the Tube from London to the RAF Museum in Hendon. There, where the remaining pilots still alive are known reverentially as "the Few," I caressed the aileron of a Spitfire and felt a mixture of elation and sadness. The museum's gift shop supplied me with a T-shirt emblazoned with a Spitfire, a coffee mug similarly adorned and a miniature Spitfire that now adheres magnetically to my refrigerator door.

Since then I've spent months learning to fly a Spitfire Mark IV, using a Microsoft Combat Flight Simulator on my computer. Day after day, joystick in hand, I bank at three hundred miles an hour and take virtual flights from airfields such as Croydon, Fowlmere or Hawkinge. Sometimes I take on the entire Luftwafta in a dogfight called "clobber college" by the computer program. I press the trigger to fire all eight cannons and destroy one ME-109 after another, chuckling all the while at my increasingly deadly prowess.

In all the years since Arnold's death I've achieved goals that are academic, musical and artistic – more than enough to rectify his incorrect assessment of my potential. I've even successfully undergone several semesters of remedial algebra. And, I'm delighted to say, not once since my report-card-forging days as a senior in high school have I been tempted to sign a document with a signature other than my own.

Magus Blacklaw

Doug and his ersatz bride vacated the apartment on Brookline Street on schedule and drove out of the city. Jerry followed in a U-haul van loaded with drums, furniture, guitars and optimism. After crossing the Massachusetts border, they traversed New Hampshire and entered what the Vermont roadmap referred to as "The Beckoning Country," a phrase that state officials have subsequently expunged after realizing (too late) that hordes of flatlanders were indeed responding to the call. The newest arrivals moved into the venerable farmhouse in Ira before the green glory of summer acceded to the inevitability of fall. A month later I departed Watchung and drove north in the MGB I'd inherited, to join them. Once in Ira, I crossed the narrow bridge that spanned a gently trickling stream – the boundary between the harsh realities of the outer world and the peaceful haven where our musical dreams would surely flourish.

To celebrate our reunion, Doug, Diane, Jerry and I each swallowed a tablet of synthetic mescaline acquired from a member of the Living Theatre, in Cambridge. Unaware that one tab equaled four doses, we soon understood why there's a law against the stuff: We tripped happily for a couple of hours before the hallucinogen's second stage kicked in – a mighty Atlas booster that flung us into orbit without the benefit of spacesuits. My brain crackled with an excessive payload of neurotransmitters; my eyes dilated as wide as ping-pong balls while my Ampex tape recorder grinned fiendishly. I watched Doug melt into a burbling puddle behind his drums. Jerry was too stoned to play his guitar. He gripped the arms of his chair as sweat poured from his brow and the floral patterns on the faded wallpaper boiled malevolently.

"Every man for himself," I muttered as I stumbled out the door clutching a jacket and a canteen filled with water. Our farmhouse lay at the foot of Herrick Mountain, a lonely, 3000-foot peak carpeted with maple, oak and beech trees aflame with brilliant autumn color. My only hope of survival lay in avoiding all traces of civilization, so I climbed into the forest's supernal embrace. Before long I could no longer distinguish between reality and the invisible jackhammer embossing Day-Glo animation on my forehead, so I sprawled on my back on a crisp carpet of fallen leaves and stared at the writhing canopy above. Spores and fungi absorbed the nutrients of my flesh. Tendrils of vegetation reached through my skeletal ribs as my bones turned to powder. The atoms I once called my own lost cohesion and were absorbed into the galactic whirligig from whence they came. Billions of years flashed by and an entirely new solar system accreted from cosmic dust. The plasma miasma disgorged a tiny bolus; the molten planet cooled...gases condensed and lightning lashed the primordial soup into a bubbling stew of amino acids. Molecules twitched and the very first living cell divided in two. Evolution kicked into overdrive; dinosaurs gave way to small furry mammals; humans climbed down from the trees, and when I regained consciousness, I'd completed one revolution on the great MG wire-wheel of Life.

11. Magus Blacklaw

We survived the psychotropic ordeal, recovered most of our wits and were just about to get down to some serious rehearsing when the mailman delivered three sinister brown envelopes, one for Doug, one for Jerry and one for me. One glance at the return address and I knew they spelled Trouble. I tore the envelope open and learned that the United States Federal Government and the U.S. Army required my presence – in Newark – for a pre-induction physical.

"Not again!" I yelped at the prospect of yet another trip to the blighted state of my origin. (I knew of only one place worse than Newark and that was Mordor.) More terrified of New Jersey than Viet Nam, the Army's explicit guarantee of lengthy incarceration (for truancy) persuaded me to comply.

In the fall of 1969, American troop strength in Viet Nam increased daily, as did the number of casualties zipped into the body bags we watched on the TV news. Confronted by Uncle Sam's order to submit to a process that could very well result in my occupying a bag of my own, I faced several options: Flee to Canada, join the Navy or find some other method for evading the draft. I didn't have the moral conviction to declare myself a Conscientious Objector; I was an objector but not the least bit conscientious. Nor did I give a hoot that the domino theory might topple all of Southeast Asia – the Communists could have the wretched place for all I cared. Defending one's country against a genuine threat, like Hitler, was one thing, but fighting and dying for some dubious socio-political cause was another. Only two things were certain: My draft card had long since gone up in flames and I knew, come what may, I would never be in the Army. Still, I needed a simple but effective means of convincing the draft board of this fact. I contacted a psychologist known for his anti-war stance.

Dr. X agreed to conduct one session a week, for a month, in his office in Summit, New Jersey. The task of convincing him that I was out of my mind was easy; I simply told the truth and blathered on about childhood beatings, low self-esteem, alienation and the ensuing emotional turmoil. "Sometimes, when I get frustrated my brain seems to explode with a shower of golden sparks, just like the computer blowing up on the starship Enterprise," I admitted.

"Hmmm," said Dr. X as he jotted something down on a pad. Not once during our sessions did I mention Viet Nam. But five minutes before we concluded my final visit I said, "Oh, by the way. I have a pre-induction physical tomorrow morning. Could you write me a letter?"

The next day dawned gray and clammy. The Federal Building in Newark looked as sinister as Tolkien's tower of Orthanc. I entered its forbidding portals armed neither with a sword nor a garment fashioned from mithril, only the letter from Dr. X. For the next eight hours, accompanied by hundreds of other Jersey apes clad only in underwear, I waited in long lines and endured a battery of physical inspections. I recognized many of my former classmates from high school – Greasers, Surfers, Future Cops and Mafia Hit-Men Trainees – all awaiting their turn to bend over and "spread 'em" so a repulsive old federal employee could inspect anal sphincters! (I had no clue what he was looking for and was not about to ask.)

The day wore on. At noon we ate a grim, starchy lunch in the federal Building's cafeteria, before moving on to still more humiliating inspections. It wasn't till four in the afternoon before I confronted an Army psychologist and handed him the terse letter. A miracle of brevity, it said, "If this man is inducted, breakdown will occur."

I received an instant 4-F. "No punji spikes for me," I said with considerable relief.

Doug had been counting on his own psychological quirks to exempt him from the draft, but the Army shrink was not impressed with his thick folder of diagnostic reports. Our drummer evaded the draft, but flat feet saved his overweight hide. Jerry also avoided conscription, I'm not sure why, perhaps due to complications stemming from the effects of Catholicism and Guilt. But regardless, we skipped through the halls of the Federal Building towards the exit like the tin-man, the scarecrow and the cowardly lion. Ira now awaited us, glowing on the distant horizon like the Emerald City of Oz.

***

Once again ensconced in our idyllic, country retreat, we congratulated one another on having avoided the Army's murderous, totalitarian clutches.

There would be no boot camp, nor a million spuds to peel, nor bayonet practice for us. And no body bags either. But now we faced the task of learning an entire repertoire, acquiring a PA system and finding gigs for our fledgling band. Howard came through with rent money and one speaker column, not an impressive piece of gear, but a start. Doug solved the problem of choosing a name for the band by suggesting "Magus Blacklaw," a character in a sci-fi paperback, a so-called "space-wizard" that reminded him of me.

The living room became our practice studio; Jerry's Twin Reverb amp and my Carlson bass cabinets stood on either side of Doug's Slingerland drums. We learned a handful of tunes – "Stone Free" by Hendrix, "Feelin' Alright" by Traffic and "You Ain't Going Nowhere" by the Byrds. I sang a Moby Grape tune called "Ain't No Use," an apt title since my voice was so thin and amorphous it wouldn't disturb a sleeping chipmunk. We played well and sounded good, but as a trio, Magus Blacklaw was incomplete. We needed a strong lead vocalist.

The city of Rutland was twenty-miles away, the second largest city in the state, large enough to support a music store. We visited Melody Music and encountered Buf Spaulding, a thin, wiry Vermonter with more imagination than common sense. The first time I saw Buf he was seated, tilted back in a chair with his roller-skate shod feet resting atop a cluttered desk, while eating pizza from atop a crash cymbal! He wore a ski-cap with a knitted appurtenance that projected five inches from his brow, like the blunted horn of a unicorn. The telephone rang. He picked it up and said, "Right here, Captain Phallic to the rescue…what's that? My terms? No money down and the rest of your life to pay!"

Jerry and I exchanged glances and a telepathic assessment, "This guy's nuts." Then we browsed around and inspected the store's merchandise – a collection of cheesy electronic organs made in Japan, Univox amplifiers, a Vox teardrop-shaped electric bass, various electric guitars, drum-kits, accordions, fiddles and, believe it or not, a treasure-trove of Gibson arch-top jazz guitars – worth a small fortune today, but completely ignored by the public then.

Buf's only claim to musical fame consisted of having once played rhythm guitar in The Rejects, a band named with uncanny prescience. We didn't know it at the time, but Buf had already reached the apogee of his trajectory and was a casualty just waiting to happen. But before his inexorable slide into the quagmire of drugs, alcohol, and schizophrenia, he ran the store with a mixture of good intentions, naiveté and dumb luck. Never a hard-nosed businessman, Buf specialized in hair-brained schemes to promote outdoor rock concerts. (Like the infamous Max's Party, held deep in the Northeast Kingdom, an event that resulted in naked, tripping hippies urinating on the lawns of the residents of East Charleston, in broad daylight).

As the nerve center of Rutland's miniature music scene, Melody Music was our only source of guitar strings or drumsticks and, with any luck, the contacts that would lead us to a vocalist. But after numerous fruitless auditions, including one with an unfortunate polio victim on crutches, we realized that finding a good singer made hen's teeth seem plentiful.

Fall drifted by and winter loomed. The sky grew turgid with threatening clouds and the temperature slowly descended. Magus Blacklaw still had no singer. We practiced less and less, although Doug and Diane were having a wonderful time nibbling on each other's ears, cavorting with their golden retriever puppy, drinking hot chocolate and tacking leather swatches onto old steamer trunks. One afternoon Doug called a meeting. "I've decided not to play drums anymore," he announced. "Diane and I are going to live here, so the two of you will have to leave."

I was stunned by the unprecedented treachery. After devoting months to finding a house, moving to Vermont and then withstanding the collective might of the U.S. Army (and the Living Theater), the band was undone by one of its own! I had no choice but to pack my belongings into the used Econoline van I'd purchased to haul the band's gear to gigs that would never materialize.

To the north lay Waitsfield, scene of my earliest days on skis, and the only other part of the state I knew anything about. It seemed the logical choice at the time, so I rented a small cabin and settled in for a lonely winter devoted to skiing and practicing the bass. Jerry arrived but stayed only briefly before returning to New Providence, to brood in the little room in the house he'd grown up in.

I never saw Doug or Diane again.

Kingdom Come

By 1969, the Dipsy Doodle had closed and that left only two places in the Waitsfield valley where one could hear (or play) rock 'n roll – the Blue Tooth and Gallagher's. Vermont groups such as Jimmy T and The Cobras alternated with The Thunderbolts and John Cassel's band, along with a dozen others from out of state, but they always arrived with a full complement of musicians. And so, I was the odd bass-man out.

As a full-time ski-bum I met others similarly addicted to the adrenalin rush derived from strapping on a pair of Head Skis – narrow, black and extremely slippery rocket sleds – then plummeting down the giddy precipices at Mad River Glen. There, I met Laurie, a vivacious blonde who also had nothing better to do than pursue flight without the benefit of wings. Laurie shared a rundown farmhouse on Route 17 with a number of ski bums, a structure that has subsequently housed two ethnic restaurants. I don't remember who came up with the idea, but someone suggested that we should convert the barn into a nightclub!

We named our enterprise "Doctor P.R. White's Music Hutchery," and I designed a poster that featured a white rabbit with hypnotic swirling eyes. We cleaned out the barn and removed pieces of rusty farm machinery and numerous bales of obsolete hay. We built a stage and I installed my stereo. Phil Lundlad set up a light show similar to Joshua's Lights at the Filmore East – a system that used glass bowls, colored oil and water to create intricate patterns that were then projected onto the blank wall behind the stage. Someone plowed the snow from the adjacent field and it became our parking lot. We hired The Texas Drivers, a local band, then fired up all three woodstoves and opened our door for business on Christmas night. It cost five bucks to get in, money we used to pay the band.

Opening night was a success, but we had no license to operate a bar, no bouncer, no fire extinguishers, no running water, no bathrooms, damn little heat and absolutely no intention of prohibiting the consumption of booze or illicit substances. We were, however, smart enough not to push our luck and opened for the second (and last) time on New Year's Eve.

Two days later, the Board of Health swooped down and nailed the barn door shut while Laurie and I watched from behind a curtained window in her house. The authorities never did learn who perpetrated such an affront to all deemed sacred by the Chamber of Commerce. It was a simpler time, to be sure, unlike today – where a similar breach would summon a swift intervention by the State Police.

***

The great blizzard of 1970 inundated the entire northeast beneath a single monstrous snowflake hundreds of miles wide and five feet thick. It hit the ground with a loud WHUMP! and provided a superb ski season – the slopes suddenly clogged with more deep powder than anyone had seen in decades.

My telephone rang one evening. It was Ron, the guitarist from the banished Prince Valiant Strolling Electric Rock Band. "Greetings from sunny California," he said. "I have a new group and we need a bass player. Would you be interested in joining us?"

"Let me think about it," I replied. "I'll get back to you."

After months of skiing and little else, my dream of becoming a professional musician wasn't getting any closer to reality. The end of winter was in sight, and perhaps now was the time to take a bold step. I told Laurie about Ron's offer. "Can I come too?" she asked. "I'm ready for some warm weather and I can help drive."

I consented, although at the time, our relationship was Platonic; the Aristotelian would have to wait. Once again I loaded the Econoline van with my bass and amp and stored the MG at a friend's. Laurie traveled light and carried only her credit card, one small suitcase, a battery-powered 8-track player and a box of tapes that included music by Pure Prairie League, Leon Russell and BB King. We set forth on a bright zero-degree morning as picturesque wood-smoke billowed from chimneys and the rising sun gilded the mountaintops. We celebrated our departure by smoking a bowl of weed and bidding good riddance to the frozen serenity of the Green Mountains. Once beyond the New York Thruway and past the swarming hive of New Jersey, we turned west and faced the vast empty expanse of America. We drove day and night, stopping only for food and gas. Too frugal to spend money on a motel, we took turns at the wheel or sleeping in the back of the van, huddled in a sleeping bag atop my Carlson speaker cabinets. The highway became an endless blur as we inched our way across the continent, through treacherous ice storms, sleet and freezing fog. I felt like the last Okie to abandon the dustbowl – enticed by the enduring bait-and-switch mythos of the Golden West – my rattling flivver heaped high with rickety furniture, dented washbasins and an empty birdcage.

Five days later we arrived at Ron's apartment in Hollywood – disheveled, grimy and exhausted. With one mighty flea-leap we'd vaulted from the pristine Waitsfield valley to the smog-choked San Fernando Valley, out of the stone-cold frying pan and definitely into the fire. From that first painful inhalation of mustard-yellow California smog, to the ceaseless torrent of vehicles congesting the freeways, I was psychologically unprepared for Los Angeles.

Ron and his flouncing partner Sean welcomed us into their apartment on bustling Barham Boulevard. Laurie and I promptly collapsed onto foam pads laid out on the living room floor, where we lay like cadavers for the next twelve hours.

The following day Ron prepared a festive Italian dinner to celebrate our arrival. We all sat around a white Formica-topped table with our plates piled high with spaghetti, steaming marinara sauce and green salad. Sean filled four goblets to the brim with red wine. Without warning, one of the table legs collapsed and our feast lurched violently. Ron and I grabbed the edges of the table but succeeded only in catapulting everything into the air. Gobs of pasta, salad and our wineglasses achieved the briefest instant of weightlessness before splattering to the floor.

"I've been meaning to fix that table leg," said Ron sheepishly.

I soon learned that the band I'd been told was waiting for me did not exist; the perfect metaphor for Hollywood, a zone where reality was so elusive I rarely, if ever, caught a glimpse. Undaunted, I registered with the Hollywood Musician's Referral Service, and then began a series of auditions that took me from one end of the San Fernando Valley to the other. Day after day, week after week, I encountered two categories of players: Well-meaning (but hopeless) amateurs, or seasoned professionals who looked at me and saw a well-meaning (but hopeful) amateur.

For three months I generated smog on the freeways and chased leads, sometimes doing two auditions in one day. It was a strange place; one day I answered a call from a group claiming to need a bass player, but they turned out to be a troupe of homosexual groupies who, for reasons beyond my comprehension, sought only bass players!

Instead of driving straight back to Vermont, I sharpened my criteria for dealing with unknown contacts on the phone. In short, I was learning. Obliged, on a daily basis, to weed out the inept, the delusional and the insane, there were times when the only way to determine a band's veracity (or potential) was to meet them in person. Like the time I ventured into a blighted neighborhood in Watts County (where wisps of smoke still curled from the rubble-strewn wreckage created by the riots). There, I met the members of Duke's Soul Band. We played rhythm and blues for a couple of hours and although I was the only white boy for miles, they hired me on the spot.

"Those guys must really like my playing," I later told Laurie, "or else they're desperate." But by then I, too, was desperate. But as the only honky in Duke's Soul Band, I enjoyed a certain degree of diplomatic immunity in the all-black neighborhood. Halfway through each rehearsal we took a break, went outside and climbed into Monty's low-slung, chartreuse Cadillac – the one with purple pompoms dangling around the rear window.

"Monty, this here's our new bass man," said Duke as we cruised slowly around the block. "I want you to treat him right." The driver smiled from beneath his mohair fedora and then handed me a joint the size of a Havana cigar, something I'd never seen before.

"It's a splif, mon," he said. Monty was the neighborhood dope dealer and quite possibly the prototype for Big Bad Leroy Brown. The splif went round and we smeared our eyes on "the crazy cult goddess" (as in Donovan's song). Then we stumbled back into the house to play the blues for an audience of slumping winos guzzling from bottles in brown paper bags.

Although Duke's Band sounded good, it didn't take long to realize that everyone involved was too stoned to actually go out and hustle up a gig.

I continued my search.

The daily auditions exposed me to another formidable aspect of the LA environment, the police. A veritable army of identical Terminators on Harleys, they had stainless steel teeth, wore shiny blue helmets and black leather boots laced to the knees. Their numbers exceeded the armed forces of many small countries – an insidious rolling militia that made Vermont cops look like a diminutive sorority of old ladies in rust-bitten Chevy Novas. There were other daunting factions on Harleys as well. An offshoot of the Hell's Angels, the Mother Nature Fuckers liked nothing better than a pitched battle with the LAPD, especially on a tranquil Sunday afternoon. It was on just such an afternoon, during an outdoor concert in a park, when the police cut off the band's electricity in mid-song. "This is an illegal gathering," an officer declared through a bullhorn. "You are hereby ordered to disperse immediately!"

The bikers responded with a "FUCK YOU!" chorus and a salvo of empty beer bottles that shattered a police cruiser's windshield into lacey filigrees. People fled as more bottles flew. Broken glass garnished the pavement with sharp glittering fragments. I raced to my van, opened the side door and pulled in as many innocent spectators as it would hold. Within minutes a SWAT truck sped into the park and squealed to a halt. The back doors burst open and out jumped a dozen fully armored combat units swinging clubs and firing tear-gas. A carpet of tire-shredding glass shards prevented our escape, so we sat and peered through the van's panoramic windshield as the conflict raged. I was reminded of having watched Roman legionnaires battling barbarian hordes on a drive-in movie screen. The matinee was a double feature, incidentally...Woodstock, followed by Altamont.

***

One predictably sunny LA afternoon the musician's referral service sent me to the palpitating heart of Sunset Boulevard – the fabled strip – where every passing vehicle was either a Porsche convertible driven by a record company PR man or a VW bus filled with stoned rock 'n rollers. The strip throbbed with every imaginable vice, plus a great many beyond my scope. The sidewalk teemed with leggy teenyboppers hell-bent on early maturation, tourists from the Midwest, hookers, hustlers, Hari Krishnas, Jesus freaks, drug dealers and demented poets in the incandescent bloom of madness.

My directions brought me into the parking lot alongside the Pleasure Dome, a boutique devoted to erotic lingerie undreamed of by Kubla Kahn. Around back, I entered a spacious studio built according to the dictates of modern architecture, but now in a state of decay – a distinctly Californian blend of the Jetsons meet the Flintstones. It looked as if I'd stumbled upon the ruins of an advanced civilization (which was precisely the case).

By now I understood that my image was as important as my bass playing; I wore faded jeans and a purple silk guru shirt with sleeves that grew wider at the wrist – a sultan's smock ideal for harem creeping, a garment that went well with my sphinx-like wedge of curly hair.

A guy with shoulder length auburn locks similar to the glossy fur of a purebred Afghan hound approached. "I'm Frank," he said, pushing aside the ear-like drape of hair that framed an aristocratic face ideally suited for a rock star. "You must be the bass player we've been expecting. Bring your gear in and I'll introduce you to my band."

It didn't take long to set up my twin Carlson speaker cabinets and switch on a 60-watt Traynor bass amplifier, a pathetically underpowered amp prone to annoying microphonic noise whenever the power tubes vibrated. I strapped on my cherry-red Gibson EB-2 bass guitar and tuned up. Frank pointed to the mysterious figure seated in semi-darkness behind a Hammond organ, a bearded individual wearing a dark suit, sunglasses and a fez.

"That's Richard," said Frank. "He thinks he's Orson Welles. And that's Sid on guitar; he thinks about guitar, dope and pussy. And that's Mitch on the drums, I'm not sure he thinks at all."

Frank handed me some charts and said, "These are my original tunes. Take a minute and look 'em over. We've been up the creek without a bass and time's running out."

"What do you mean?" I asked.

"We've only got eight days left to prepare for the arrival of a hotshot producer, flying out from New York to hear us. If Mr. Big likes my material, he'll sign the band."

"Nothing like a little incentive," I replied.

For the next two hours we played all ten of Frank's tunes. The lyrics were interesting. He sang well and gyrated like a properly debauched rock star. I supplied an energetic combination of foundation and embellishment on the bass. One song featured an anthem-like chorus and a memorable hook that sank in and has yet to let go.

"Far fuckin' out," said Frank. "You seem to know exactly what's right for my tunes. Consider yourself hired. Now all we have to do is decide on a name for the band. I've narrowed it down to Soma Crayola or Kingdom Come. Which do you prefer?"

"Kingdom Come," I replied. "It has a majestic quality."

"So be it," Frank decreed.

12. Kingdom Come

The afternoon elapsed and Frank departed. Richard and I went outside to sit under the trees bordering the Pleasure Dome's parking lot. "There are empty rooms behind the studio," he said. "You're welcome to move in. Leave your van where it is. No one will bother it."

Just then a dirty white Dodge van rolled in and parked nearby. The door opened and a rotund, older woman with a horsetail of lanky gray hair emerged. "Where's Frank?" she asked, "squirtin' around, drinkin' and whorin' with Jim, as usual?"

"Hi mom," said Richard, and then to me, "Frank and Jim Morrison are buddies."

The woman moved closer and sized me up with a formidable glare.

"This is Peter, our new bass player."

She scowled and continued to stare.

"My mother used to be one of the nurses in the asylum made famous in Ken Kesey's novel, 'One Flew Over the Cuckoo's Nest.' She knows too much about what went down so they shit-canned her. Now she's a gypsy and lives in her van."

I pointed to my Econoline and said, "I'm a gypsy too." She swiveled her eyes to my van, then fixed them on me once more.

"Peter is going to sleep in one of the extra rooms in the studio," said Richard. A wry smile creased the woman's face. I had not yet read Kesey's novel, so I didn't know what to make of the reference, but that night I discovered its implications – the crazy old cow thought she was still working at the asylum and locked me in my room! From then on I slept in my van.

And where was Laurie during all of this? She'd moved to Topanga Canyon to inhabit a tiny hut that had once housed beehives. I visited her and relished the peaceful alternative to Sunset Boulevard. The hut had an odd feature; every morning a parade of ants entered through a window, marched across the floor in an undeviating column, then up and out through the opposite window, a commuter's procession that ended at dusk.

Back in the Pleasure Dome; after honing Frank's songs to a razor's edge – enough songs for an album – I recorded them on my trusty Ampex

600. But on the day before the arrival of Mr. Big, I made the mistake of loaning the tape to Frank, after first extracting his solemn promise to return it the next day. Twenty-four hours later, on the evening of our big break, a Porsche crashed into the hydrant out front, which sent a 75-foot geyser jetting into the sultry air. An amusing sight but a bad omen. Mr. Big and his entourage arrived at the appointed hour; the band was ready but Frank never showed. We waited while the producer snorted coke and grew angrier by the minute. Finally, he looked at his Rolex and said, "Time's up." Then he stormed out the door.

Richard informed me that this wasn't the first time Frank had pushed a project to the brink of success before screwing it up. I left the Pleasure Dome the next morning and never saw Frank, or my tape, again. "I will never lose another recording," I vowed.

Manna

Drawn by an intriguing call from the musician's referral service, I again cruised the freeway's hydrocarbon-slicked ribbon. I'd become skilled at navigating the LA grid but when eight freeways intersected in a disorienting skein of bridges, loops, ramps and overheads, I felt like a tiny metal bolus descending into the belly of an asphalt whale. After an hour's drive through bumper-to-bumper traffic I turned off at the Anaheim exit and followed my directions to the gate of a vast automobile junkyard.

"So this is where the elephants go to die," I muttered as I viewed a blighted terrain of crumpled steel, shattered glass, oozing transmission fluid and one chained up "meaner than a junkyard dog" dog. The auto graveyard's northern border abutted Disneyland, the fountainhead of my television-addled childhood – the flickering font that introduced me to Davy Crockett and Donald Duck. Mythic and unapproachable till now, Walt's magic kingdom sprawled from the Foothills of Fractured Flivvers (at my feet) to the Matterhorn's artificial, snow-capped peak. It was as close as I'd ever get; in 1970, the Disney Authority denied entry to hairheads like me.

A wooden barn loomed amidst the automotive wreckage. Four figures stepped out and squinted in the late afternoon sun. Mechanics? No. Musicians. After the introductions, I set up my amp in the barn amidst the unknown potential of Hammond organ, electric guitar and a set of drums. Angled sunlight stabbed through myriad knotholes in the wall, piercing the dim interior with golden, pencil-thin shafts. We began to improvise. I whittled the air with a flat pick, carving fluid bass lines that pushed the music forward.

I realized that these were talented players, because when I shifted the tonal center or introduced rhythmic variations, they responded instantly.

Tall, thin and suave, Dennis played his Gibson Stereo guitar with effortless fluency in both jazz and rock idioms. Swain hailed from the Deep South and looked like a modern-day Tom Sawyer who'd traded in his raft for a Hammond B-3. He was a monster player and must've had six fingers on each hand, because he always persuaded that ponderous instrument to dance. Bobby, the drummer, bore a face-full of unkempt beard and hair down his back. He looked like a barefoot hillbilly from the Ozarks (with a name like Cousin Fernbelt) but he played drums with primal ferocity one moment and great delicacy the next.

Chuck, the group's lead vocalist, was a combination of Marine drill-sergeant and born-again, Bible-thumping Jesus freak. He was a teetotaler with a voice that cut like a plasma torch, and it was his idea to name the band Manna, no doubt inspired by the biblical nourishment he claimed to prefer.

The audition went very well. After an hour we stepped outside for a breather. "Check it out," said Cousin Fernbelt, pointing to an object dangling high above the Great Wall of Disney. I watched as a woman gripped a harness in her teeth and hung twirling in midair while she slid the length of a cable stretched from the peak of the Matterhorn all the way to Fantasyland. The twilight deepened as fireworks exploded high above the junkyard's crumpled metal corpses.

"This is fantastic," I said. "I've always wanted to visit America."

***

A week later Chuck called to say, "We've been looking for a bass player for a long time and so far, you're the closest we've come to finding our ideal. But since we need a strong high voice to complete our three-part harmony, we'd like to hire you on a temporary basis, while we continue auditioning."

"Fair enough," I said, all too aware of my weak vocal prowess.

So began a month of daily rehearsal in the perforated barn, surrounded by acres littered with latent automotive trauma. Since a gig's worth of material required at least thirty tunes, we learned current Top-40 hits as well as a jazzy arrangement of "Eleanor Rigby," "Gypsy" by The Moody Blues, "Make Me Smile" by Chicago and "Light My Fire" by The Doors. I was still homeless, but content to retire to my van each night, parked amidst mountains of crumpled metal that glinted in the moonlight.

When at last we were ready, Manna made its debut at Mr. Fat Fingers, a rock club in Garden Grove. I was under the impression that the gig had gone well until the corpulent club owner waddled over and said, "Your band sounds good, but the bass ain't heavy enough."

True, my Carlson cabinets and 60-watt Traynor amp were woefully insufficient to fill the room with vision-blurring low frequencies. The Ampeg SVT was the heavy artillery of the day (with eight 10-inch speakers and enough power to stun a mule), but they were expensive. To make matters worse, my Gibson bass lacked the authoritative punch of a Fender – even after the installation of a pickup custom-made by Doc Kaufman (Leo Fender's earliest partner).

The band rented a house near the ocean in Laguna Beach, a single-story dwelling flanked on all sides by marijuana dealers. Everyone in the band got to live inside except me; my blue van continued to be a rolling bedroom and I had to be content to eat and shower in the house, swim in the Pacific and play as many gigs as possible before they cut me loose. Is it any wonder I felt as insecure as a bug clinging to a windshield? I had little money, my bass wasn't "heavy" enough and I expected to be fired any day.

13. Manna playing an outdoor party

This state of limbo persisted for the next few months, a time when Manna played all sorts of bizarre venues; such as "Daisy May's," a strip club where the dancer's bobbling boobs were a distraction, but infinitely preferable to the hideous dive in Ventura where a drunken motorcycle gang decapitated live chickens and cheered uproariously as the poor headless creatures flapped around and bled all over everything.

Manna scored a regular gig at a club in Newport Beach. Feliciano's (yes, owned by Jose) featured two bands that played simultaneously at opposite ends of a large L-shaped room. The other group, a Vegas style showband, wore bouffant hairdos, rhinestone-studded, white jump suits and specialized in music such as "The Age of Aquarius." We, on the other hand, staggered onstage reeking of the black hashish known as "primo" to play Top-40 tunes that included spacey, twenty minute jams that sounded like Pink Floyd meets Frankenstein.

The band auditioned bass players before each gig at Feliciano's, drawing upon an inexhaustible supply of musicians that brought with them models of every bass guitar ever manufactured…Fenders, Gibsons, Epiphones, Harmonys, Carvins, Rickenbachers and a Hofner or two. Each night I sat and listened as the contestants auditioned.

"Nope!" I shouted. "Next!"

My time with Manna was fast running out.

Inevitably, the ideal bass player showed up and Manna hired him. Bruce wasn't at all insecure. He had perfect hair, a beautiful blonde girlfriend, played flawlessly, sang like a bird and owned, you guessed it, an Ampeg SVT. By that time, I'd had enough of California. LA was too crazy. There were too many people, too many cars and way too many cops. I'd grown weary of one never-changing season, so rather than pursue another band, I decided to head back east.

On the night before my departure, I went to a party in a house in the hills above Laguna Beach. Someone at the party, under some dubious pretext, persuaded everyone there (except me) to write his or her name and address on a sheet of paper. The air quickly filled with hash smoke, music and laughter. The phone rang and we received a tip that a police raid was imminent. People immediately dove through open windows, climbed down tree limbs from the second story and sprinted into the darkness. I jumped into a VW bus and we sped away.

"What about that list of names and addresses?" I asked. "It's still on the table in the living room!" We turned around and raced back. No sign of the police, so I dashed into the house and grabbed the incriminating document. After a second clean getaway, the party reconvened in a different location and we celebrated by smoking more opiated hash.

Eventually I collapsed into an empty bed and fell into a deep, dream-polluted sleep. When I arose the next morning, the new bass player's beautiful blonde girlfriend greeted me in the kitchen, handed me a cup of hot coffee and said, "Good morning, Peter. Too bad you missed the orgy last night. We tried to wake you, but you were dead."

The Antelope Band

The hazy ocher smear of air pollution gradually faded in my rearview mirror as I left the LA basin, headed east. It was December and winter pursued me at a gallop as I crossed the Mojave Desert and threaded my way through Needles, then up into the mountains of northern Arizona where the air grew cold. My Ford Conestoga contained everything I needed for the journey except whiskey, a Winchester and a wench.

At dusk I rounded a sharp bend and entered the lonely outpost of Jerome. A ghostly full moon rose above a canyon wall and bathed the empty town in cold reflected light. Nothing moved except tumbleweed – the silence broken only by an extinct saloon's weather-beaten sign creaking with each gust of wind. The dust-whipped street reminded me of a scene from High Noon after the climactic shoot-out. No horses though, only a derelict police car up on blocks, as if the victim of tire-eating vultures. The skeletal remains of a house of ill repute stood on the far side of a gulch, inhabited only by forgotten memories. I imagined what it must've been like a century ago when the mine produced ore, whiskey flowed, chorus girls kicked their legs and a piano player earned his keep in the saloon. But in 1970, only a handful of stubborn souls eked out an existence in Jerome, clinging to the rocks as stoically as lichen.

There was no live music being played in Jerome, so I drove on.

Alone, thousands of miles from any familiar point of reference, as itinerant as an armadillo, I had nary a clue where I might find a friend, a home or a band. The isolation grew oppressive. I swept the dial but the radio offered no relief. Caught between the choice of thundering evangelical zealots and traditional country and western, I chose silence.

The tedious hours behind the wheel gave me ample time to stew in my own juices. Still undeterred, I looked upon my latest musical fiasco as one more valuable lesson in how to be a professional musician. But the question remained, where to look next?

"What the hell," I said. "I'm twenty-one years old, bursting with rude, animal health, as independent as a rattlesnake and as resilient as a prairie dog. Something will turn up. It always does." (Unless, of course, the prairie dog falls victim to the snake, at which point the latter enjoys a good meal at the expense of my analogy.)

Fortunately, a safe haven awaited back in New Providence. At that time my friend Rob, from The Owsley Elevator, was in England, playing bass in a folk duo, so when his father offered me a place to stay while I caught my breath and sorted things out, I gratefully accepted. (Bob has always treated me like a second son, God bless him.)

I pushed on through the cold, yawning emptiness of the southwest. All color had drained from the land, leaving only a lifeless dun carpet traversed by countless tractor-trailer trucks that buffeted my van with ferocious windblasts as they hurtled past. I still slept in the van, unwilling to fork over a single greenback for anything except food and gas, regardless of my need for a hot shower, a home-cooked meal and a real bed.

State after state unrolled before me on an asphalt conveyor belt of tedium – Arizona, New Mexico, Texas, Oklahoma. Somewhere in the frozen wastes of Kansas, I spotted a stranded hitchhiker lying on his back, head pillowed by the curb. Too tired and hungry to stand, he merely raised one arm to display a beseeching thumb. The dispirited pilgrim was about my age and had been traveling for days – mostly on foot – watching as car after car driven by devout Christians zoomed by without stopping. I pulled over, gave him a ride, fed him and eventually asked, "You wouldn't by any chance happen to know of a band looking for a bass player?"

"Sure do," he replied.

Hundreds of miles later I halted my eastward progress in Indiana to deposit the hitchhiker at his door in Terra Haute, a house he shared with an incomplete rock band. The next morning I met them and we played. They weren't bad players and I was tempted to stay. But after a brief tour of the grim, industrial city of Terra Haute, I was dissuaded when I encountered a sobering demonstration of virulent anti-longhair sentiment by one of its many blue-collar residents, who yelled, "Get a haircut, you fucking pervert!"

Back on the interstate, I traversed Indiana, Ohio and then one of the more interminable states – Pennsylvania – before crossing into New Jersey, the land of yellow peril, exemplified by smog-yellow license plates. I finally arrived in New Providence, where Bob greeted me warmly. Rob was still touring England, so I moved into the basement room that had been the Owsley Elevator's spawning ground. My first order of business was to find work as a bass player, so I answered ads, met all sorts of musicians and tried to determine which, if any, had prospects.

The ensuing auditions took me to East Orange, Montclair, Newark and Jersey City, but finally, I met a band from Flemington called His and Hers – a quintet that played regulation Top-40 every Friday and Saturday in a bar in West New York, called, of all things, the Hangout. Gloria fronted the band and did most of the singing, while her brother, Danny, played rhythm guitar and sang harmony. I quickly learned their repertoire and made my debut, playing tunes such as "After Midnight," "Black Magic Woman" and "Burnin' Love." One night the manager took me aside and said, "Do me a favor, will 'ya. Tell the others to ignore anything that sounds like a gunshot."

The band was competent – not particularly creative – but professional, the only thing that really mattered. While the drummer appreciated my attempts to add greater rhythmic drive to the music, Danny felt threatened. In Manna, I'd grown accustomed to flights of spontaneity with musicians who could play circles around these guys, and therein lay the primary distinction between East Coast and West Coast bar bands in the early seventies. In California, the audience appreciated improvisation, but in New Jersey, it was strictly taboo.

The gig became memorable only after two in the morning, when a gorgeous black stripper leapt onto the bar to strut, shimmy and kick baskets of pretzels into the customers' leering faces. A superb tigress, I asked if she might allow me to caress her perfect derriere – just once – so I could die a happy man. His and Hers fired me soon thereafter. I still had a lot to learn.

***

It wasn't long before Rob returned from England with Jim Metzner, the other half of his folk duo. In those days, Jim had an unkempt beard and frazzled hair that gave him the look of a misplaced goat-herder from Afghanistan. (Yes, the same Jim Metzner heard on "Pulse of the Planet" on National Public Radio all these decades later.) Jim spent a week scouring Vermont's ski resorts in search of work for his duo. He approached the owner of the Broken Ski in Killington, a quintessential rock 'n roll ski bar, and

Marty, the owner, booked the duo to play for the après-ski crowd – five afternoons a week for the entire ski season.

Jim returned to New Providence to deliver the good news.

At which point Bob had a brainstorm. "Why don't you let Rob play rhythm guitar, since Peter's here and he plays bass?" Jim agreed that a trio would indeed be better than a duo. Jerry, another former member of 'Elevator – who now resembled a cross between Cochise and Mike Bloomfield – showed up with his Mosrite guitar. Jerry was an excellent lead player and we sounded so much fuller as a quartet that Jim decided to hire him as well. But without drums we would never achieve our full potential, so Jim said, "Why stop now?" We advertised for and hired a drummer from Long Island, an amiable soul who played well enough, but exhibited so little personality that I've forgotten his name.

Jim suggested we christen our five-piece group the Antelope Band. What had been a simple folk duo was now a rambunctious, full-blown rock band!

Laurie returned from her idyll in the beehive in Topanga Canyon, moved in with her aging parents in nearby Madison and became the band's first and only fan. She was an excellent fabric artist and created a magnificent satin banner to hang on the wall behind the band when we performed. It featured an antelope leaping heroically across a deep blue sky filled with stars and a crescent moon. Too bad the antelope's head faced backward – twisted 180 degrees – therefore unable to see where it was leaping.

Nor would it be long before I grasped the image's true iconographic significance.

14. Jerry Williams, Rob Norris and Jim Metzner of the Antelope Band

With a month left before the start of the gig at the Broken Ski, we assembled a rudimentary PA, an obsolete Bogen amplifier and two inadequate speakers. Although we'd been rehearsing diligently, our repertoire consisted of the most inappropriate tunes for a rowdy, hard-drinking ski crowd – endless verses from "Long Black Veil," plus Jim's equally unsuitable original songs. In "Bike Boy," an incomprehensible ditty about a guy who steals bicycles from children, the music crashed in and out of common and waltz time in absurd, lurching transitions guaranteed to annoy anyone foolish enough to venture onto the dance floor.

When at last the big day arrived, we drove north for six hours and hit the stage at the Broken Ski not as the innocuous folk-duo they were expecting, but as a raucous, schizophrenic quintet. The audience sat speechless as Jim emitted peculiar stuttering, buzzing noises between song lyrics. My bass sounded like a giant tubular metal insect stalking angrily through a Japanese science-fiction movie. The drummer thumped bravely but collided with his cymbals at the most inopportune moments. Jerry's guitar stung the ear like an enraged hornet. Rob played rhythm guitar with the manic intensity of a Mayan priest about to gouge a living heart from a sacrificial chest. No doubt about it, we were awful (and I have the tape to prove it.)

After our debut performance we stormed through the Broken Ski's kitchen like a Mongol horde, swallowing everything in sight. "It's okay," we told the befuddled cook, "We're the band."

When we descended into the bowels of the building to our quarters, we entered a veritable black hole of Calcutta – a dark, windowless chamber of doom into which no flicker of daylight ever intruded. There, to our surprise, we found six other musicians already encamped, the members of The Spittin' Image, a polished cover-band that played tunes by Chicago and Santana and enjoyed great popularity with the nighttime dance crowd.

The Antelope Band's pay amounted to a hundred bucks a week for all five of us. "Wow, a hundred dollars!" we gloated naively. But after a celebratory feast in a nearby restaurant, we were broke. There would be no further dining in restaurants. Instead, I set up an emergency kitchen in our subterranean grotto and cooked up a vat of spaghetti on a Coleman stove. It didn't take long before our claustrophobic barracks became hopelessly cluttered with guitars, practice amps and dirty-clothes littering the floor between our sagging metal bunks. Worst of all, when the switch was thrown to extinguish the 40-watt bulb mounted in the ceiling, we were instantly smothered in impenetrable Stygian darkness.

All that week we played to fewer and fewer people as word spread of our ability to repulse. The Spittin' Image took a shine to Jerry's guitar playing and hired him out from under us! Suddenly he was making more money than ever before and squandering it just as fast. Marty sobered up just long enough to fire us, and the Antelopes (minus Jerry) scattered like a herd on the Serengeti that smells a lion approaching its flanks. Rob and I had no choice but to return to his father's house in New Providence.

Now, at that point, any normal person might've seriously questioned the wisdom of devoting additional energy to becoming a professional musician, but not me. "Surely, the law of averages has to swing the other way," I reasoned. But till then, I grappled with the problem of how to escape the dreaded garden state, once and for all. To counteract my profound abhorrence of suburbia, I sought refuge in the Great Swamp, a cloistered wetland filled with vine-choked trees, wilted ferns and the rumor of quicksand. There, skulking like the elusive Jersey Devil, I yearned for the crystal silence of Vermont.

I had no choice but to find a job. The Kemper Insurance Company in Summit hired me to work in the mailroom, where I performed a task any self-respecting chimpanzee could manage. Day after day I punched the clock, sorted the mail and seethed with discontent. After reaching the limit of my tolerance for drudgery, I barged into the president of Kemper's office, handed the startled CEO a carefully drawn blueprint and said, "Here's a plan for a machine that will sort all your mail for the minimal cost of the bananas required to feed the chimp that propels the conveyor belt." The executive stared silently at the blueprint.

"There is one other thing," I said. "I quit."

The Trailriders

Laurie had left her parents' house in Madison and now lived three hundred miles away in Pittsford, a small town in central Vermont, not far from Rutland. We wrote to one another and I relished her description of the cheerful apartment she inhabited in a beautifully restored farmhouse known as Split Rock Farm. To my surprise and delight, she invited me to join her. I thanked Bob for his unflinching hospitality and left New Providence, vowing never to return. I sped north on the Garden State Parkway and emitted a juicy Bronx cheer as I sped past my all-time favorite billboard, the one that says, "You Are Now Leaving New Jersey."

Split Rock Farm sat on the side of an idyllic hillside, surrounded by fields, forest and mountains. A magnificent red barn sheltered Laurie's VW bug and a trio of horses; I soon became proficient with a shovel. Nearby, Bald Mountain and an adjacent conical hump jutted into the sky like twin breasts of stone. Laurie taught art in the local elementary school and had become a respected member of the community, but I suspect her reputation suffered when the news leaked out that she had "taken up with a hippie musician." Yes, we lived together in glorious sin, right under their parsimonious noses, snapping our fingers at the indignant gossip engendered by the members of the school board.

Once again, I needed a job, so I visited Buf's music store in Rutland and persuaded him to hire me as a part-time assistant. Melody Music still attracted every guitar totin', spoon-playin', country yodeler and small-time rock star for miles around and I met them all. Beau and Sabra, a husband and wife duo, were among the glittering cavalcade of talent. But unlike the majority of our clientele, they were excellent musicians. Sadly, Beau's distinction resulted from his extinction. As an overindulgent consumer of Columbia's most notorious export, and I don't mean coffee, he became the first drug-related casualty among my peers in Vermont. (The rumors concerning the discovery of his coke-frosted corpse in a bathtub may not be entirely accurate.)

Buf's store hadn't changed much since my first encounter in 1969, still a profitless, albeit zany enterprise. We tried to sell a brand new Japanese-made 12-string electric guitar, and lowered the price every month, but to no avail. The shiny red instrument hung on the wall till the day it committed suicide. With a sudden, nerve-jangling twang, the guitar neck tore loose from the body, but rather than send the pieces back to the distributor for a refund, we left the wreckage dangling there as a reminder of the transience of all things.

One day I answered Buf's phone and a guitar picker named Ted asked, "Where kin I 'git me a good bass player?"

"I'm your man," I replied, without hesitation. And before you could say Folsom Prison he'd hired me to play in a country and western outfit called The Trailriders. (In those days, country and western groups were always "outfits," never bands.) The following Saturday, without any rehearsal, I showed up to play my first gig at The Golden Horse – a squalid watering trough for saddle-weary cowpokes and truckers – easily recognizable by the life-size, gold-painted concrete nag that stood near the entrance to the parking lot.

The Trailriders consisted of Ted singing lead and playing a refrigerator-white Telecaster, an electric guitar that rode atop his potbelly like a rodeo-rider on a bucking bronco. We had a peddle-steel player who sounded like he used a raw potato on the strings instead of the traditional steel bar. The drummer was a shifty-eyed, chain-smoking used-car salesman named Hank, a guy who liked nothing better than chasing other people's wives, drinking while driving and tossing his empty Budweiser cans out the window. And then there was me – a skinny hair-head so desperate to play that I ignored the revulsion engendered by the band's repertoire (which, incidentally, consisted of only the most cloying, tears-in-your-beer country dirges imaginable – songs about unfaithful spouses, wrecked pickup trucks, getting fired from the mill or watching your old dog die of loneliness and sorrow).

The Trailriders scaled the peak of surrealism the night a 300-pound woman named Mary Beth joined us onstage to sing a rendition of "Tiny Bubbles." Her voice was so powerful she didn't need amplification. But nevertheless, she gripped the microphone in her meaty fist and belted out the lyrics while the beer-soaked mob sang along. Mary Beth sang the chorus over and over again, "Tiny bubbles, in the beer," each time a bit louder, "TINY BUBBLES, IN THE BEER!" Suddenly the tormented voice coils in the PA's distortion-wracked speakers melted and the amp fried a transistor. The fuse blew and the woman's debut performance with the Trailriders shuddered to a dreadful, dissonant conclusion.

After playing four grueling sets of three-chord progressions in the key of C in a poisonous, smoke filled barroom, I succumbed to a nicotine-raddled horror so profound that the only option was to burn my clothes, smoke a bowl of homegrown and then immerse myself in a tub of hot water, while "Dark Star" played on the stereo.

Mercifully, my tenure with the Trailriders lasted only six months, although it felt like six years. In all fairness, playing music I loathed taught me to keep my mouth shut, except to say "thank you" at the end of the gig when Ted handed me my meager pay. The Golden Horse has since burned to the ground and nothing remains except weeds, a few patches of crumbling asphalt and the rectangular indentation in the ground where a heavy cement statue of a horse once stood.

***

Three decades later…on a cool, sodden, dreary evening, I stood onstage at the Addison County Field Days, under a huge empty tent, playing in a western swing band that should've been called The Drought Busters. (Every time we played an outdoor venue that summer it rained like a million racehorses pissing from on high.) Water dripped through holes in the canvas overhead and fell into strategically placed buckets. We faced row upon row of bleachers, empty except for one lone figure sitting in the top row, all the way to the left.

Ayup, it was Ted.

The Monks of Weston Priory

One afternoon I answered a call at Buf's music store and encountered a horse of a different color. "Good day," a mellifluous voice crooned in my ear. "My name is Brother Gregory and I'm calling to inquire if you might know where I could find an accomplished bassist?"

"Allow me to introduce myself," I replied. "I am a professional bassist." (I did, after all, earn fifty bucks a week playing with the Trailriders on Saturday nights).

"How providential," said Brother Gregory. "We are an order of Benedictine monks, currently preparing to record our second album, here at the priory in Weston. We need a bassist, a string bass preferably."

I explained that my electric bass could easily be adjusted to provide a suitably mellow tone. (It would be another three years before I acquired my first string bass.)

"Splendid," said Brother Gregory. "Can you come to Weston this Sunday, at nine, to rehearse with the ensemble before we record?"

"Yes, it sounds very interesting. I'll be there."

On the appointed morning I set out for Weston and drove the approximately thirty miles from Pittsford, south on route 7 and then east on 103. I'd been up late the night before, having played at the Golden Horse, and arrived at the priory's chapel only slightly haggard from insufficient sleep. The contrast between the two could not have been starker: The 'Horse was dark, fetid and harbored all venial sins, while the chapel was airy and clean and aglow with righteous sanctity.

At first glance, the Monks of Weston Priory appeared to have insulated themselves from the harsh rigors of the outside world. They watched no television, preferred silence during meals, and, as you might imagine, never drank booze or danced in honky-tonks. Instead, they devoted each day to a life of simplicity, spirituality and organic gardening. In addition to their collective skill in disciplines such as the restoration of ancient documents and repairing the tractor, the Benedictines in Weston recorded original music. They'd released an album entitled "Locusts and Wild Honey" the year before. The new album would be entitled "Wherever You Go." (To which Brother Gregory had wisely chosen to omit the second half of the phrase... "There You Are.")

Sunday's rehearsal began promptly at nine. Brother Gregory handed me a dozen charts, compositions that can only be described as liturgical folk songs. We went over each song till Brother Gregory was satisfied that my bass lines were suitably restrained and that I was cognizant of all dynamic subtleties, then we adjourned while the monks conducted the traditional Sunday morning mass. A pious flock of worshippers shuffled in and filled the pews, and I began to feel like a wolf in sheep's clothing. After the usual mumbo-jumbo about eternal this and divine that, the prior invited the congregation to remain after the service to quietly observe the recording session. A clutch of little old ladies, freshly scrubbed of whatever sins they'd mustered since the previous Sunday, accepted the offer and watched as the recording engineer positioned an array of condenser microphones. When he was satisfied that they were optimally placed to capture the sound of eighteen male voices, acoustic guitar, piano, flute, cello and my bass, he then switched on a Studer tape machine and said, "Rolling."

The monks sang and the ensemble played, imbuing the tape's ferrous oxide with the miracle of electromagnetism. In 1972, a recording produced beyond the confines of a studio did not generally allow a separate track for each voice or instrument. In other words, there would be no overdubbing. Instead, the performance of each song had to be flawless. If a take wasn't pristine – if someone hit a wrong note or sang a semitone flat – we began again and repeated the song until perfection was achieved. Upon completion of that session, a short, sprightly octogenarian with blue hair and an ecstatic smile rushed forward and gripped my hands fervently in her own. She gazed up into my eyes and said, her voice quavering with rapture, "Brother, you're doing such a wonderful job!"

Little did she know I was neither a monk, celibate, nor even Catholic as I placed my right hand on her bowed head, smiled beatifically and said, "Bless you, my sister."

15. The Monks of Weston Priory

The process of recording the entire album required several weekends, and each time I visited the priory I was assigned a tiny room in which to sleep – a cell – as they are called in both monastic and penal institutions. The monks retired at eight every evening to sleep in narrow, ascetic beds, but I was accustomed to staying up till three or four in the morning and this left me with a large block of time to kill. Having observed where they kept the ceremonial apple wine, I poured myself a brimming goblet and haunted the chapel like Lon Chaney in the Phantom of the Opera. Outside, the wind whistled through skeletal branches and the moon emerged between scudding clouds. Midnight found me quaffing a third glass of apple wine while playing eerie diminished chords and flat fives – the devil's interval – on the chapel organ.

Eventually, I crept up to my cell and fell into a fitful, wine-soaked sleep, only to dream that I'd been sealed inside a hollow metal tank. I awoke in the pitch-black, pinioned by my twisted sheets and utterly convinced I was, in fact, entombed. I cried out for help and began to hammer on the wall with my fist. A moment later I was wide-awake, cackling like a madman. The next morning the Prior broke the traditional silence at breakfast by saying, "You know, there was a hell of a bang last night." I burst out laughing and all eyes turned upon me. I confessed to being the cause of the commotion and explained my dream-induced provocation, leaving out the details concerning my copious consumption of ceremonial wine.

When at last we'd finished recording all the songs for the new album, Brother Gregory thanked me, handed me a check and said, "I hope the amount is sufficient."

I glanced at the check, assured him it was indeed satisfactory and bid him good day. At the time, a hundred and twenty-five dollars was a small fortune and I felt like a rich man.

I'm still a rich man.

I've always been a rich man.

I just don't happen to have any money.

Sweetbriar

I broke Laurie's heart when I announced my decision to leave Pittsford and move to Brattleboro to form a band with Jerry, my guitar-playing friend from high school days. Thank God her suicide gesture was just that, a gesture and unsuccessful. The emergency room personnel at the Rutland hospital pumped out her stomach to remove the pills she'd swallowed, then sent her home. Undeterred, I left Split Rock Farm, selfish brute that I was, driven by an unquenchable desire to play in a band. I was twenty-two years old; I had no parents, no ties to the community and no one to whom I could turn for advice. My life was nothing more than a canoe adrift on a tide of self-indulgence, but at least I had a paddle...my bass.

Jerry had emerged unscathed from his stint playing in the Spittin' Image at the Broken Ski, and now lived in Guilford in an ancient green trailer that resembled a huge sardine-can. By day he ran a music store on Flat Street in Brattleboro, a struggling enterprise owned by Buf, that consummate master of free enterprise. Although poorly stocked and consequently doomed, the store provided a focal point for local musicians, such as the lanky guitar player and vocalist named Stuart Norton who strolled in to buy a set of strings for his Gibson ES-335. Jerry and I conducted an impromptu audition and discovered that Stuart played well and sang with a genuine Hank Williams twang in his voice, exactly what we needed for our nascent country-rock band. Jerry made the pitch and Stuart said, "Okay, I'm in."

Stuart lived in the woods of Westminster in an extinct school bus fitted out with a stove and bunks, a yellow automotive artifact so mired in hardened mud that not even a lightning strike could ever make it roll again.

We still needed a drummer, but they are problematic, perhaps as a result of the incessant pounding that rattles their brains. We searched high and low before we found Ratso, a student at the now defunct Wyndham College in Putney. Short, dumpy and Jewish, Ratso was the most profoundly neurotic human being I've ever encountered, as riddled with quirks and phobias as an abused lab-rat, but a good drummer nevertheless.

It was Jerry's idea to name the band Sweetbriar, a plant endowed with prickles and thorns. Our goal was to exploit the country-rock trend then being established by the Byrds, Poco and the New Riders of the Purple Sage. Stuart's bus had no electricity so we squeezed the band into Jerry's sardine can for rehearsals – cramming the drums into the kitchen, the guitar amps into the living room, my bass amp into the dining area and a forest of microphone stands in between. We built a repertoire based upon our favorite songs from various albums released by our musical heroes, blissfully unaware that the listening public in Brattleboro would prove to be stubbornly unreceptive to anything other than full-tilt, head-banging rock.

In 1973, the biggest musical act in the Brattleboro area was an unbearably loud, quasi-religious rock band known as "Spirit in the Flesh." The band (and their apostles) lived in a commune in Putney and traveled around in a shiny, silver bus. They were decent musicians, but I was mortified by the fusion of spirituality and rock 'n roll. (To this day, I consider Christian rock to be an abomination, as pointless as drinking non-alcoholic beer.) The expression "drugs, sex and rock 'n roll" clearly omits any reference to Jesus, and for good reason…the rebellious hedonism of rock was never intended to share a pew (or the dance floor) with the Holy Ghost.

The only gig Sweetbriar played occurred in a dive called Alice's Restaurant, the ideal place to commit musician-assisted suicide. The clientele consisted of the most homely women in town – frowzy, snaggle-toothed creatures that lived on food stamps, alcohol and the grace of God. Typical of all such nicotine-clogged haunts, the stage was accessible only by ladder, resembled a boxing-ring and stood five feet above the dance floor.

"Dance with me," implored a crone, clutching my ankle like a supplicant seeking alms.

"I can't," I explained, wrenching my foot free. "I have to play the bass."

The real action, or so we believed, occurred around the corner in a rock club known as the Red Barn, so we talked our way into a gig there one Thursday night. Sweetbriar opened with "Mama Tried," "Me and Bobby McGee" and "Six Days on the Road," our heaviest tune. We played energetically and sang three-part harmony on key, but the glaring stage-lights prevented us from observing the audience as they sat, sullen and vastly unimpressed as they stared at us with ill-concealed contempt. Had we played "Born to be Wild" we would've been honky-tonk heroes. But instead, we subjected them to "Lovesick Blues," "Mr. Spaceman" and "Glendale Train," precisely what the hard-bitten, hard-drinking, hard rock clientele did not want to hear. We finished our set and swaggered off the stage, pleased with our performance.

The Red Barn's owner sidled out from behind the bar, handed Stuart a wad of greasy singles and said, "Here's 'yer pay, fellers. You can go home now. Don't play another note."

Brickbush

Sweetbriar withered and died not long after its ignominious dismissal from the Red Barn. Ratso's neurosis flared up and intervened like a flock of invisible ducks orbiting his head, each duck quacking instructions that only he could hear, but which resulted in his decision to quit the band. Without drums, we couldn't hunt for gigs, not that there were any. The bands that played at the Red Barn were usually from Massachusetts, and I realized that Brattleboro offered little opportunity for an aspiring bass player. Other than an upstairs café where women with hairy legs played dulcimers on the weekend, the town was dead. Jerry's music store had yet to fold, although the crease had become apparent to everyone except Buf.

I met an attractive brunette in Jerry's music store; I listened as she sang and played an acoustic guitar. "This is Kathy," I said, introducing her to Stuart, "she sings like an angel." We spent the day talking and playing and later she echoed our frustration at the limited musical options in Brattleboro. By now, I knew that the most critical element in a band was its vocalist, so when Kathy expressed an ardent desire to form a working group of her own, I heard the faint yet unmistakable knock of opportunity on the door. We already had the essential core of a band, and so, in yet another naïve gambit, Stuart, Kathy and I decided to transplant ourselves to the alien soil of Fitchburg, Massachusetts, where she knew a drummer also looking for work.

Bidding good riddance to Brattleboro, I felt no remorse the day I vacated my chilly bohemian flat – four schizoid rooms whose windows and doorframes were anything but 90 degree angles – a crooked Bohemian apartment in which the floor sloped this way and that, allowing a dropped marble to wander aimlessly before coming to rest beneath the refrigerator at the far end of the kitchen. It was a noisy place. Directly above lived a pack of heavy, shambling humanoids that wore hobnail boots as they conducted square dances on the hardwood floor while I tried to sleep. Not only that, the apartment overlooked Brattleboro's fire department, and their response to every alarm activated a siren identical to those of the Blitzkrieg in London.

Our arrival in the gritty industrial city of Fitchburg marked the beginning of collaboration with two of its native sons – a pair of nervous, wiry Italians with dark eyes and pointed black goatees. Tony played a Chordovox, an electric accordion that sounded exactly like a Hammond organ when pumped through a Leslie speaker. In those days, accordions, even electric accordions, dwelt at the bottom of the rock 'n roll prestige ladder and Tony felt ashamed of the instrument's unglamorous reputation. He solved the image problem by building a large wooden façade that looked exactly like a Hammond organ, a ridiculous piece of furniture that he hauled to every gig. The audience was none the wiser as he sat behind the prop with the Chordovox strapped to his scrawny chest.

His brother, John, was an excellent drummer but missed his true calling as a comedian. John loved to smoke weed, turn off his television's sound and then slowly rotate through all thirteen channels (long before cable) while spouting hilarious impromptu dialog based upon the silent, on-screen action. Whenever John played "television roulette" his imaginary plots evolved into epics – a display of agility that reminded me of the old vaudevillian on Ed Sullivan's show, the guy who kept a dozen dinner plates miraculously spinning atop long wooden sticks.

When Kathy admitted that her nickname in high school had been Bonita Brickbush, we pounced on the latter as the perfect name for our band. We hired a jazz sax player and a conga-drummer, to further fill out our sound. Brickbush rehearsed every day and built a repertoire.

We didn't know it yet, but the key to breaking into the music scene in Fitchburg lay in a band's ability to duplicate every nuance of a current hit song from the radio. If a band didn't sound exactly like the record, it didn't work. When this sad fact finally dawned on us, we tried to recreate the Top-40 fodder of the day, songs like "Witchy Woman" and "Listen to the Music," but Brickbush was much better playing "Cloud Nine" by Mongo Santamaria. Consequently, we never made the slightest dent in the club circuit. We survived by scrounging up the odd gig here and there – salivating like emaciated curs on the frozen sidewalk outside a fabulous restaurant where the succulent aroma of prime rib blew across our muzzles on a fan-driven gust. (Woof!)

Brickbush disbanded after six months of hunger, frustration and sleeping on various couches, one of which was in a decrepit farmhouse owned by an equally decrepit farmer – a domicile infested by a gang of unscrupulous ex-physicists that had dropped out and gone back to the land, I kid you not! John and Tony remained in Fitchburg to resuscitate their duo, the Posco Combo. Eddy and Jose kept their day jobs toiling in some loathsome factory that manufactured screwdrivers. Stuart and Kathy moved to Illinois and got married. (Today, more than thirty-years later, they are still happily married and Stuart's blues band, The Cooler Kings, performs regularly.) And me? I returned to Vermont for more musical self-flagellation.

Forest

Stuck in Brattleboro once again, I did not see the writing on the wall, even though the spelling was correct and the words were quite luminous. The Brickbush fiasco pitched another pail of gasoline onto the fire of my resolve; I stubbornly adhered to the belief that with enough perseverance, I'd eventually forge an incredibly eclectic ensemble, play for enthusiastic crowds and record brilliant albums. I had not yet read of the trials of Odysseus, nor did I suspect that the pursuit and attainment of my goal would consume the next thirty years of my life.

I was still learning, and Brickbush had taught me some valuable lessons; a seven-piece band was too large and Afro-Cuban conga rhythms in a Top-40 band were an unaffordable luxury. It seems obvious in retrospect, but a Hank Williams style singer (with a twang and a yodel in his voice) did not mix at all well with jazz saxophone.

In 1973, Brattleboro wasn't just a sleepy little town – it was comatose. The apex of available culture appeared onscreen in the Lachis Theater, a crumbling art-deco movie palace in the heart of town. "The Night of the Living Dead" played as I sat in the empty balcony watching the newly deceased lurch to their feet in pursuit of living flesh. I lit a pipe stuffed with illegality as ghouls consumed human entrails, amused by the perfect analog to my own musical and social morbidity formed by George Romero's staggering zombies.

After the movie I, too, stumbled out in search of my next meal. The Lachis bar beckoned on some subtle wavelength so I went in to investigate. Sure enough, my antennas still functioned and I met Jonathan Whitaker, an itinerant troubadour who resembled a wandering minstrel from the time of Shakespeare. I ordered a beer and listened as he played a Martin guitar, warbled songs and blew into a harmonica held in place by a device worn around the neck. (Performing solo can be a lonely task, especially when the audience is absent or devoted exclusively to its grog.) I introduced myself and we spoke at length of gigs and women and how best to pursue them.

Jonathan said he'd be back the next evening and invited me to bring my bass and accompany him. I showed up with a bass and an Ampex tape recorder and then recorded our first set – tunes by Cat Stevens, John Denver and Neil Young. Once again, the bar's patrons were oblivious, hunkered down on stools with their backs to us as Jonathan sang in a pleasant tenor voice. He was not a master technician on the guitar, although his simple strumming and finger-picking allowed me to embroider freely on the bass, to alternate between a traditional supporting role and melodic counterpoint that might best be described as overplaying.

An idea occurred to me, and like so many others before and since, it amused me, thus making its implementation mandatory. Instead of playing another set, I piped the recording I'd just made through the PA, filling the room with the sound of guitar, voice and electric bass as the two of us stood idly by, beers in hand, instruments untouched. From time to time we set our glasses down and made absurd, grandiose gestures as if we were, in fact, performing before a multitude of adoring fans. No one even noticed.

***

In Vermont winter is never very far away, even at the height of summer. When fall loomed on the horizon yet again, Jonathan packed up his guitar, both cats and drove his wheezing VW bug (named Brunehilde) to the Mad River Valley (also known as the Bad Liver Valley). I loaded up my MGB and followed, hoping that the valley would be ripe with opportunity for a folk-slinger and his trusty sidekick.

Winter slowly tightened its grip around our throats and the only lodging Jonathan and I could afford was a mobile home, a dreadful metal sarcophagus that alternately baked us with arid blasts while the furnace cranked, and then chilled us with cold drafts the moment it switched off. This resulted in desiccated sinuses and a sore throat so persistent that I swore I'd rather live in a tent than to subject myself to a mobile home. Little did I know how soon I'd get my chance.

Jonathan and I found a regular gig in the Red Nose Room, a cozy little den where the unlikely sound of Caruso's voice (on scratchy 78 RPM records) filled the gap between our sets. The promise of work was fulfilled, however meager the pay, but unattached women were rare and I was unwilling to delude myself with thoughts of romance without finance. Tourists always import their own women, and those that lived in the valley were on the lookout for well heeled, or at very least, dependable breadwinners. (Life in a ski-town can be tough when you can't afford the cost of a lift ticket – to say nothing of skis, poles, boots and the latest in designer sunglasses.)

Jonathan and I expanded our geographic radius, and this lead us to an après ski gig in Killington, not far from the scene of the Antelope Band's grizzly debacle.

Blizzards struck with ferocious regularity that winter. Trees shattered in the sub-zero cold as coyotes loped across the crusted snow-pack in search of something to bite. We loaded our instruments into Brunehilde, and then drove fifty miles through wind-blown whiteouts and snowdrifts large enough to swallow the beetle. And like every VW ever driven in Vermont, the wretched machine had no heat and no defroster. My job was to scrape the ice off the inside of the windshield while Jonathan peered into the darkness through a saucer-sized clear spot. As ridiculous as a Laurel and Hardy skit, we stomped our feet to prevent frostbite while I chiseled the ice and Jonathan spun the steering wheel from one prolonged skid to the next. Miraculously, we always made it in time to Killington, only to repeat the mad scramble after the gig, swerving through Stygian darkness to our evening performance in the Red Nose Room.

By the end of March the starlings had returned to loiter in the naked branches, a sure sign that spring was near. In April the snow melted and another ski season came to an end, and with it our employment. In May we left the mobile home and moved to the Rutland area, where summer resorts offered more gigs. Jonathan pitched a tent in a campground in Mendon, which he shared with two Siamese cats, while I sought a commodious campsite of my own.

I visited a creaking old couple I'd previously met in Pittsford. Jack and Catherine Crockett lived in a magnificent house they'd built fifty years earlier, using timber from a 200-year old barn, rebuilt on acreage that included a field, a pond and a swiftly flowing brook. I explained the purpose of my visit – seeking a summer-long campsite – and they consented, pleased with the thought of having a vigorous young man around to help with the chores made increasingly difficult by their advancing age.

After selecting a promontory alongside the brook, the ideal spot, I constructed a tent using polyethylene plastic, nylon rope, wire and duct tape; the finished structure resembled a rocket nosecone. Incredibly simple, yet elegant, my outdoor kitchen was protected by a rain flap and featured a Coleman stove and a small wooden shelf for my utensils. A circle of stones enclosed a campfire. A nearby spring supplied me with the most delicious water imaginable, water that remained at a constant forty-two degrees summer and winter, which allowed me to fashion a humble but effective refrigerator. Sheltered by conifers, cheered by chipmunks and soothed by the continuous sound of rushing water, my hidden glade was a wonderful place to spend the summer.

Reaching my peaceful, secluded haven entailed a short hike across a wide, grassy field, over a wooden bridge and then upstream a hundred yards along the edge of the Furnace Brook, named after one of the earliest smelting furnaces built in Vermont. My campsite sat near the remains of the furnace's massive chimney, hidden within a dense thicket of sumac, an odd sight as it loomed in the green gloom like a sacrificial altar.

Jonathan and I enlarged our duo into a chlorophyll-enhanced trio the day Barbara Cox arrived with her Fender Rhodes electric piano and excellent singing voice. She moved into Jonathan's tent, quite a change from Manhattan, but one that demonstrated her adventurous spirit. Our instrument amplifiers required electricity, so we sought permission to rehearse in a stone church in downtown Rutland. There, our repertoire quickly expanded to include songs by Roberta Flack and Carol King. We now faced the age-old problem of choosing a name for our ensemble, something simple yet declarative. After tossing hundreds of suggestions into the air, which blew away like chaff, we hit upon the perfect name – Forest – a name that resonated with the nuts-and-berries sensibility we embraced. After all, we lived in the woods like gypsies, literally ensconced on Mother Nature's breast.

16. Newspaper ad for Forest

Next, we needed a demo tape and a promo photograph, so I shot a roll of Tri-X with the Leica inherited from my father. Looking back at those photos, I resembled the wild child of Avignon grown to a noble savage, although some might think I looked like an escaped lunatic. I wore a deerskin shirt, an unruly wedge of long, curly hair and a bristling Manchu mustache. If I frightened the locals, I didn't give a hoot; I was a free man and roamed the hills at will, so far off the beaten track as to be invisible.

Forest enjoyed a modest degree of success. We played often enough to be able to rent indoor living quarters during the winter and to buy food – a definition of success that persists to this day. Forest lasted longer than any other group I'd been in up to that point, but ended when Barbara abandoned the bucolic splendor of Vermont and moved back to Manhattan. Jonathan eventually pulled up stakes and left too. And, like the majority of my musical associates over the years, once a band ceased to exist, all communication between its former members ended.

The Furnace Brook still flows as cheerfully as ever, but Time's heavy hand swept away not only Catherine and Jack, but also their magnificent house of bone-dry, silvered tinder, I mean timber. Tragically, fire utterly consumed the structure.

Southern Exposure

It'd been one hell of a weekend. I'd driven hundreds of miles to hear the 'Dead, broken up with Laurie for the second time and then vacated an apartment in order to join a band that inhabited a chalet on Hawke Mountain…only to be fired the very next morning! In spite of the perfectly reasonable explanation for my sudden and temporary incompetence on the bass guitar – a potent blend of sleep deprivation, too much weed and simmering emotional turmoil – the bastards fired me. Once again I loaded my bass and amp into the MG and roared away, forced once again to acknowledge the ephemeral nature of all Utopian societies.

I was now twenty-four years old. The future loomed as nothing more than an abstraction, a wavering mirage that never seemed to move any closer, no matter how I tried to approach it. With two hundred bucks in my wallet and no responsibilities, I was as transient as a grace note, my stratospheric independence circumscribed only by the radius imposed by the cost of gas.

No better time for a leisurely drive, I decided. The early morning showers had ended. Skeins of vapor rose from the wet pavement as blue sky and sunshine insured a superb day in the offing. I pulled over at the bottom of Hawke Mountain and faced Route 100. The only question… which way should I go, north or south? After folding the MG's convertible top down, I climbed back in and turned left, simply because the scenery was better in that direction.

Steep wooded hillsides rose on either side as I rallied through the Granville gulf towards the Waitsfield valley. My red roadster hugged the serpentine curves of Route 100. Shafts of sunlight pierced a canopy of dense green foliage as I downshifted into third. It was no accident the Abarth exhaust growled with a throaty roar reminiscent of a Spitfire Mark IV – my father's favorite aircraft. The Lucas instruments in the dashboard were round and their needles bore a coating of phosphor, exactly like the gauges in a 'Spit. Arnold had equipped the car with other vaguely aeronautic frills – fog lamps, compass, air horns and a powerful short wave radio. All it lacked was a brace of cannons and a firing button atop the gearshift knob. Ten miles on I stopped at a café in the Waitsfield Commons.

"By the great god Rotor," I mused over a cup of coffee, "what should I do next?"

The one constant in my life was the awareness of a deep core of untapped creative energy, a hidden flame seeking release. I desperately wanted ribald camaraderie, that delirious esprit de corps that only a professional band seems capable of generating. I sought the fraternity of hashish assassins, in other words, regardless of how illusory such a surrogate family might be. Lost in thought, I sipped a second cup of java and floated like a bladder of seaweed on my own Sargasso Sea. I felt poised for whatever opportunity might present itself. In short, I didn't have a clue. Anything could happen, anything at all. Always had, always would. I simply had to be patient and appeal to the beneficence of a higher power…but which one?

"Excuse me," I said to the waitress. "You wouldn't happen to know of anyone around here looking for a bass player?"

"See that condo up there?" she said, refilling my cup a third time and pointing towards a building that clung to the side of a hill like a barnacle on the hull of the Queen Mary. "There's a guy living up there in one of those condos, a songwriter named Russell Dexter. You should talk to him. Head south, then turn right at Doc Quimby's, go all the way up the hill and follow the sign to Top of the Valley Condos."

I thanked her, finished my coffee and left a generous tip.

Five minutes later I looked down upon the Waitsfield Commons, now just a miniature shopping center sharing God's ping-pong table with a dozen HO-scale toy cars. As I circled the 6-unit building on foot I heard a 12-string acoustic guitar releasing clouds of notes into the air like pollen from a blooming lilac bush.

"HEY RUSSELL!" I shouted. "I hear you're looking for a bass player!"

The music stopped abruptly. A figure leaned out over a deck railing high above.

"Come around to Unit #2 and I'll let you in," he said.

The door swung open and Russell, who looked more like the square-jawed captain of a football team than a songwriter, invited me in. Within minutes I'd set up an amp and plugged in my bass. He taught me his original songs and we sounded good. Later, he invited me to spend the night in one of the condo's extra bedrooms. I accepted the offer and stayed a year.

The view from our outdoor deck was spectacular. Russell and I shared Unit #2 and lived like the benign rulers of some wind-swept duchy – isolated and aloof – content to gaze down upon our diminutive subjects from the giddy heights. It was an interesting place to live. Our four-story aerie contained endless flights of stairs; every square inch had been painted white except the hardwood floors, and snow-blindness remained a threat. An inefficient, circular woodstove heated the living room and the walls bore enough switches for track lighting and outdoor floodlights to warm the heart of a nuclear engineer.

"What an incredible country this is," said Russell. "Where else but America could two penniless musicians inhabit a luxury condo, lounge around on the deck all day with guitars in hand, drink Genesee and listen to Red Sox games on the radio?" Russell's girlfriend must've liked the idea of nurturing such uncompromising artists, because she supplied us with bread, tuna, hot dogs, frozen vegetables and beer. Russell and I put in a couple of days of manual labor from time to time in exchange for rent, but it was not the first nor the last time I felt like the violin-playing grasshopper that enjoyed life while the ants busted their humps preparing for winter.

We played exactly one gig, a total disaster. Russell's song-lyrics spoke of life in "the valley" as a place where the rich and the poor dance hand in hand with deceptive nonchalance. His melodies conveyed a deep melancholy, and we learned that such poignant sentiments should not be expressed in a bar packed with drunken rugby players. The boisterous louts drowned us out with their raucous clamoring. Russell was not used to being ignored when he performed, and took it badly. "Should I stay here another year, or leave this goddamn valley behind?" he sang.

"Whadaya' mean 'this goddamned valley?'" shouted an irate codger in the audience.

Russell vowed never again to perform in public.

Every year, the Waitsfield valley absorbed an influx of transients. Most departed in the spring, driven out by the limitations for employment inherent in a seasonal resort town. A few always remained, however, to work on construction sites, find a spouse and build a house of their own, and eventually raise a family – but not Russell. By the end of October he was gone, out of the valley and out of Vermont, never to be seen by me again.

Now alone in Unit #2, the days and weeks drifted by like cumulus clouds. I spent my time practicing the bass, hiking the mountains or taking long rides on my 10-speed bicycle. My driver's license and the registration for the MG expired and I couldn't afford to renew either one, so I snuck around on back roads under the cover of darkness, driving on bald tires. I honed my sense of irony by living on Food Stamps and playing tennis with millionaires, bigwigs who owned entire mountains and soared above them in gliders, when not playing polo.

Around that time I acquired my first string bass, after receiving a surprise birthday check from Bob Norris, who still lived in New Providence. That first upright bass was not the hand-carved German instrument I would someday own, but a humble doghouse made from plywood. Nevertheless, it started me on the long, arduous road to competence demanded by such a cumbersome instrument. There wasn't much work for an itinerant bass player, although I met Peter Cover, the jazz pianist who introduced me to reading charts. One night we joined two venerable jazz legends, Jonah Jones and Cozy Cole, onstage in the Sugarbush Inn. I played well, in spite of my nervousness and the limitless depth of my musical ignorance.

One day a guitar-toting cocaine-cowboy pulled into town (on his white horse, Mescalito). News travels fast in the valley and it wasn't long before Don and I joined forces to play a few gigs. Tall and skinny, with shoulder-length straight hair, Don hailed from the South, and so we named our duo Southern Exposure, and culled a repertoire from the songbooks of Hank Williams, Jesse Winchester and John Prine. Don was a wily operator and somehow finagled a job managing a slightly disreputable motel while its owner vacationed in the tropics for a month. I agreed to help. Every morning I cooked breakfast for dozens of ravenous ski-bums. Sometimes, for special customers, I garnished the omelets with magic mushrooms, a meal guaranteed to pack a wallop.

At night Don alternated between tending the bar and playing guitar. If someone wanted a beer, they had to wait till we finished a song. Inevitably, Don and I ate some of my psychotropic cuisine before going onstage. Carlos Castaneda only knows what we sounded like, but no one complained, probably because our rollicking audience was equally whacked out on 'shrooms. The room melted but no one seemed to mind our hysterical laughter, the bungled lyrics or the bass notes that hit the wall and exploded like squibs on the Fourth of July.

17. Southern Exposure

I've heard it said that God protects small children and idiots. If it's true, the old boy must've been working overtime that month. Because, less than half a mile away, the Sugarbush Inn hosted a brigade of vacationing Police Chiefs and Narcotics Officers – a veritable hornet's nest of Law Enforcement. Fortunately, they were too busy skiing and drinking to be anything other than off-duty. But had they been paying attention, they would've intuited the flaunting of all they held most sacred – the psychedelic auras illuminating the night – and then descended on us like a ton of very indignant bricks.

The New Leaf Band

My luck changed abruptly on the first day of spring in 1975. "Just this once," declared Zeus, weary of tormenting me, "I'll grant this pathetic mortal his most ardent desire."

All of my previous attempts to create or join a stabile, working ensemble had yielded little more than fleeting glimpses of my goal. The experience had been educational, certainly, but equally frustrating. And so, after a year of austere luxury (or was it luxurious austerity?), I bid farewell to the pristine isolation of Unit #2 and left its barren white walls, track lighting and superb mountaintop vistas. I moved into a drafty old barn in the heart of the Northeast Kingdom – a crumbling, ramshackle structure that reeked of creosote, cow manure and chicken shit – but in many ways it was an improvement. Perhaps I'd better backtrack a little.

Somehow, from deep within the 'Kingdom, Lucy Horton and Dan Fath learned of "a hermit bass player living on a mountain in Waitsfield." Determined to find me, they drove ninety miles, parked at the foot of Bragg Hill and then, unable to locate the road to the condo, struggled up the steep, snow-covered incline, on foot, to stagger, half frozen, to my door. I responded to their unexpected knock and confronted what appeared to be two Tibetan Snowmen, or possibly Sasquatch and his mate. I invited them in, thawed them out and listened as they described "the farm." For a moment I was certain that Jesus was about to enter the conversation and then dominate it, without ever once contributing to it. But instead, Dan wiped away the icicles clinging to his beard and said, "We're starting a band and we need a bass player."

"Yes, and I'm going to sing," said Lucy, smiling broadly – her round, coke-bottle glasses opaque with vapor. "Dan has a wonderful voice and plays electric guitar. We also have a great drummer; he's in Colorado at the moment but is supposed to return in a couple of weeks. "

I knew nothing about the Northeast Kingdom – a zone as blank in my mind as it looked on the map – I agreed to accompany them to the farm for a visit.

"Why not?" I asked. "Perhaps it's time for a change."

The March sun shone brightly as we wended our way north in Dan's battered Toyota, past Montpelier, Hardwick, Glover and Barton, into ever-wilder terrain. After two hours we arrived in East Charleston, site of the funky microcosm known as Frog Run Farm, a genuine hippie commune carved out of the howling wilderness, home to twenty-seven granola-crunching, pot-smoking, urban expatriates determined to live simply and coexist peacefully.

Lucy, Dan and I entered the farm just in time to observe the weekly meeting – a forum for airing concerns large, small and microscopic. Two-dozen hairy communards sat on rough-hewn, tree-stump stools placed around a low circular table. Some drank herb tea; others blew marijuana smoke-rings into the air. Mary, Martha, Doodles, Simon, Turtle, Chris, Mary Ann, Polly, Sky, Cb (pronounced ceeb) and many others listened attentively as Lydia described a dream she'd recently had. (As the holder of the farm's deed, Lydia's words carried weight.)

"I dreamt there was a band living here at the farm and practicing upstairs in the barn. It was called The New Leaf Band."

"Quite a prophecy," I thought, realizing that it would be wise to listen when Fate spoke.

18. Frog Run Farm

Frog Run Farm offered few modern conveniences. No electricity in the house but plenty of kerosene lamps. No telephone or indoor plumbing, either. Day or night, summer or winter, a trip to the outhouse entailed a brisk hike up a wind-scoured hill. The only source of heat in the old farmhouse was a massive woodstove, the heart of the kitchen; with so many people living under one roof, a hot bath required considerable planning and effort. Cold water poured continuously from a spigot in the kitchen sink – a pleasant sound and an excellent metaphor for the flow of humanity that swirled in and through Frog Run. (The name, incidentally, had nothing to do with Frenchmen, but referred to the countless amphibians spawned in the nearby Clyde River.)

I'd been living alone in the glacial sterility of Unit #2 for so long that the sight of twenty-seven frazzled toothbrushes jammed into one jar gave me pause. If anyone caught a cold, I realized with a shudder of apprehension, it would spread like the plague. A simple matter to isolate my own toothbrush, I ignored my germ apprehension and agreed to join the new band.

I returned to Waitsfield to collect my few belongings and inform the condo owner of my impending departure. Knowing I'd be safe once I got beyond Montpelier, I waited for darkness before departing in my illegal MG, still without license or registration. There was a tense moment on the outskirts of Montpelier when a police car pulled up behind me, but I spotted a coin-operated carwash and deftly avoided the cops by pulling in to give my salt-encrusted roadster a scrub. When at last I arrived at the slumbering farm, the constellation of Orion dominated the western sky. Winter lingers in the 'Kingdom, but in spite of the frigid air I relished the stillness, a silence more profound than any I'd known.

The insulated practice room on the barn's second floor was to be my temporary bedroom, but when I entered it that night I discovered that the woodstove had been allowed to overheat. The stovepipe radiated an alarming shade of red as it passed through a circular aperture in the ceiling. Curious as to what might be up above, I took a flashlight and climbed a ladder to investigate. To my horror I saw dozens of hay bales stacked within six feet of the red-hot chimney-pipe – hay as dry as tinder, the entire barn as flammable as a powder keg! I immediately shut down the stove's air intake vents to deprive the fire of oxygen. I had no idea where to find water. The ground floor was poorly illuminated and full of large, sleeping animals so I dashed to the house, stumbled from one dark room to another – the air resonant with snoring – until Mary awoke to heed my warning.

We sprinted across the barnyard, up the stairs and into the practice room, where the stovepipe still glowed brightly; a trickle of creosote ran hissing down its length, filling the room with a woody stench. There was nothing we could do except watch and pray.

By two o'clock in the morning the metal stovepipe had cooled to its usual dull gray color. The danger had passed, so I crawled into my sleeping bag, unaware that the barn also sheltered an implacably loud and determined rooster set to go off at four.

A few days later, as spring showed signs of becoming more than a theoretical abstraction, the drummer returned from Colorado with a set of Rogers drums and a teepee. David Weaver was not only a gifted percussionist, but also a terrific vocalist. Either of these talents would've enabled him to earn a living, but the combination gave our new band enormous potential.

It had been a hard winter in the Waitsfield valley for the members of The Heart of Gold Band. With no gigs on their calendar, and the snow melting fast, they reluctantly called it quits. As soon as news of the breakup reached Lucy's ears (via the mysterious grapevine) she pounced and returned with Tom Ross in tow – a talented, blind guitarist who spent every waking minute practicing his finger vibrato on a plastic ukulele, inverting knuckle-busting chords on a Trini Lopez model guitar, or harmonizing the strange melodies that played incessantly in his head.

Frog Run Farm offered Tom a new band and a place to live, and gave us the missing element necessary to complete our lineup. Our new lead-guitarist was tall, as strong as an ox and possessed the ears of a bat. He wore a scraggly beard and a bowl-cut of unruly brown hair that gave him the look of an inebriated monarch from medieval time. Tom moved into the farmhouse and quickly learned to negotiate the 100-yard ascent to the outhouse, aided along the way by his heightened sense of smell. (Sooner or later, everyone at the farm earned a nickname; Tom became "King Snee," David insisted on being called "X," Dan became known as "Farnsworth" and for reasons I've never quite understood, I got tagged as "The Renegade Prince.")

Tom presented an amusing sight as he shambled around in an unraveling wool sweater, dirty jeans, shoelaces hopelessly adrift and a plastic ukulele clutched to his chest. Invariably, a length of dental floss straggled from a hip pocket. He was born with clouded corneas, severely limiting his sight, but he could discern a greenback's denomination by holding it close to his left eye, although I was sure he could smell the difference between a five and a ten.

19. Tom Ross playing his Trini Lopez Gibson

Much of the farm's once magnificent old barn had caved in under the sheer weight of time, but the remainder loomed large and stable. (Pun intended.) The barnyard resembled an 18th century painting by Constable, replete with cows, horses, chickens and a welter of toiling peasants. Unlike the farmhouse, which had no electricity, our practice room hummed with electronic technology. A snake's nest of wire connected electric guitars to wa-wa's, flangers, distortion-pedals and phase shifters – more than enough glowing gizmos and saucer-shaped cymbals to convince an old Vermont farmer that the Martians had indeed landed.

The unsuspecting livestock loitered in stalls directly beneath our practice room. At the sudden eruption of electric guitars and drums, the horses snorted in fear, reared up on hind legs and kicked the walls. The cows lurched in terror, bleated piteously and rolled their eyes to reveal bloodshot crescents of white. Milk output plummeted drastically. As my Fender Jazz bass shook the rafters, fronds of Fiberglas insulation drifted down amongst the chickens in a gentle, pink flurry. The birds pecked it up like so much cotton candy, which induced a bout of constipation that immobilized the entire flock, including the rooster. To a bird, they clenched their cloacae and refused to squeeze out any more eggs. The hens slumped with heads bowed, eyes shut and feathers ruffled, sadder than a bunch of Woolworth's parakeets on Christmas morning.

Eventually the chickens built up enough internal pressure to again meet their daily egg-quota, but I shudder to think of the insulated omelets that resulted from those first-laid eggs. After the initial shock wore off, the cows adjusted to the daily noise and milk production returned to normal. The horses also adapted to the booming from above and life in the barn settled into a new routine: The New Leaf Band practiced eight hours a day, five days a week and the animals learned that rock 'n roll was here to stay.

20. New Leaf in 1975. Tom Ross, Dave Weaver,
Peter Williams and Dan Fath

As a child of the 'sixties, my generation was the first since the time of Emerson to actively embrace Transcendentalism – a philosophy that emphasized the intuitive and the spiritual in favor of the empirical. Clearly, the proliferation of communes across the land demonstrated an intense desire among the young for Utopian alternatives. The Northeast Kingdom spawned other communes (such as Madbrook and Entropy Acres) in addition to the outlaw anarchy that existed for a time in Earth People's Park, in Norton, thirty-miles further north. The inhabitants of Frog Run Farm, on the other hand, embraced horse-powered organic farming, the sexual revolution, home-groan marijuana, live music and dancing (which, even now, still sounds Utopian to me.)

Winter in the Northeast Kingdom arrives early and lasts longer than in other parts of Vermont, but April slowly bowed to May and four feet of rapidly melting snow sent torrents sluicing to further engorge the Clyde River. Spring brought glorious renewal to all living things.

21. Doodles and Martha

Every successful commune invariably included an individual who lived apart from the clamoring throng. At Frog Run Farm, I became that outrigger – its counter counter-culturalist, so to speak. My decision to live alone in the forest had its foundation in the festering swamp of adolescence, when a sorely vexed English teacher introduced me to *Walden*, never dreaming the seed would fall upon such fertile soil. Possibly the most subversive book ever written, old Henry's deceptively innocent volume hit me right between the eyes. I loved his loquaciously poetic good sense and instantly grasped the wisdom of simplicity. There would be no life of quiet desperation for me. Quite the opposite; mine was amplified through 15-inch woofers! Nor had I any need to lament my previous good behavior, as did Thoreau. There hadn't been any!

With Henry's advice to "live deliberately" rattling in my gourd, and the weather improving every day, I decided to get away from the rooster's relentless reveille. Unhindered by the slightest trace of Hawthorn's Puritanical fear of the woods, I set out to explore the hills behind the farm, determined not to choose the spot for a campsite, but to allow the spot to choose me. I soon found a harmonious glade where four stately conifers demarcated a rectangular zone of level ground. "I'm home," I announced to the trees.

I returned with a borrowed staple-gun, a wheelbarrow full of two-by-fours and a ten-dollar roll of polyethylene plastic. After lashing support beams to the tree-trunks (thus avoided their enmity, had I used nails), I stapled plastic sheets to the frame and installed mosquito netting for windows. I built a plywood door, a platform for my foam-pad mattress and then a shelf for my Coleman lantern and an FM radio that picked up late-night jazz out of Rochester, New York. The passenger side bucket seat from my MG became an easy chair and the fragrant mat of pine needles underfoot pleased me more than an oriental carpet.

Dubbed Plasticland, my translucent abode was comfortable, quiet, waterproof and bug-proof. For the next six months I lived in my homemade plastic palace. Many times I trudged up the hill at dawn, after returning from a gig, to be lulled to sleep by the wind soughing through the pine boughs overhead. All that summer I inspected everything that came within my province; the great swathe of the Milky Way, fog rising from the valley at sunrise and the distant flicker of lightning that aroused the fireflies. Beneath the glare of a full moon's stare, I listened to the serenade of a 600-pound, testosterone-driven bull as it bellowed for a mate. Similarly inspired, I howled a few times myself, our calls mingling harmoniously with a chorus of peepers.

22. Plasticland

No longer the stuff of dreams, the New Leaf Band took off like a rocket. Soon we were onstage more nights of the week than off, playing music we enjoyed, earning a living. Hitherto, we'd been a bunch of misfits scrambling around in vain, but now we were a working band – essential for individual musical growth, while also providing much-needed entertainment for the community dispersed throughout the immense brooding solitude of Caledonia County.

The secret to our success lay not only in our ability to sing and play well but also in our mastery of various musical idioms. Eventually, New Leaf acquired five separate repertoires, each an entire night's worth of material – music as diverse as C&W, Top-40, R&B, disco and jazz. We never revealed our chameleon-like personas, so the folks who listened to us play the music of Bobs Wills and the Texas Playboys in the Woodland Ballroom on Saturday never dreamed we'd be playing Thelonius Monk's compositions in Jaxon's Jazz Club, in Stowe, the following night.

But, as anyone who's ever been in a band knows, there comes a time when a particular member becomes flaky, unreliable or simply loses interest. The reasons are as varied as the people involved. New Leaf underwent its share of personnel changes, but each time the replacement strengthened the band.

Lucy was the first to go. She had enormous enthusiasm but not much rhythm, a fatal flaw for a singer. Perhaps we were too critical, but our intense motivation to push ourselves forward and improve never relented. Six months later we faced the sad fact that Dan had become psychologically unstable. He had the habit of drifting up to the ceiling and hovering there like a helium-filled balloon. When we needed him for a gig someone had to snag him with a pole and pull him back to earth. It got so bad we fired him; a small tragedy for two reasons – he had a good voice and his father owned the company that supplied raw vinyl to album-pressing facilities.

We advertised for a replacement vocalist in the Green Mountain Trading Post and the Boston Phoenix, which resulted in an onslaught of amateurs and various people entirely without musical talent. Some contestants drove up from Boston, only to stumble ineptly through the tunes they were supposed to have learned by heart, prior to the audition. There was, however, one notable exception. I remember the day an immaculate crimson Dodge van pulled into the farmyard – a fur-lined rolling bedroom driven by a tall black man accompanied by an enormous dog that peered through one blue and one yellow eye. The beast was half Siberian husky, half wolf and only responded to commands in Portuguese! Skip strode confidently into our practice room, glanced at our song-list and said, "I know all these tunes."

For the next two hours we played hit songs by the Spinners, Otis Redding, Sam and Dave and concluded the session with a knockout rendition of "Get Away," by Earth, Wind and Fire. It was a flawless audition; Skip sang like Stevie Wonder, strutted like James Brown and had a falsetto that could etch glass. "So, where've you been for the last six months, Skip?" I asked, expecting to hear about a band somewhere.

"In prison," he replied.

"What landed you in the slammer?"

"I killed someone."

A long pause...

"Care to tell us what happened?"

"Some white cat was hassling me in a bar," he said. "So I crushed his windpipe."

Dave paled. Tom blinked. I stared. We'd never auditioned a murderer before and for once I was at a loss for words. A look at the clock told me it was time to load our equipment into the van and prepare for the night's gig. "Why don't you come to Newport and hear us?" I suggested. "We're playing at a place called Gantry's."

But first, a word from our sponsor...

The 'sixties may have ended seven years earlier, but it endured in East Charleston and lingers still, I suspect, if you know where to look. Along with music and booze, marijuana also provided a dependable, albeit illicit, form of entertainment. (A so-called Northeast Kingdom Breakfast consisted of a joint rolled from consciousness-crushing Colombian weed accompanied by a mug of coffee laced with cream and maple syrup. Bacon, eggs, toast and home fries came later.) The law of supply and demand gave rise to a small but fanatical cadre of enterprising albino Rastafarians – smugglers – guys who distributed large quantities of the sacred herb, but who lived off the beaten track, deep in the 'Kingdom's mountain fastness. As a result, the woods were full of connoisseurs, people who called each other "mon," listened to Bob Marley and the Wailers and discussed the bouquet and metaphysical properties of each new shipment.

I include this psychotropic preamble simply to clarify the ensuing events.

Halfway through New Leaf's second set at Gantry's, on the day we met Skip, someone in the audience spotted him as sat quietly nursing a beer. Their eyes met and it was obvious that they recognized one another. Quicker than you can say the word "narc," Skip's cover was blown sky-high. Apparently, our fabulous vocalist was the same undercover agent who'd busted the guy for dealing drugs in Boston, the previous year! Waves of paranoia rippled out amongst the weed-barons in the crowd and our audience quickly evaporated. Skip finished his beer and departed, leaving us to play for an empty house. The band convened the next afternoon.

"Skip's a great vocalist," I said. "I say we hire him; he can bust whoever he wants as long as he shows up for the gig on time." Not too surprising, my idea did not fly. We faced another problem; no one wanted to be the one to tell the guy his services would not be required, so we drew straws. And who do you think drew the short straw? That's right, me. So, with "I crushed his windpipe" still echoing in my mind, I met Skip in the farmyard and stumbled through some lame excuse as to why we weren't going to hire him. He listened quietly and then, without a word, climbed into his crimson van and drove away.

The ploy had come very close to succeeding. What better way to infiltrate our little Shangri La than to join a band, get to know the dealers and then bust 'em?

I saw Skip one last time, later that day, as I drove towards the northern end of Lake Willoughby. I glanced at the water at the northern end of the lake and there he was, floating just offshore in an inflatable raft, eating sardines while his blue and yellow-eyed wolf sat on the sand and gazed wistfully at its master.

***

On warm, silky nights in August New Leaf played outdoors on a wooden stage built deep within the forest's verdant domain. We generated our own electricity and muffled the Briggs and Stratton engine's roar by enclosing it in an insulated doghouse, then isolated it still further at the end of a 200-foot extension cord. A bonfire cast a ruddy glow as exuberant young women danced and whirled beneath the Milky Way's gauzy ribbon, a delightful smorgasbord of feminine wiles and guiles. Truly, the halcyon days of my youth.

A petite parlor panther with a tawny mane caught my eye; her name was Betty but everyone called her Boop. She lived with her young daughter, Lakota, in a house at the end of a dirt lane lined with Lombardi poplars. The woods were alive with bears.

23. New Leaf in 1977. Lee Clark – keyboards, Pat Austin – vocals, Howdy DeHoff – guitar.

Nearby, Lake Willoughby's deep water lay between the cloven humps of Pisgah and Wheeler – sliced in half as if by a monstrous electric carving knife, a realm where ravens ruled the air and nested in the cliffs. Boop and I became an item and eventually she invited me to move in. We shared a lively sense of humor and this brought out my playful streak, and much nimble jousting in the boudoir. Sometimes we were awakened at dawn by the eerily human cries of a rabbit being killed by a fox.

The idyll didn't last, alas. One afternoon, while cavorting in the bathtub, Boop said, "Winter's coming and I'm moving to Austin. But don't worry, you can still rent the house."

One punch to the solar plexus and the relationship was over.

A month later she was gone. With remarkable timing, the heating system in the house seized up on the very day she left. The furnace looked like some mad plumber's idea of a perpetual motion machine – a baffling array of pipes that froze, valves that jammed and switches that didn't. Apparently, the wretched contraption deeply resented the departure of its owner. I did too, but unlike the furnace, I never saw Betty again.

24. New Leaf's final lineup: Charlie McDougal, Peter Williams,
Pat Austin, Lee Clark, Dave Weaver

The Road

Drive a million miles to and from gigs across this well-paved country and strange things are bound to happen. Not just mechanical problems such as melted wheel bearings, worn-out kingpins or a brake pedal that goes all the way to the floor and stays there during an ice storm, but instead, all sorts of strange and treacherous encounters with man, beast and machine.

An automotive breakdown in the Northeast Kingdom in January at two in the morning is not a predicament to be taken lightly. The temperature can be twenty-six degrees below zero with a howling gale. Nevertheless, this is Winter's favorite time to administer a test of survival – the SAT's of adversity – a multiple-choice exam in which the wrong answer can result in severe frostbite. Regardless of one's aptitude or score, it pays to keep alert. And so, when not threatened by drunks behind the wheel, moose, deer, skunks or suicidal owls that fly headlong into the windshield, I have come to expect the unexpected, regardless of where I happen to be.

Like the time I walked through a parking lot in downtown Burlington on my way to a gig at Nectars. I heard a loud, scraping noise and spun around to face an Oldsmobile that had jumped the curb and now bore down upon me. I quickly leapt aside and caught a glimpse of an old man slumped behind the wheel as the car zoomed by and smashed broadside into a parked Chevy. Apparently, only moments before, two young idiots had pelted the Olds with rotten apples, so enraging the driver that he promptly suffered a fatal heart attack. His foot tromped the gas pedal and for the briefest of moments, a corpse pursued me!

Fortunately, not all encounters with auto-motion are so grim.

To celebrate the year of the Bicentennial, 1977, the tiny village of East Charleston held a Fourth of July parade. The New Leaf Band set up its equipment on the back of a flatbed trailer truck and rolled leisurely through East Charlie's blink-and-you'll-miss-it center of town, playing "Hot Rod Lincoln" for the hundred or so patriotic spectators that lined our route. We sailed by at five miles an hour and a minute later rounded a bend in the road and left all traces of humanity and civilization behind. A splendid summer day unfolded as we rolled past thick forest on our right, while the Clyde River meandered through lush fields on our left. We continued to play as our driver looked for a place to turn the big flatbed around. Another vehicle approached as we rolled to a halt. A moment later Jimmy T and his band Boogie Beast pulled up alongside in a van. Their eyes bugged out when they saw us playing on the flatbed, amidst the vast emptiness of the 'Kingdom. "What the hell do you think yer' doing?" hollered Jimmy.

"Practicing," I replied.

25. July 4th, 1977

A few years later I made the mistake of buying an exhausted VW Microbus from the trumpet player in a band called Nightwatch. I spent days patching the vehicle's salt-perforated body with metal screen and a dripping pancake batter of Bondo. When I had done all I could to restore the bus, ·I bolted on plates and drove to a gig. So far so good.

The bus gave every indication of running dependably, but late that night, when I pulled into a driveway to make a U-turn, I cut the wheel a little too sharply and the right rear tire rolled off the edge of the narrow bridge I'd inadvertently chosen in the darkness. The bus tilted back, rotated 90 degrees and slid – ever so slowly – into a ravine! The bus came to rest on its tail, pointing straight up, while I sat and faced the constellation Cygnus through the windshield like an astronaut awaiting liftoff. I climbed out and cursed my stupidity. Suddenly a tow-truck roared up, hooked onto my bumper and pulled the bus out. I started the engine, paid the guy my night's earnings and then drove home as if nothing had happened. Incredibly, the entire cycle of chaos and resolution had taken less than five minutes.

The bus ran smoothly until the day I crossed the Vermont state line; the engine promptly died when the Volkswagen realized that I intended to drive it all the way to Texas. Fortunately, I'd armed myself with socket wrenches and a book appropriately entitled *The Complete Idiot's Guide to the VW Microbus*. After poring over a chapter brimming with glib advice, I approached the engine with a fist-full of tools and adjusted a critically misaligned wing nut, for which I was rewarded with the chugging sound of the pathetic eggbeater known as an engine. On and on I drove, but every 150 miles or so, the motor belched, wheezed asthmatically and died, forcing me to read another psalm in the VW Bible and administer what I hoped was the appropriate fix. This happened so often my knuckles bled and my nerves frayed. By the time I broke down in the sweltering Arkansas outback I was ready to insert a fuse in the gas-tank and ignite it. But instead, I read another chapter in *The Idiot's Guide* and performed yet another repair.

I made it to Austin, but not before experiencing a new wrinkle in the tedious sequence of automotive death and resuscitation. Two guys pulled over to help, or so it seemed, but while one deliberately destroyed the contact points in the distributor with a screwdriver, the other one rifled the glove compartment and stole my watch! I should've taken the time to determine once and for all the cause of the VW's breakdowns, but I didn't, perhaps because it ran beautifully as long as each excursion was less than a hundred miles.

Once in Austin, I adjusted to the urban heat, investigated the numerous venues for live music on Sixth Street and auditioned with a number of bands. I could've joined any number of country and western groups the day I arrived, as there was a shortage of bass players willing to endure the tedium. Instead, I kept auditioning till I found a band I liked. I met "Portable Trainwreck" on Tuesday and by Friday I'd absorbed their entire repertoire, prior to playing a four-set gig in The Double Eagle, a club spacious enough to house the Concorde.

It was an interesting, albeit hot, summer in Austin. I resisted the pressure to wear cowboy boots and speak with a drawl in a city home to at least fifty thousand college students, but in spite of their ameliorating influence I grew tired of the Texas redneck mentality, as demonstrated when I rode a bicycle and underwent the risk of bombardment with empty beer cans thrown from passing cars. I could've stayed and made a go of it, but I decided to leave Texas and return to the green, moist coolness of Vermont – a trip marred by another round of inexplicable breakdowns and inconclusive diagnostics performed by inept grease monkeys wielding wrenches. The bus rattled through state after state until my luck and my money ran out. The wretched machine expired in New Jersey, wouldn't you know, moments after limping into Howard's driveway in suburban New Providence. I spent the next six hellish weeks living in his basement and working on a nearby construction site, pulverizing rocks with an air-hammer in the noonday sun, an activity that will strengthen one's body, but is murder on the fine-motor coordination required to play an instrument.

When at last I'd earned the exorbitant sum needed to pay a local VW specialist to replace the so-called "computer" in the microbus ignition – the cause of all the trouble – I polished the wretched vehicle to a blinding gloss, advertised it in a New York City newspaper and then sold it to an unsuspecting stranger during a thunderstorm…at midnight.

Good Fortune

Getting back into chronological order once more…

After the fall of New Leaf, which resulted from the simultaneous resignation of the drummer and the keyboard player, key members impossible to replace, I began searching for the next band, aware that it would be very difficult to duplicate the musical eclecticism I'd grown accustomed to. In the course of one fruitless audition after another, I met a blues guitarist, a Top-40 band and a composer of melodies so convoluted as to be unplayable. The blues guitarist wanted to form a band but the thought of starting all over, from scratch, seemed too onerous. The Top-40 band was a working ensemble but entirely too stolid. The composer, Muff Ruth, wrote music that made a 12-tone composition by Schoenberg sound like a sea-chanty in comparison.

I spotted an ad in the Burlington newspaper: "Trained vocalist and versatile pianist seek bass and drums." I responded and met Alison Fortune and Flip Casey. Alison was good-looking, friendly and sang (on-key) with relaxed self-assurance. She'd studied music in college and possessed oodles of stage-presence. Flip resembled a suave, young Cary Grant; he sang well and played piano, synthesizer and saxophone. They hired me and Alison suggested we call ourselves Good Fortune, a name that conveyed an entirely positive vibe. Finding a good drummer proved so difficult we were forced to settle for a weak-wristed specimen whose snare drum sounded like a fish flopping in the bottom of a rowboat.

The drummer had access to rehearsal space in a loft above an auto repair shop – a dusty attic cluttered with dozens of stacked cafeteria chairs and a pile of cardboard boxes full of plastic duck decoys. In an inevitable synthesis, I arranged the chairs in semi-circular rows and then deposited a mallard on each one. From then on, our captive audience listened attentively to every note, like dowagers at the opera. Alison did most of the singing, although Flip and I chimed in with our golden chipmunk voices to create solid three-part harmony. Our vocal prowess gave us an edge over the competition and we became a fixture at the Holiday Inn.

For the better part of a year we endured the drummer's insipid playing, his annoying know-it-all personality and his misguided attempts to micro-manage the band. Finally, we couldn't stand it any longer and fired him – letting him have it with both barrels at point blank range. He left with tears in his eyes. Maybe we were a bit ruthless, but he deserved it.

A drummer by the name of Chris Bennett stepped in to replace him; a tasteful player in spite of his size-fourteen feet and an astonishing lack of coordination in all things except playing drums and swallowing single-malt whiskey.

26. Good Fortune

As consummate lounge lizards, we provided whatever style of music the gig required – be it ancient acorns like "Lullaby of Broadway," jazz classics such as "When Sunny Gets Blue," or the gilded thump of Donna Summer's disco hits. (The disco craze may be looked upon as an odious musical transgression, but the songs always featured strong bass lines. Say what you will, to me, disco will always be infinitely preferable to karaoke.)

Flip and Chris and I understood one of the great Truths for success in the commercial music biz – dress well and you'll earn more and work more often. We each invested in revolting, three-piece beige polyester suits and peach-colored shirts, with ruffles that cascaded down our chests. As a result, Good Fortune played more gigs than most other bands I've known.

The income allowed me to buy an Alembic bass, the Rolls Royce Silver Cloud of electric basses. Handmade in California, the instrument was gorgeous but weighed 40 pounds, with another 15 for the hard-shell case and the power supply for the onboard electronics. The Alembic's pickups featured active preamps, virtually unprecedented in 1979. Instead of a simple decal on the headstock (like a Fender bass), the Alembic bore a sterling silver medallion shaped like a hand reaching down from the clouds to grasp an alchemist's alembic. There was just one problem with Good Fortune... the repertoire. We still played jazz standards from time to time, but Alison preferred to sing lachrymose songs like "Feelings." (Playing "Raindrops Keep Fallin' on my Head" on an Alembic was like swatting flies with an H-bomb.)

27. The Alembic bass

Today in Plattsburg, instead of a rubble-strewn vacant lot where the L&M Lounge once stood, one encounters a snazzy new "touchless" carwash. But in the L&M's heyday, Good Fortune played there five nights a week for a month at a stretch. The steady work was welcome even though we played to an empty house more often than not. Live music was, presumably, a tax write-off for the owner. "Good evening tables and chairs," I quipped at the beginning of each gig.

Tedium became our worst enemy. I missed the ducks. The L&M Lounge became, in my mind, the S&M Lounge. Sometimes we amused ourselves onstage by throwing Poppers at one another, those little white paper packets that contain a pinch of fulminate of silver – tiny nodules prone to implosion on impact. When things got particularly dull during the bridge to "Misty," for instance, a fusillade of Poppers was followed by grim-faced concentration as if nothing unusual had occurred. Sometimes the drummer raised an eyebrow to signal the addition of an extra beat to a measure. Then, the trio accented the new downbeat with a resounding crash, invoking a shriek of mock outrage from Alison.

The boredom got so bad one night that I wound up on my knees on the dance floor with one of those rubber lobsters that leaps every time you squeeze a bulb. Another time I concluded a melodic bass solo by laying the Alembic on the floor and then giving the strings a good lashing with my leather strap!

Good Fortune also played in The White Lantern, in Milton – a dark, malodorous restaurant run by a hatchet-faced chiseler named Steve, a guy who trusted no one and often lurked in the walk-in cooler, where he spied on his employees and made damn sure the cash went into the register and not into their pockets. The place reminded me of an enormous hamster cage, lacking only a layer of absorbent wood chips on the floor.

There was one gig at The White Lantern I'll never forget, try as I might – the most awful wedding reception I've ever played (and I've played a lot), followed by an even greater horror. It's safe to say that no one in his or her right mind gets married in Vermont in the dead of February, but the unfortunate couple in this instance were both mildly retarded (and quite possibly their guests as well). How do I know this, you ask? Well, to begin with, the groom resembled a demented orangutan, and all doubt vanished from my mind when he removed his false teeth and chattered them in my face like a novelty item from the Johnson Smith catalog. His leering bride had a face like an angry pudding, topped by a hairdo that resembled a lemon meringue pie. An unusual couple; I shuddered at the thought of offspring.

Steve stood guard over a buffet table amply stocked with a turkey, cheese, fruit, salad, vegetables and rolls, but the food was not for consumption. It was a strictly "look but don't touch" wedding feast. Instead, a sullen waitress snapped her chewing gum belligerently as she doled out glutinous lumps of cold tuna-macaroni on paper plates, accompanied by fistfuls of stale potato chips and watery grape Kool-Aid!

Outside, the fading blue light of a bitterly cold winter afternoon succumbed to an endless arctic night. The temperature plummeted towards absolute zero and only the distant yelping of some misbegotten mutt broke the deathly silence. Good Fortune had been booked to play for the reception, and then again for the restaurant's Saturday night regulars. I was trapped. It was too cold to venture outside and too early to go home. But as frightful as the afternoon had been, the evening was worse. At nine o'clock, only six forlorn customers sat in the candle-lit gloom. They sipped Wild Turkey and amused one another by poking Marlboros into their mouths, ears and nostrils. Good Fortune played a set and concluded with "You Make Me Feel Like Dancing." No one danced and I knew it was going to be a long night, especially when Time itself ground to a halt. We took a fifteen-minute break, then went back on and played "Get Ready." No one could've imagined what they were supposed to get ready for, especially Mr. Henry Mulcoux, an elderly gentleman who sat nearby with chin in hand, arms propped up on bony elbows. Our next song was the Stevie Wonder hit, "You Are the Sunshine of My Life."

"I feel like this is the beginning," sang Alison.

I glanced over at Henry. Our eyes met and I nodded a friendly greeting. Suddenly he clutched his chest, tumbled headlong out of the chair and sprawled facedown onto the dance floor! Steve gestured frantically from behind the cooler's glass door. "Keep playing," he shouted. The headquarters for the Milton Rescue Squad was next door and someone must've called them, because moments later a team rushed in and tried, unsuccessfully, to revive Mr. Mulcoux. We looked on helplessly and played verse after cheerful verse. Fifteen minutes later they carried his body out on a stretcher and the show biz phrase "knock 'em dead" took on dire significance.

Steve was determined to extract his every penny's worth of music from us, and so, rather than send us home early, he ordered us to keep playing. We dutifully cranked out one insipid song after another till one in the morning. I manipulated the strings of my bass and contemplated life's caprices, and swore I'd never play "You Are the Sunshine of My Life" ever again.

The room grew darker as the evening wore on. The candles guttered. A chill not entirely the result of the subzero temperature just beyond the wall seeped into my bones. I sank into a deep, introspective funk. To whom or to what does one turn when the façade of normalcy has been abruptly torn aside to expose Life's fragility? Booze? Religion? What?

The answer was not forthcoming and I knew that without the elusive balm of faith, prayer would be nothing more than hypocrisy.

The hours crept by at a pace that made the downhill migration of a glacier seem hasty in comparison. The two listeners remaining in the audience leaned forward to stare hypnotically at a candle's diminutive flame. They looked like a couple of Cro-Magnons huddled in a chilly, flame-illumined cave – an appalling grotto that none of us are likely to abandon anytime soon.

The Mike Martelo Band

My allotment of Good Fortune ran out when I lost the battle against tedium. The money was good but the repertoire was driving me crazy. (You try playing "We've Only Just Begun" five nights a week to an empty house and see how long before your head caves in.) The desire to burn my three-piece polyester chipmunk suit and ruffled shirts had been growing for months; I longed to drench the odious garments in kerosene, ignite them, and then dance around the flames, howling and gibbering like a baboon. I gave Alison my notice and she soon replaced me with a bass player named Tom Buckley, a good musician who has subsequently filled the slot left vacant by my departure from other bands. I was relieved to never again have to endure the sight of floor-to-ceiling mirrors reflecting uninhabited leather upholstery in the L&M Lounge.

The next gig materialized when Mike Martelo hired me to play in his Top-40 band, a booking he'd had at the Sheraton in Burlington, every weekend for the preceding 8 years. By the time I joined, Mike's keyboard player, Reed Loudon, had left, but I'd heard him with the band before and he always reminded me of the pilot of the Enola Gay – seated behind a bank of synthesizers, wearing a baseball cap, aviator's sunglasses and a pair of Koss headphones.

In addition to Mike on electric guitar, the group featured two female vocalists, Bonnie and Diane, a blonde and a brunette. Our "groovy chick singers," as Mike liked to call them, were easy on the eyes as they shimmied onstage. Diane's husband played drums and used a separate PA to amplify his kit. Mike never sang, but preferred instead to cultivate his image and his chops on the electric guitar. He could easily have been mistaken for the Italian ambassador to the UN, or perhaps the mafia's favorite guitarist. And although he presented a moderately refined appearance, he was as tough as a stevedore and could scorch the paint off the walls with a stunning outburst of foul invective, delivered in a gravel-edged, nicotine-ravaged whisper. Annoy him in public and he'd curse a blue streak; piss him off in private and he'd break your arm.

In those days my quest for the perfect bass sound resulted in a system that included a preamp with parametric equalization and a Crown amplifier that drove four Electro-voice 15-inch woofers. I, too, crooned a song from time to time, such as "The Other Woman," a ditty reputed to have tormented all the lonely widows in the audience.

Every Friday and Saturday night we packed the Sheraton's dance floor with tourists, traveling vacuum-cleaner salesmen, wandering wives, straying husbands, itinerant insurance agents, hungry divorcees and a small coterie of loyal fans. We played whatever was hot on the charts that week, as well as our big production number, "Rocking the Paradise," by Styx.

This regular exposure at the Sheraton led to other bookings. One July afternoon we played a wedding reception in the spacious Knights of Columbus Hall. Inevitably, there came the moment when two hundred guests looked on as the happy couple entwined their arms and gazed tenderly into one another's eyes. The newlyweds held elegant flutes of champagne aloft as the best man stepped forward to deliver a toast. But in that moment of perfect silence, a split-second before the best man could utter a word, Mike delivered a toast of his own… "Here's lookin' up your ass." The phrase hung in midair like a bad smell, followed by a flurry of embarrassed titters from the guests. I, on the other hand, was delighted. Here at last was an unscripted moment in an otherwise tediously predictable ceremony, an event neither the bride nor the groom would forget for the rest of their married lives.

28. The Mike Martelo Band

Mike's band rehearsed every Sunday morning at the Sheraton until the day an unscrupulous employee stole his guitar. (A black, semi-hollow body Gibson jazz guitar, in case you hear of one obtained under suspicious circumstances.) For years he'd been safely locking the instrument in the Sheraton's basement, along with the booze. He went wild with rage when he discovered the theft. Initially, the hotel manager refused to do anything about it, but finally agreed to invoke an insurance policy to replace the guitar. There were other unfortunate occurrences at the Sheraton: Late one rainy night the roof above the stage leaked and water ruined Mike's expensive PA amp. Once again the recalcitrant manager refused to take responsibility, but this time Mike responded with cunning: On Friday evening, just minutes before we were to play for a full house (with a rented PA), Mike went to the manager's office and calmly said, "Listen, you cheap son of a bitch; if you do not agree to replace my PA amp, first thing Monday morning, the band walks and you can tell your full house there won't be any entertainment tonight or tomorrow night either!"

Mike's power play worked but after that, things started to slide. On Saturday night a car hit a power-transmission pole on the street out front and snapped it in half, plunging all of South Burlington into darkness. Our electric instruments were abruptly silenced, prompting a wag in the crowd to shout, "Drum solo!" I peered through the window as brilliant purple arcs of electricity flared from the end of the severed power cable. The hotel's emergency lights came on and we went home early.

Around that time the Sheraton began a massive construction project, one that resulted in the complete demolition of the nightclub. But before its destruction, Dave and I inspected the new, unfinished structure during one of our 20-minute breaks. We entered a room where I noticed a small cone-shaped object attached to the ceiling. I reached up and gently touched it, unaware that my curiosity would set off the hotel's entire fire alarm system. The blaring, nerve-jangling sound filled the air as we scurried away. Once again onstage, we played a tune by the Pointer Sisters called "Fire," just as three fire engines careened into the Sheraton's parking lot with their sirens screaming and red lights blazing. Dave and I suppressed guilty chortles and kept playing.

A week later the word came down from the manager. "It's been nine years," he said, "so we've decided to make some changes…you're fired!"

No testimonial dinner. No gold watch. Mike took the news philosophically. After all, what can you say after a nine-year gig? I was only mildly disappointed when the group fell apart. The Sheraton had paid me only a measly fifty bucks a night, the absolute bottom of the scale, so I added another name to my list of bands and began looking for the next.

The Mood Elevators

A brilliant full moon illuminated the icy cliffs that loomed above the town of Bristol. The snow-bound fields alongside Route 116 resembled the Siberian tundra as I drove to the gig. It was the sort of night on which not even the dumbest rodent would dare stick its nose out of the burrow. Bristol's little hub of commerce included a Laundromat, a pizzeria, an auto parts store, a liquor store, a TV repair shop and a bakery – a typical one-horse town where, in this instance, the horse took the form of a lumber mill. The Village Gate was my destination, a bar in the basement of the auto parts store, a frontier saloon that bore no resemblance to its namesake in Manhattan.

I spotted an identifying sign, parked my car and then stumbled down a crude wooden gangplank like a steer on its way to meet Ronald MacDonald. Inside, the other members of the Mood Elevators were setting up their gear in the dim glow of a buzzing neon beer sign shaped like an electric guitar. Chuck Setzer sat at the keyboard of his Wurlitzer electric piano and looked like a missionary about to deliver a sermon to pygmy headhunters. Tim Searles plugged his Stratocaster into a Twin Reverb amp, hit an E-chord and then adjusted the dials like a technician fine-tuning the device used to administer electro-shock therapy. Pat, his brother, assembled the drum hardware with the weary resignation of a plumber fixing a clogged sink.

Peering into the gloom, I observed the collection of staves, scythe blades and bucksaws that adorned the rough wooden walls. The temperature was ninety degrees, the air so thick with wood-smoke, cigarette-smoke and body-odor it would've killed a rat. Had I farted, it would've been an improvement. All around me, hulking forms gripped beer bottles in callused paws the size of catcher's mitts. I realized we were no longer in the presence of human beings... these were trolls! Trolls at the bar, trolls standing around the woodstove, trolls wearing bloodstained leather aprons and pork-pie hats pulled low over their prognathous brows. The Village Gate wasn't a saloon, it was an uncouth lair filled with denizens of a noisome bog where a demented Oslo Philharmonic played the Peer Gynt Suite perpetually out of tune.

We were a bit late getting started but chose to ignore the club-owner's glowering gaze. When at last we were ready, we opened with "Satisfaction," "Johnny B. Goode" and "I Heard it Through the Grapevine," sure-fire crowd pleasers.

The trolls sat and stared. No one danced. No one clapped.

We played "Ain't That Peculiar." No response.

"Here's a cheerful little song about old age and lonely death," said Tim, moments before launching into a rocking rendition of "Eleanor Rigby." Still no reaction from the trolls.

"I see you didn't dance," said Tim. "If you don't get up for the next one, the hell with you...one, two, three, four!" He hit the opening chords to "Hang On Sloopy" and then bellowed the lyrics as if belching forth lava. Chuck pounded the piano keys with the heel of his foot. Pat hit his snare drum so hard he broke a stick. I thwacked my bass strings hard enough to produce a metallic clang reminiscent of manhole covers being used for a game of tiddlywinks. And still the trolls sat as inert as felled timber. We persevered, nevertheless, and walloped them with one chart-busting hit song after another. By the end of the second set, I could've used some pharmaceuticals myself.

When at last we finished our show and switched off our amps, the audience didn't seem to notice. We packed up our gear and collected our pay.

"Don't ever book us here again," said Chuck.

"You needn't worry about that," Tim replied.

Outside, a throng of swaggering young trolls demonstrated their hardiness by loitering in T-shirts that actually steamed in the frigid air. When I tried to start my car the starter yelped, but eventually the engine caught. I allowed it to warm up, then pulled out and rolled past the TV repair shop where six color televisions flickered silently in the window, each set displaying an identical image of Ronald Reagan's face. I accelerated away as the Gipper's head bobbed and his eyes shone with moral rectitude, no doubt pitching an endorsement for Hostess Nuclear Twinkies, America's favorite. Driving north on Route 116, my clothes reeked of nicotine and my brain was as numb as a coelacanth that has spent its life in a dioxin-laced cesspool. The unblinking moon shone with icy clarity as it cast harsh blue shadows across the road. There was only one thing to do. I donned a pair of headphones, pushed the button marked "play" on my Walkman and listened to the Van Williams symphonic tone poem entitled "The Lark Ascending."

29. In an elevated mood

Jon Hendricks

Most gigs glide smoothly by and offer little that is memorable. The occasional brutish episode is to be expected, but every now and then a gig comes along that is so rewarding that all previous musical perturbations pale to insignificance. The forces responsible for these wondrous events are capricious and involve the players, the venue, the repertoire, biorhythms, the weather, sunspots and the phases of the moon. An example of a miraculous conjunction occurred the day I answered the phone and was asked, "Do you know who 'Lambert, Hendricks and Ross' are?"

"Yes," I replied. "They were the first jazz vocalists to write lyrics for compositions by Ellington and Basie and then sing them in three-part harmony, at breakneck speed, using the melodies originally played by the instrumental soloists. Jon Hendricks invented scat singing."

"That's right," said my unknown inquisitor. "Okay, you passed the test. This is David Millstone, the owner of the Millhouse Restaurant and Gallery in Waitsfield. I'm bringing Jon and his group in to do a series of concerts and we need a bass player to complete the rhythm section. Your name came up. Are you interested?"

"Does Godzilla like Tokyo?" I replied. "Of course I'm interested."

Lambert, Hendricks and Ross released their first album, Sing a Song of Basie, in the late fifties, and Jon has kept the tradition alive by performing around the globe, accompanied by his wife, daughter and a young vocalist who, although unknown in 1982, has since become a household name – Bobby McFarron.

30. Jon Hendricks singing, with Skeeter Camera on drums

I showed up for the first rehearsal with an electric bass. Jon took one look and said, "Bring your upright bass, man." (Somehow he knew I owned one without having to ask.) At the time, I'd been building my chops on the upright for only seven years and felt a bit green, but I knew I'd rise to the occasion. The rhythm section included a skinny young drummer named Marvin "Smitty" Smith, pulled out of the Berklee School of Music to travel north and play the dates. (No longer skinny, for years now Smitty's broad smile has been visible behind the drums as he played and responded to Jay Leno's smutty jokes on the Tonight Show.) Our pianist was the late Alex Ulenovsky, a music theory professor at Berklee and a jazz pianist who evoked majesty from a Steinway. The ensemble also featured Vermont's preeminent jazz guitarist, Paul Asbel.

Jon handed each of us a book of charts and we began rehearsing under the hairy eyeball of the notorious (and the late) David Millstone. I say notorious because of his unflagging ability to insult practically everyone he came into contact with – his chef, his staff and even his customers. Millstone was arrogant, overbearing and bolstered by entirely too much money. Everyone in Waitsfield has at least one apocryphal David Millstone story. For instance...

He once hired a string quartet to perform during the reception for the opening of an art exhibit in his gallery. Resplendent in black tuxedos, the musicians rosined their bows minutes before playing the first movement of Mozart's Eine Kleine Nachtmusik. Suddenly Millstone placed a condenser microphone in their midst and said, "I'm going to record this so I can play it back later during regular gallery hours."

"No, that's illegal," said the cellist. "You are not going to record us."

"Oh yes I am," said Grindstone. "And if you don't like it, you can get up off your fat ass and leave right now."

The musicians conferred and decided that since the gallery had filled with ticket holders, an abrupt departure would reflect very poorly on the quartet. There was only one thing to do – they played as scheduled, but every time they reached a pause in the music, one of the musicians leaned in close to the microphone and whispered, "Fuck you, David."

***

On the afternoon of our final rehearsal, Alex shocked Millstone by asserting, "It's a well-known fact that there's never been a really good wine from California."

"Don't move," ordered Millstone, aghast at the denunciation. The self-professed wine expert scurried to the cellar and returned with an eighty-dollar a bottle Burgundy from a west-coast vintner. Millstone uncorked it, poured a glass and handed it to Alex. He took a sip and swirled the liquid around in his mouth before swallowing. "A tediously bumptious domestic with a deplorable deficiency in breeding," he said, scowling deeply.

Millstone dashed off and returned with another bottle, one so expensive that had I been wearing a hat, it would have flown off my head at the mere mention of the price. And so, while the rest of the band happily quaffed the remaining contents of the first bottle, Millstone poured the new contender into a clean glass and handed it to Alex. "Hmmm," he said after taking a sip. "Intriguing metaphysical tendencies, but definitely not on a par with the best from France."

"Just you wait," muttered Millstone as he trotted to the cellar for yet another bottle of an increasingly costly West-Coast vintage. This went on for an hour and each time, the rhythm section polished off the remains of the previous bottle. Finally, a thousand dollars worth of fermented grape juice later, we all sang, "Gimme' that wine... I can't get well without Muscatel!"

Alex's flushed face beamed a cheery grin and his eyes twinkled mischievously as he sampled another glass of heavenly elixir. The pianist raised his glass to Millstone and said, "I'm delighted to have my low opinion of California's vineyards proven to be so woefully inaccurate."

Our final performance occurred on New Year's Eve, on what proved to be the coldest night of the entire winter. But in the Millhouse Gallery, warm and snug between the Steinway and the drums, I watched condensation on the windows bloom into icy fractal bouquets. The room was electric with anticipation and filled with jazz aficionados, a mixture of high rollers from out of state and indigenous jazz-buffs. We went on at ten and played a terrific set that included classics such as "Every Day," "Whirlybird" and "Avenue C." Then a gentle, haunting Jobim song in which a lover woos his paramour, "In summer, I love you more than any other season. Without you, it's like winter in my heart."

Our first show finished at eleven and I mingled with the crowd until it came time to play again at midnight. At five minutes to twelve a distinguished-looking gentleman wearing the costly raiment of an investment banker approached me, held out his right hand and said, "You're doing a terrific job." We shook hands and I thanked him, cognizant of the small flat object he'd just palmed into my hand. I knew exactly what the little pouch contained, even though I'd never before had the slightest interest in cocaine. "Why not," I decided, "Sigmund Freud was crazy about the stuff." I disappeared into the men's room and locked the door. Sure enough, the leather pouch held a tiny glass vial, a small mirror and a razor blade. I laid out what is known by aficionados as "a couple of lines," lowered my nose to the glass and Hoovered up the white powder. The alkaloid overran the blood-brain barrier in my head and suddenly I felt invincible!

Yes, a miracle cure, just as Ziggy claimed! I wiped the loopy grin from my face and returned the pouch to its owner using the same adroit handshake technique, then thanked him for a profound pharmacological insight. The stroke of midnight found me onstage, literally coked to the gills. Then something unexpected happened. Big Joe Burrell arrived with his mellow saxophone. He and Jon had not seen one another in thirty years and their joyous reunion guaranteed a triumphant set. The New Year now upon us, we played like dervishes. (And ever since, I've never felt the slightest compulsion to try cocaine again.)

After the show we discovered that the temperature outside had fallen to a dangerous thirty-six degrees below zero. The heaters in our vehicles were useless. Any thought of driving for an hour under such conditions was out of the question, so the entire band spent the night in guest rooms in Millstone's spacious house. Our rooms were comfortable but we became aware of the unmistakable sound of Millstone beating his wife. No one intervened. A mistake perhaps, but we were guests, and who knows what consequences such an intervention might've triggered?

The next morning Jon and I sat at the kitchen table wearing luxurious bathrobes while we sipped coffee, ate croissants and read *The New York Times*. We discussed Man's boorish penchant for violence, a topic motivated by the previous night's domestic brutality.

Jon described to me his first encounter with the Dalai Lama, how they'd stared silently at one another for ten seconds, and how the latter then reached out and delivered a surprising bop on the top of Jon's head. I listened as if in the presence of the reincarnated Avalokitesvara himself.

Jon returned to Waitsfield the following summer for more concerts and I was invited to participate once again as a member of the rhythm section. The performances took place in the Bundy Center for the Arts – a spectacular Bauhaus cube of brick and glass perched amidst eighty acres of manicured fields – also owned by Millstone. We played to a packed house, and played very well indeed. But during our last number the door swung open and in walked Art Blakey accompanied by all seven members of the Jazz Messengers! Our performance now over, we basked in the ensuing applause.

Then, without a word, we handed our instruments to the 'Messengers. They played magnificently and delivered a message that plunged me from the pinnacle of acclaim one moment, to the depths of obscurity the next.

Ah well, such is the nature of reality when jazz is being spoken.

Champlain

"Oh crap!" said Muppet after hearing an ominous clank from deep within the Plymouth's automatic transmission. The needle in the temperature gauge crept into the red as the car lost velocity. "We just lost high gear."

I groaned as the crippled Fury slowed to a crawl. We were screwed, no doubt about it; too far from home to turn around, and no chance of finding a transmission specialist open for business in the wilds of Maine on a Sunday afternoon. Trapped, I slumped in the backseat, ankle-deep in a crackling tide of empty Styrofoam coffee cups, donut wrappers and burger cartons.

I pondered my fate – an entire week on the road with a band I hated. Champlain was an industrial-strength band – a rock 'n roll SWAT team that crushed everything in its path and left a swath of incandescent wreckage in its wake. I had no business being in a stadium rock band, but only I seemed to be aware of this fact.

"With a top speed of 23 miles per hour," said Muppet, "We'll get to the gig in about five hours. We'll have just enough time to tune up."

My journey into the heart of dissonance had only begun.

Our destination lay upriver in deepest, darkest, mosquito-infested Maine – the Outer Mongolia of the Soul – in Lewiston, a factory town where the inhabitants all had moss growing on their north sides. It was mid-July. The sun hammered down and the asphalt bubbled as the Fury ambled along, overtaken continuously by little old ladies who glared at us for driving so slowly. "Sorry, lady," said Muppet with a helpless shrug.

"Give 'em the finger," said Pat, our lead singer.

Norbert, our guitarist, stared out the window at an endless corridor of pine trees. Covered from head to toe with a mat of curly black hair, he resembled a Stratocaster-toting bear. He was, however, a master in the art of guitar feedback, for which I dubbed him The Gentle Cyclone.

"Hey Pat," said Norbert, "What do you know about this gig?"

"Not much. The motel's got a club in the basement called the 'Pink Flamingo.' But don't worry. It's not a gay-bar. Ted said it was 'lively,' whatever that means."

"Lively, huh? If that little twerp double books us once more I'm going to mummify him in Duct tape." (Our agent's last name was Malahoit, incidentally, which I changed to Maladroit.)

"Ted's not so bad," said Pat. "He may be flaky but he's honest, most of the time."

As the leader of the band, Pat's philosophy was simple – never go anywhere without a briefcase full of drugs and cash. Nothing more than a happy-go-lucky party animal, his straggling blonde hair and smiling mug brought to mind Huckleberry Hound, the old Hanna-Barberra cartoon character. Every night Pat jumped onstage wearing purple spandex pants, a T-shirt torn in half to reveal a slightly protuberant belly and a pair of running shoes, even though any real running would've killed him.

Muppet steered the car with one knee as he held a cup of coffee in one hand and a gooey, crème-filled doughnut in the other. A skinny, native Vermonter, his pinched Yankee nose poked out from beneath a curtain of auburn bangs. His glossy shoulder length tresses were the envy of Breck girls everywhere. Onstage, he bobbed back and forth behind a phalanx of keyboards, visible only from the waist up, hence his nickname.

Pat twirled the radio dial until a tune from our own repertoire filled the car.

"Dirty deeds and they don't come cheap!" snarled the chorus over and over again.

Short, speedy and rapacious, our drummer – the Blur – was in mid-nap and temporarily inert. And me? I was known as the TV repairman from Mars because I went onstage in an Air Force flight suit emblazoned with NASA, Yin-Yang and American flag patches. I always wore a pair of Ray Ban's to shield me from the glare of a follow-spot and to ensure that no one ever recognized me on the street.

Our perpetually pot-addled roadies, Bigfoot and Sheik, schlepped the gear, ran the lights, the sound, ignited the pyrotechnics and, in a gambit that makes drilling for oil look like a sure thing, persuaded their parents to mortgage their house to raise the funds to buy the band's equipment! These unbelievably naïve parents often showed up at our gigs wearing official Champlain warm-up jackets and baseball caps. True to his nickname, Bigfoot resembled the immense shaggy creature once caught on a jittery home movie. He and Sheik took turns driving the truck and were supposed to have arrived at the Pink Flamingo early enough to unload all seventeen tons of amps, speaker cabinets, instruments, drums and the hydraulic scaffold that held our stage-lights aloft.

Hours later, stunned by our incarceration in the spent Fury, we sat and waited for one last red light to turn green. The Pink Flamingo was in sight; a flickering neon sign portrayed a long-legged bird standing alongside a tilted martini glass. Suddenly our truck veered past. Ignoring the red light, it swerved through the intersection – narrowly missing a police car –

accompanied by a terrible grinding noise and a geyser of sparks from the front axel. The truck shuddered to a halt and we watched, spellbound, as the right front wheel continued on. It rolled through the intersection, across the parking lot and into the motel's office window, shattering it to smithereens! Pat smiled nonchalantly and said, "Well, boys, we've arrived."

One look at the Pink Flamingo and I smelled trouble. Every lamppost in the parking lot tilted at a different angle, no doubt after having been pin-balled repeatedly by drunk drivers. At the base of each metal pole lay an indelible stain left by a thousand furtive, midnight urinations. Cooked by the summer sun, an acrid stench rose from the gooey asphalt and I began to feel like one of Dante's hell-bound Florentines. "Why am I doing this?" I asked myself for the hundredth time. The answer was simple, for the money. Champlain was the only band I've ever been in that paid me a salary, whether we worked or not.

The Pink Flamingo's two-story façade appeared normal upon first glance, but I soon learned just how thin the veneer of normalcy could be. The Bird, as it was known locally, housed a rock club on the ground floor, around back, while the motel's second floor contained a ghoulish sorority of aging prostitutes! We stepped gingerly around the broken glass and checked in while our roadies dealt with the truck, the police, an accident report and the motel's hysterical manager. We were given keys to our accommodations – three dingy, stifling rooms that smelled like incipient suicide and came equipped with air-conditioners that hadn't functioned since the Korean War. I'd brought along an extra rack fan and placed it on the windowsill to get the air moving.

Usually, we walked onstage to find our instruments waiting, tuned and ready. This time, however, we were so far behind schedule we all pitched in to unload the truck and assemble the complex system. It took an hour and a half, but at last we were ready and began our show with an ear-splitting rendition of "Neon Nights" by Black Sabbath. An expanding crowd of grinning yokels listened, the advance scouts sent by their peers to determine whether or not the band was worthy of their attention.

Pat shrieked the lyrics in a vein-distending falsetto guaranteed to snap anyone else's vocal chords. Our second song was an anthem called "Rock of Ages," followed by "Fantasy." My bass thundered like a B-52 strike. Our volume was deafening, but I wore heavy-duty earplugs and resorted to a technique I'd mastered in order to preserve my sanity: I closed my eyes and achieved a serene Zen-like state, a tranquil plateau of transcendent bliss where my mind was as calm as the unruffled surface of a pond.

Meanwhile, the Blur writhed and pounded atop an immense gibbet of drums, cymbals and microphone stands. Bathed in sweat and drumsticks twirling, he froze for a millisecond in the strobe light's staccato blink. The Blur may have been fast on the drums, but he'd earned his nickname as a result of an unrelated talent. I had never met anyone who could survey an audience seething with young women and select the one most eager to accompany him outside to perform fellatio in the bushes during intermission! His accuracy in selection was astonishing. His stamina was impressive, as he sometimes demonstrated – twice in one night – with two different females.

Halfway through "Another Thing Coming," Muppet climbed atop his Hammond organ and exhorted the crowd, beating time with his fists like some deranged air-traffic controller conducting mid-air collisions. Bigfoot threw the switch to activate the fog machine. The device hissed malevolently as it spewed a carcinogenic cloud of white vapor into the air. I grabbed my World War II gasmask, pulled the ugly, canister-snouted apparatus over my head and began to sweat like old dynamite. Slithering tendrils of fog engulfed the crowd.

Timed to coincide with the first ear-splitting chord of "Party on the Patio," Sheik pushed a button and the gunpowder-charged flash-pots at the foot of the stage exploded like Claymore mines. They shattered my inner tranquility and plunged me to the seventh bardo of musical hell – that infernal region reserved for all musicians who have the temerity to think they should be playing "The Pines of Rome" instead of the sound track for Armageddon.

31. Champlain

Without warning the electricity cut off and the stage went black. All the instruments were silenced, except for a measure or two of solo drums, then blessed silence.

"Yes," I realized, "there really is a God."

The befuddled crowd milled about in the fog-choked blackness, then began to whistle like an entire prairie dog village on high alert. A moment later the lights came on and Verne, the little ferret that owned the place, pushed through the audience barking, "Too loud! Too loud! You're too goddamn loud!" He approached the stage and glared at me. I leaned over until my lips were an inch from his ear. "Go away," I said, slowly and distinctly. He continued to peer at me through watery eyes as opaque as poached eggs, and then heeded my advice. When the power came back on a minute later, Pat picked up his wireless microphone and said, "We can all thank Verne for that timely interruption. Anyone out there think we're too loud?"

A terrific cry of "NO!" erupted from the mob.

"What a' ya' say," said Pat. "Let's hear it for Verne!"

Another hearty cheer went up, laced with hoarse shouts of "Fuck you, Verne!"

No question about it, Champlain was ridiculously loud. A four-foot high stack of PA amps delivered 8000-watts to two towering banks of speakers, enough sound pressure to slam the needle in Sheik's hand-held DB meter to the peg and keep it there.

After the show, each member of the band drifted away to seek solace in his own way. Muppet unwrapped a Ring Ding and sipped his tenth cup of coffee of the day. The Blur lit a joint and then opened a tiny glassine envelope containing a gram of coke. Norbert uncorked a bottle of Jack Daniels. Pat intoned a mantra – "Let's party" – then set to work with a bong in one hand and a beer in the other. I stepped outside to eat a cup of strawberry yogurt and gulp fresh air. A blizzard of bugs swarmed in the bright nimbus cast by each tilted lamppost in the parking lot. High above, only the brighter stars pierced the sweltering blanket of humidity. I saw a meteor zip through the constellation Cygnus, a streak of white against the velvet sky.

"Ah," I sighed, "peace and quiet at last."

But it was not to be. A screen-door burst open and Bigfoot lunged through carrying a television in his arms. He stumbled several paces, fell headlong and pitched the set into the air. The Zenith scribed a shallow arc, hit the ground not ten feet from where I stood and imploded with a shattering crunch.

"They don't make 'em like they used to," said Bigfoot, snickering as he got to his feet.

"What's going on?" I demanded.

"I tried to rearrange the furniture in our room," he replied. "I thought the TV was screwed down so no one could steal it, but it wasn't. I yanked it off the table and lost my balance. Don't worry. We already know the motel has insurance."

***

Our week at the 'Bird coincided with the hottest days of the summer – a succession of humid, sweltering days during which the sun beat down like a thousand Moslem devils tapping on my cranium with ball-peen hammers. The motel's swimming pool contained a slimy green broth that had never known chlorine, but the overhanging trees created a shady oasis where I spent my afternoons reading Conrad and writing in my journal.

The days dragged on and we played every night till two in the morning. It didn't seem possible, but every day grew hotter and muggier than the one before. By the end of the week Pat's endless party had left him with dark half-moons beneath bloodshot eyes; Norbert's second bottle of Jack Daniels was empty; Muppet was a nervous wreck after over-amping on caffeine and sugar; the Blur ran out of coke and subsequently exhibited personality fluctuations that made those of Dr. Jeckyll and Mr. Hyde look like simple mood swings in comparison. And although Bigfoot and Sheik suffered from sleep deprivation and poor nutrition, they still managed to toke-up every hour. Compared to the others, I was in good shape: I'd brought along a foam pad, sheets and a pillow, which enabled me to enjoy a good night's sleep in the quiet seclusion of the band's empty truck.

Sunday finally rolled around, my last day in Purgatory, and with it came the 'Bird's annual Wet T-Shirt Contest, generally regarded by the clientele as being better than Christmas at Disneyland. This year's contest attracted over two hundred hicks, a sweaty horde that salivated at the thought of glistening female flesh on display. Few had been near a naked breast since infancy and judging by their looks, none were likely to get closer anytime soon.

Half an hour before the band began its final performance we heard a loud roar as a wolf pack of Harleys filled the parking lot, their noisy engines belching and sputtering ominously. A platoon of grizzled, leather-clad Visigoths switched off, leaned their hogs on kickstands and entered the club. The name "Beelzebub's Brothers" was embroidered in red on every leather jacket; the human equivalent of black flies, they too had detected the imminent presence of female flesh. The tension in the air was palpable as the 'Brothers bellied up to the bar to guzzle Penobscots. It dawned on me that we now had a volatile mixture of heat, humidity, thirsty hoodlums, alcohol and lust. The safest place was onstage, so I donned my bass and waited. Soon, we opened the first set with "The Kid is Hot," followed by "Eminence Front" and then "Trooper."

Faint purple flashes of distant lightning punctuated the deepening twilight. Inside, our stage lights illuminated tumbling nebulas of dust and nicotine molecules as they coagulated in mid-air. Halfway through our set, the moiling throng grew impatient. "Enough music already," someone shouted. "Bring on the bitches!"

Verne elbowed his way to the stage, grabbed a microphone and shouted, "Welcome to the seventh annual Wet T-shirt Contest!" (Cheers from the crowd.) "But before we begin, I just wanna' say it's been a real pain in the ass having this band here." (Cheers from the band.) "And even though they're a bunch a wild animals, they're the best goddamned band we've ever had and I'd personally like to invite them back again!" (A tumultuous cacophony erupted as every chimp on the rock let out a scream.) Pat smiled, put his arm around Verne's rounded shoulders and said, "Not a chance in hell, Verne old buddy."

Undaunted, Verne said, "Okay! The moment you've all been waiting for. Let's start the contest. Bring out our foxy contestants!"

The walls reverberated with the sound of unbridled simian joy as nine young women sauntered across the dance floor. "Remember ladies," said Pat, "you're competing for 250 dollars in prize money."

I grabbed Norbert's microphone and said, "Step right up, ladies! Now's your chance to indulge in some good, old fashioned exploitation!"

"Get that mike away from him," ordered Verne.

"Now you know why we never let him have one," Pat explained.

Bigfoot slewed the 1000-watt follow-spot like a turbo-laser on the Death Star as the women entered the dazzling arena created by dozens of PAR lamps overhead. Some of the contestants glanced nervously at the bikers, while others knocked down last minute shots of tequila. One exultant Amazon exuded so much confidence that I wondered if she might consent to mate with Beelzebub himself, right there on the dance floor.

"Drum-roll, maestro," said Pat.

The Blur played a press roll on his snare as Dawn stepped forward. She was a supple vixen with raven-black hair, and might've been a trapeze artist. I couldn't take my eyes off her lithe torso. Bigfoot swiveled the spotlight and pinned her like a deer in the high beams. Sheik hit a button and a tape played "Hit Me with Your Best Shot." Pat grinned lasciviously as he emptied a pitcher of ice water on her heaving bosom. Dawn gasped and her eyes grew wide as the liquid coursed between her breasts. Her nipples sprang to attention and the crowd erupted with a cheer.

The next contestant was a bubbly blond named Ginger who wore a brassiere that cupped her breasts with a pair of Union Jacks. Pat leered for a moment and said, "Hail Britannia!" Ginger pulled on a dry T-shirt; but now, protected by a double layer of fabric, the ice water failed to produce the desired effect and the audience booed.

"Remember ladies," said Pat, "No skin, no win." The mob roared its agreement. With 250 bucks on the line, the remaining competitors sluiced more tequila down the hatch, while outside, lightning pulsed brighter and with greater frequency.

The contest gathered momentum. The bikers pressed in and filled the air with an aerosol haze of testosterone. Knuckles dragged across the floor. Saliva dribbled from a dozen hairy chins. The event took on the Sybaritic splendor of a victory revel for Genghis Khan's army after a hard day of conquest and pillage. (Could rape be far behind, I wondered?)

Every male in the room felt an electric tingle in the scrotum when Mandy slinked into view. The little minx had the soul of an exhibitionist, the heart of a narcissist and the body of an Olympian. She began a lascivious strip tease to the taped sounds of "Feel Like Makin' Love," then draped herself on a chair and arched her back to receive the unholy baptism. Pat ogled her magnificent endowment and said, "Quite a team you've got there."

Mandy gasped when the water hit, but when she tore off her T-shirt to reveal a pair of golden, devil's food cupcakes with cherries on top, I knew the contest was over. The crowd voiced its agreement with a roar of approval, but after sensing that they'd become dangerously aroused, several of the contestants changed their minds and wriggled away.

With only two remaining, the women knew their only chance to win hinged upon a bold stratagem. And so, after a brief huddle, they offered a double dip and Pat obliged with a pitcher in each hand, but when they too yanked off their T-shirts and then rubbed their nipples against one another's, the king of the bikers lunged forward and tried to bury his face in the naked cleavage of quadraphonic breasts!

"Get away you brute! Where's your fuckin' manners?" yelled one woman while the other slapped him upside the head. The 'Bird's bouncer – a guy named Tiny and anything but – waded in and yanked the biker away by the scruff of the neck. The thwarted, lust-maddened lout turned and decked the bouncer with one punch. The crowd went berserk. In an instant every T-shirt in the club had been torn off and held aloft like a victory pennant. The women screamed and ran through the grappling throng, their breasts jouncing wildly as they dashed for the door. The vortex of chaos expanded when, out of sheer frustration, Beelzebub's Brothers began to pound one another. All allegiances collapsed as everyday, rank and file thugs knocked one another senseless. The approaching storm continued to gather strength and a thunderclap shook the building. The Wet T-Shirt gods were angry!

Verne scuttled out a side door clutching the cash register in his arms. A minute later he reappeared empty-handed, fought his way to the stage and yelled, "This is all your fault. Get off my stage. You're fired!"

Bigfoot chose that moment to set off the flash-pots and to activate the fog machine. A head-splitting blast stunned the crowd, followed by an evil hiss as the machine wafted choking vapor. I'd seen enough, so I put my bass in its case and shouted, "Hey Pat! Grab my stuff in the room and look for me on the road when you head out. I'm leaving now."

I skirted the edges of the writhing, pummeling fray and leapt out a window. A monsoon-like downpour instantly drenched me as I darted beneath the wind-lashed trees. Vast electrical discharges coruscated through the heavens, turning night into day with lurid flashes, followed by instantaneous detonations of thunder. A squadron of police cruisers swerved into the parking lot with their gumball machines flashing angrily. The cops took one look at the nunchakus being clamped around the combatants' throats and smiled grimly as they drew their batons.

I paused at the boundary of the 'Bird's perimeter and watched as swarms of unsated satyrs staggered through the door and into a parking lot jammed with motorcycles, pickup trucks and police cars. Another blinding electrical discharge was followed by a shuddering clap of thunder that sounded like Charles Atlas tearing in half every Manhattan phone book ever printed!

There, illuminated by the purple glare, a clutch of mascara-streaked harpies stood on the motel's second floor balcony and cackled gleefully. I turned and set off at a brisk pace towards the interstate highway, determined, if need be, to walk all the way back to Vermont. Forked lightning skewered the clouds and I welcomed the torrential rain's cleansing wrath.

At a bend in the road I turned for one final glimpse of the 'Bird. A fortuitous lightning strike had set the roof ablaze! Although soaked to the skin, I smiled with infinite satisfaction as fire engines sped past. I strode purposefully into the wind-lashed darkness. The rain subsided and the thunder faded, although the fiery orange glow in the sky behind me did not. Eventually the clouds dispersed, swept away by incoming high pressure from the west. High above, the Milky Way shone with bright indifference.

I walked on.

Nightlife

The following winter, on yet another night dominated by glacial arctic air, I drove the winding Stowe mountain road towards the propane-fed flames that flickered atop the torch placed at the entrance to the Top Notch Resort. I parked my '74 Camaro in the distant corner of the lot, amidst a rusted task force of duct-taped jalopies belonging to the resort's employees, far from the fleet of gleaming Mercedes with out-of-state plates owned by the guests.

One more Saturday night and I was looking forward to inaugurating my new, hand-carved German string bass with Nightlife, an ensemble that featured the singing of Penny Towers, Steve Young on piano, Brian Kent on saxophone and Steve Adler playing the drums. We were a jazz swing band and our repertoire consisted of classic tunes such as "I Get a Kick Out of You," "All of Me," "Darn that Dream," plus some original tunes written by Penny. We began our first set in the cozy atmosphere of the Buttertub Room, an intimate, barn-board-paneled, thickly carpeted lounge furnished with couches and plush easy chairs. Penny sang lustily, cracked jokes and made the listeners feel as if they were enjoying a concert in their own living room.

As we were about to begin our second set, I decided to introduce our vocalist to the audience. I stepped up to her microphone with every intention of saying, "And now, the starlet of our show," but my neurons misfired and out popped, "And now, the harlot of Stowe." The audience gasped in astonishment. Penny stared at me, speechless, then laughed brightly and recovered control of the stage (another example of why bands never let me have a microphone.) We quickly sidestepped my verbal gaff – best described as a vowel movement – by playing a soulful rendition of "Moonlight in

Vermont." Our set proceeded smoothly until halfway through "Gimme' a Pigfoot and a Bottle of Beer," when I noticed tentacles of smoke pluming silently into the lounge, at ceiling height above the door. I left the stage, approached the bartender and said, "Excuse me, but I think we're on fire."

Sure enough, a massive chimney fire had erupted in the freestanding stone fireplace in the main lobby, a blaze that quickly filled the air with densely roiling white smoke. Moments later, a number of fire engines roared into the parking lot and disgorged dozens of helmeted smoke-eaters wrapped in yellow plastic and carrying axes. They swarmed through the building and rousted every guest, diner, drinker and employee and herded us all outside into the frozen darkness. "Jack Frost nipping at your nose," sang Penny as we loitered in the cold, each syllable accompanied by a puff of vapor. Huddled under the piercing stars like so many demented penguins at the South Pole, we were safe, but my magnificent new bass was still inside, onstage.

"What if the entire building goes up?" I wondered. Plenty of other resorts had met such a fate – the Hillwinds in Franconia, for instance – so I dashed through the main entrance, then towards the Buttertub Room. I saw no signs of actual fire, although there was plenty of thick smoke. Suddenly Paul Bunyan's great grandson loomed before me in a yellow slicker, blocking my path. "Where'd you think you're going, buster?" he demanded.

"My expensive new bass is right over there," I said, pointing to the stage.

"You're not going in there."

"Apparently not," I muttered, turning and retreating towards the door. Not so easily thwarted, however, I hurried to the far end of the parking lot and reentered the building through the kitchen, then ran the length of a long corridor, past the game room and the imitation farmhouse parlor and on towards the Buttertub Room.

Suddenly that same enormous fireman appeared before me.

"What are you doing back in here?" he shouted. "I should arrest you right now, get out!"

Still no flames visible anywhere, so I tried to reason with him. "Look," I said, "my hand-carved bass is right over there. Just let me grab it and I'll be out of here. It won't take a second."

The big yellow galoot was really angry now and lunged at me like James Arnes as the alien in "The Thing from Another World." I deftly outmaneuvered him and sprinted down the corridor. Once outside I merged into the shivering crowd – some clad only in pajamas, slippers and bathrobes. We waited nervously for either an all-clear signal or a spectacular inferno. It didn't take long to extinguish the chimney fire, or to disperse the smoke with large fans. Half an hour later we were allowed inside, the guests to their beds, Nightlife to the stage.

32. Nightlife: Steve Adler, Penny Towers, Peter Williams and Steve Young

Seven months later, on a balmy summer evening, Nightlife was again performing in the Buttertub Room. We played as well as we ever would, somehow producing a sound greater than the sum of our parts. Penny sang with her usual gusto, Brian wailed on the sax, Steve clattered happily on the drums, the other Steve rippled the keys adroitly and I kept my mouth shut.

After the gig we packed up our gear, said goodnight to one another and went our separate ways. At a quarter to two I steered my Camaro north onto the empty interstate. It was a perfect summer night: A current of warm, fragrant air caressed my skin, a full moon sailed between puffs of cumulus and the radio played the pastoral music of Delius. It felt good to be alive; my third year at the University of Vermont was about to commence and I was looking forward to another semester devoted to oil painting, Shakespeare and making the Dean's list.

And then it happened...

There, blocking my lane lay the smashed remains of a car! I jammed on the brakes, pulled over and switched on my flashers. I took my flashlight and hurried over to the crushed metal husk as it lay upside down amidst fragments of shattered glass and an expanding pool of oil. Dreading what I might find, I peered in but the wreckage was empty. The only sounds were the somnolent rustle of leaves and the chirp of a weary cricket. The driver had to be near so I searched the vicinity, but found only a pair of broken wire-rim glasses and a wallet, empty except for an insurance card. Aided by the light of the moon, I searched the grassy median and found the twisted remains of the driver. Something about the angle of the limbs left no doubt in my mind that he was dead. But to be sure, I aimed my flashlight at a human head that had been crushed like a grape. There was nothing I could do. Within minutes, other vehicles approached and pulled over. When a State Trooper arrived, I departed. Although my idyllic drive had turned ugly, the tale gets even weirder.

The next day I read in the newspaper that a 21-year old driver had blown his brains out with a 45-caliber pistol while on the interstate, prior to hitting a rock abutment at high speed! An entire year would elapse before the dark smudge on the pavement finally disappeared, and many more years before I would be able to pass the spot without recalling the grim scene.

I spent the next few days trying to erase the gruesome image of the dead youth from my mind, doing little except swim in Lake Champlain, bask in the sun, guzzle Molson and listen to the restless slap of water hitting rock. It's the best remedy I know and I highly recommend this sort of Paleolithic therapy – regardless of the provocation – especially in August when humidity turns the setting sun into an orange billiard ball and the rising full moon into a cue ball, a time when God calls his next shot…"Blue planet in the corner pocket."

Bands that Never Got Off the Ground

For every fledgling band that succeeds in vaulting the hurdles that guard the stage, many others fail. Those that do get airborne must then confront a daunting gauntlet of unforeseen hazards. Some bands break up as a result of an ultimatum delivered by the bandleader's wife, conveyed with a withering glare, arms folded across her chest and the toe of one foot tapping impatiently on the linoleum. "You can have the band or you can have me," she will declare, "but you can't have both, so what's it gonna' be?" (The hubby always acquiesces to the wifey.)

A band can fold when a key member, usually the singer/songwriter, packs up and moves away (as with Martin Groswendt and the Home Wreckers, or Chip Wilson in the Style A's). Other bands throw in the towel after years of successful collaboration, but must then hire a bassist for one or two final performances (as happened to me with The Chet Arthur Five and Bongo Moon). Nimbus redefined "evanescence" by performing only once before vanishing quicker than a charmed quark in an atom smasher. Most dire of all, a band can cease to exist when Death – that most implacable of impresarios – cancels a musician's contract (as in The Len Ghendal Trio.) Chapter Eleven lived up to the name's dire connotations when Andy Shapiro, the keyboard player and vocalist, died of a brain tumor after unwittingly ingesting a toxic chemical in his tap water.

The source of band drama is usually far less appalling. (Absurd runs a close second, with Ridiculous gaining fast.) The singer in Sheri and the Blue Collar Band hated me, for reasons unknown. The drummer in Aquafuge quit when the bandleader informed him of the remote possibility that he might

200

someday be required to wear a bow tie onstage. "A bow tie?" he gasped in horror. "No fuckin' way. I'm outa' here." One band chose the name Syzgy, a term that none of its members could pronounce or spell, let alone remember. (My Random House Unabridged Dictionary defines "syzgy" as "the conjunction or opposition of two heavenly bodies.")

33. Syzgy: Peter Williams, Penny Towers,
Jeremiah McClain, Steve Adler

Some bands fizzle out due to sheer incompetence. The Jokers fell flat after endless basement rehearsals that never brought them any closer to the stage. The lead guitar player was tone-deaf, which didn't help. I remember carefully tuning his instrument, and then watching as he strummed a chord, frowned and detuned it to his satisfaction. Sometimes a band disbands because key members are unable to put aside their personal differences. The group may create excellent music, such as the Parisian style jazz played by Swingshift, but unfortunately, David Gusakov did not get along with Chip Wilson and this doomed the group.

34. Swingshift

Nightwatch is an example of a band that had strong vocalists, superb instrumental soloists and a crackerjack rhythm section, but a group that failed because of a simple economic reality; a seven-piece ensemble costs a lot more to hire than a trio or a quartet.

35. Nightwatch: From left to right - Jack Phipps, Peter Williams, Shamms Mortier, Howie Mitchell, Peter Smith, Jim Cheney, Dave French

Musicians and lemmings have much in common. When young, their fur is sleek, their eyes are bright and gigs are plentiful. Yet, both species are prone to a cycle of boom and bust. An abundance of food (or gigs) is invariably followed by overpopulation and the inevitable crash. Exceptional specimens may persist beyond the usual allotment, but sooner or later, all will succumb to a bite from the jaws of Time...even Mick Jagger.

Lemmings are not durable. Cats eat them; owls swoop down and carry them off. In times of hardship the little buggers will consume one another. And don't forget their alleged penchant for hurling themselves over a cliff and into the sea, for which the only analog for musicians is the abuse of drugs. Bands are not durable: Friendships sour, goals change and entropy kicks in. While no predators lie in wait to cull the weak, the inept or the stupid, attrition remains high. And as my experience has shown, there are few endeavors among humans as prone to disloyalty as a band, the only possible exception being marriage. With few exceptions, any member can be booted out at any time, for reasons that are as diverse as the people involved. But regardless of the reason, there's always a replacement ready and eager to take over at a moment's notice.

If you are blessed with youth, a photogenic face and a head of hair malleable to unorthodox styling, and in addition, you write catchy tunes and sing on key, then and only then will you be allowed to purchase a ticket for the Rock 'n Roll Lottery.

But in spite of the astronomical odds for winning, the great lemming Iditarod continues and the headlong sprint towards the abyss never ceases. At this very moment hordes of riffing rodents tumble head-over-heels clutching guitars. Listen carefully and you'll hear the chunking of dominant seventh chords, the sibilant squeal of rodent harmony and the pentatonic licks that mingle with the pattering of a million furry feet.

All heed the call, "Onward! Ignore that precipice up ahead!"

The Nashfull Ramblers

The leader of The Nashfull Ramblers – Rick Norcross – was a jocose, guitar-toting circus ringmaster with ginger-colored muttonchops, a twenty-gallon Stetson and a talent for marketing. When I joined, the Ramblers had already been in existence for decades, cruising from one outdoor music festival to the next like a vintage Rambler Ambassador hitting potholes and crushing armadillos. During my seven years with the band, we played venues that would've made Federico Fellini ecstatic; from the redneck roundup in the beer-pavilion at the Champlain Valley Fair – right alongside the racing pigs – to the elegant black-tie soirees held to celebrate Howard Dean's gubernatorial election victories (where we alternated sets with Sterling Weed's Imperial Orchestra, an ensemble that has performed, in one form or another, since before the First World War. Mr. Sterling Weed recently passed away at the age of 105, but was still playing gigs with his orchestra at 103!) The winning pig, incidentally, received an Oreo cookie for its effort; the winning politician earned an attaché case full of 'em.

On the evening of July 3rd the local TV weather-clown donned his propeller-driven beanie, looked at the sky and said, "Just a stray chance of a thunder-boomer on the Fourth." Good news because the Ramblers were scheduled to play the next evening on a baseball diamond in the heart of Hinesburg, just prior to the town's annual fireworks display.

Independence Day dawned sultry, the air heavy and oppressive. At noon the sky churned with enough negative ions to signal the onset of the apocalypse, but with no hint of rain. I arrived at the baseball field late in the afternoon and drove across the infield to a stage erected atop the pitcher's mound. A pyrotechnic crew behind home plate attached fuses to dozens of canisters loaded with high explosives. The temperature hovered at ninety-two degrees. Not a breath of air stirred. The sky modulated from cobalt blue at the zenith to purple at the horizon, where the hills faded into the azure dream of a painting by Maxfield Parrish.

A column of spectators marched across the outfield clutching folding chairs like so many bearers on safari. Soon the entire field would be inundated by thousands of moms, pops, teens and tots fidgeting on blankets or wandering amongst the junk-food vendors. The afternoon wore on, but still no threat of rain, even though the humidity level defied the laws of physics by exceeding one hundred percent.

Kevin Healey and Doug Pomeroy arrived and busied themselves setting up guitar amps and drums. Nearby, Rick stocked a concession table with cassettes, T-shirts, key-chains and official plastic Rambler beer mugs. Junior Barber, our crack Dobro player (and a Viet Nam war vet), arrived next. Tall and thin, he reminded me of a TV cowboy gunslinger – the silent stranger who comes to rid the frontier town of outlaws, rustlers and varmints. Junior approached with a worried look on his face.

"Howdy, Sheriff Twang," I said. "How're things in Dodge?"

"I'm concerned," he said. "I got a letter from the IRS ordering me in for an audit."

"Don't worry," I replied. "I have the perfect solution to your problem. First of all, be sure to wear your best suit when you go in for the audit. Be calm, be polite, but whatever you do, don't make eye contact. Look out the window with your best thousand-yard stare. And most important, every time the IRS agent says the word 'income,' you holler 'INCOMING!' and throw yourself to the floor. Do that and I guarantee you'll be out of there in less than ten minutes."

"Thanks," said Junior. "I'll bear that in mind."

Just then our lead guitarist pulled up in a battered pickup and began to unload his gear. Larry Beaudry had a stocky build, long black curly hair, a beard and a slight limp – the result of a shotgun accident that necessitated the attachment of an artificial foot. He was a terrific guitar player and a commanding vocalist. When Larry sang, people dropped everything and turned to listen. I liked him because he gave the impression that at any moment he might run amok. Not only that, but I was impressed by the tattoo on his upper arm – a masterpiece of ink that featured a grinning skull in a cowboy hat, a dagger embedded deep in one eye and the word "Mother" etched beneath in blood red!

By seven o'clock the baseball field swarmed with every stump-jumping weed-bender for miles around, all eager to observe the undisputed cultural high-water mark of the year.

I'd waited as long as possible before donning my official Rambler stage duds – an itchy, long-sleeved, black polyester cowboy shirt spangled with machine-embroidered roses that resembled gunshot exit wounds. A gritty patina of sweat and dust coagulated on my skin even before I'd finished buttoning the damn thing, a scratchy varnish that did nothing to impede the mosquitoes beginning to arrive from a nearby swamp.

At seven-thirty Rick strutted onstage tightly corseted in a fringed buckskin jacket, jeans, a string tie with silver bolo, Stetson and a pair of alligator skin cowboy boots; to all eyes a heroic figure just slightly larger than real life. He basked in the stage lights clasping an acoustic guitar inexplicably known as "The Wonder Guitar." But after so many years of neglect, his pudgy fingers were as inflexible as cucumbers and the guitar had devolved into a prop, to be donned and then beaten into submission. (Our soundman made darn sure it never went out over the PA.)

We opened the show with "Ramblin' Fever," a tired old war-horse long overdue for the glue factory. The intro hadn't even finished before the frogs in the swamp dove for deeper water. Clouds of mosquitoes homed in on the stage as evening settled. The little fiends plummeted like kingfishers, stabbing their pointy little beaks through polyester and into flesh. I fought valiantly, swatting my attackers with one hand while pounding on my bass with the other, but the more bugs I mashed into a greasy smudge, the more determined they became.

The light of day slowly expired and the swamp exhaled an eerie fog that crept slowly closer at knee level. "Thank you, ladies and gentlemen," said Rick after a desultory round of applause. "Our first sitting ovation of the evening."

We took advantage of the pause between songs to douse ourselves with bug repellant. Our next musical offering was "Rolly Polly," an up-tempo western-swing number about a ravenous kid who eats everything except oats and hay – the perfect song in view of the lowing herd assembled before us, all greedily scarfing down hot dogs, beer, cotton candy and ice cream.

The Ramblers were a good band: Rick sang in a voice once described by the local media as "a friendly tenor." Kevin looked like an attorney from the firm Strato, Castor and Pollex, but he played his Stratocaster just like ringin' a bell. Junior never missed a note, ever. Larry played lead guitar with the maniacal focus of an amphetamine-crazed trucker highballing his eighteen-wheeler straight to hell. Tony's fiddle provided down-home authenticity. Doug's drums and my bass were, as usual, so deep in the pocket we encountered lint.

Halfway through a Cajun tune called "Down in Louisiana," we were startled by a loud WHUMP! as the first rocket soared into a sky not yet sufficiently dark for fireworks. The projectile tumbled end over end, high into the air. Then a bright flash, a deafening explosion and a drizzle of glowing embers that fell onto the stage and singed our scalps. Another rocket went up. WHUMP! Then another punch to the solar plexus and more glowing cinders. The skyrockets went up at a frugal pace, about one a minute. (What small town fireworks displays lack in tactical throw-weight, they make up for with unabashed patriotism.) The crowd rose to its feet and sang along when the mayor played a scratchy old recording of Kate Smith singing "God Bless America" through an equally antiquated speaker. This was followed by the Pledge of Allegiance, accompanied by a ground-display in the shape of Old Glory – a geyser of silver sparks that burned brightly for about twenty seconds. The shimmering cascade fizzled out but left an enormous curtain of cordite smoke that drifted ever so slowly through the humid air. The launch crew used flares to ignite more rockets, prancing like Satan's roadies to illuminate the cloud with a hellish red glow. Larry sang "Six Days on the Road" as a fusillade of explosions hammered us with shuddering impact concussions that threatened to derail the song.

When the cordite cloud drifted onto the stage, I took one breath, coughed and yelled, "It's toxic! Run for your lives!" I abandoned my post, dashed across the infield and outflanked the deadly smokescreen. A rocket exploded prematurely and Junior hit the deck as purple streaks went zinging by. Children screamed, women fainted and grown men panicked as the creeping cloud engulfed everything. Fistfights broke out amidst rumors of an armed desperado holed up in a nearby house, defying the State Police's attempts to apprehend him. Packs of snarling dogs attacked one another in a vicious tornado of fur. And finally, as the fireworks hit their climactic peak and the sky blazed with dazzling colors, the weather forecast for "a stray chance for a thunder-boomer" became a reality. A wind-whipped deluge soaked everyone to the skin. Vast dendrites of electricity slashed the heavens as thunderclaps drowned out the fireworks explosions. Torrents of water sluiced down as we struggled to unplug our guitars and amps before they electrocuted us. Suddenly the stage lights blinked out and darkness prevailed. Another flash of lightning briefly illuminated the chaotic scene; water dripped from the brim of Rick's Stetson as he gazed at the fleeing crowd. His only comment, "Aye, caramba!"

***

Every August, the Ramblers played in the beer pavilion at the Champlain Valley Exposition – two nights of raw-boned barnyard vitality, an event that inspired even the most implacably introverted farmers to abandon their hardscrabble fields and gather for a beer-soaked hoedown with their peers. Each year the members of Rick's band swore they'd never play there again, but I loved it. Medieval in its simplicity, the gig afforded a good long look at the vanishing breed that is rural Vermont.

Fresh from the timeless drama of hurling baseballs at wooden pins to win a Kewpie doll, or tossing plastic rings to win a shiny trinket, or gazing covetously at spotless new tractors, the beer pavilion's patrons frolicked with giddy abandon. As thirsty a pack of gomers as you'd ever hope to see, they quaffed pitchers of beer, downed fistfuls of fried dough and a gut-distending blitz of "Eyetalian sawsitches."

Saturday night in the cacophonous beer tent: A half moon rose above the Ferris wheel as the month of August slipped away. The discordant, shrieking clamor of the midway rang in my ears. Garishly lit rides clattered and whooshed as hydraulic machinery flung cotton-candy-smeared children through the warm air in giddy, nausea-inducing arcs. The barkers barked and the racing pigs squealed competitively. The air was rich with the aroma of greasy corn dogs, popcorn, candy apples and Philly steaks sizzling alongside green peppers and onions. The tantalizing smell mingled with the aroma of equally nutritious animal by-products from the agricultural exhibits. Above it all I heard the distorted boom and sizzle of canned music blaring from the Tilt-a-Whirl, the Whip, the Bumper Cars and a dozen other death-defying attractions.

I'd arrived early and had ample time to wander through the fair's tawdry neon splendor. An enormous painting at the entrance to one attraction caught my eye – a portrait of a deathly pale man with long disheveled hair and staring, bloodshot eyes.

"SEE THE DRUG ADDICT!" shouted the barker. "Step right up and for only one dollar you can see with your own eyes what drugs can do to a man!" The "addict" in the painting looked a lot like our lead guitarist, Larry.

I entered a large wooden building for a look at the hundreds of exotic hens that pecked disconsolately at one another, at the rabbits the size of golden retrievers that moped listlessly in their wooden pens and at the African gray parrots that looked as if they'd seen it all before. I checked my watch – almost time for the Ramblers to begin – so I started back towards the beer pavilion. Halfway there, Willie Nelson's nasal voice rang out through the best sound system half a million bucks can buy. "Crazy…"

So close yet so far, I thought, as Willie and his band performed on a stage the size of a tennis court, before a grandstand packed with thousands of adoring fans.

The Ramblers, on the other hand, played on a tiny platform amidst the raucous clamor of drunken farmers stomping the beer-soaked straw underfoot into a muddy porridge. The ambient noise in the beer tent was so loud it drowned out Willie's show. We were forced to turn our own amps up, but still couldn't compete with what I call the barnyard effect, the ceaseless din generated whenever humans congregate in large numbers, a sound akin to that created by a head-on collision between two trucks, one bearing pigs and the other empty milk canisters.

Without warning, an airborne invasion struck – dozens of praying mantises! – a buzzing tactical wing that rode into the tent on a current of warm air. Some of the goggle-eyed predators whizzed by, others smacked into our faces. One landed on Rick's microphone, but he kept singing, oblivious, as the little monster snatched at his mustache with scissoring claws.

The noise and the drunken bedlam made for a long night. Invariably, tempers frayed and fights erupted, similar to the combat of bighorn sheep butting heads to determine dominance. At each outbreak, the security goons dragged the scuffling combatants apart and then ejected them unceremoniously into the outer darkness. Disaster was narrowly averted when one of our metal light-towers collapsed and crashed to the wooden dance floor, narrowly missing the head of one crazy old geezer who capered about holding a live chicken in his arms for a dance-partner!

Willie and the boys finished their concert hours before we finished ours. They received thirty thousand dollars for their show. I earned a hundred bucks for mine. Willie retired to his luxurious motor home to relax and smoke weed with his cronies. I rattled away in a Bondo-swathed Toyota that had traveled more miles than the distance from the Earth to the moon.

The Ramblers played a gig at the automotive racetrack in Barre. Thunder Road racetrack looked ludicrously small, especially with a dozen muscle cars orbiting in a tight, angry cluster. There were no straight-aways, as in Daytona, just a diminutive asphalt donut fit only for NASCAR-fixated motor heads dreaming of the big-time. We arrived early in order to set up our gear on a flatbed trailer parked safely, or so we thought, below the brow of a hill, well away from the track. We were told that once the race was over, a tractor would tow the flatbed onto the track and position us facing the grandstand. Till then, however, it was a classic "hurry up and wait" scenario as a thousand fans watched the distinctly American spectacle of noisy, brightly painted vehicles zooming around and around in second gear, each driver's cheek distended by a nasty wad of Red Man chew.

The relentless howl of tortured engines set my teeth on edge. The sweet summer air was tainted with the smell of burning oil and carbon monoxide. Suddenly a wheel flew high overhead and crashed into the woods a hundred feet away, shattering tree limbs and our sense of safety. We posted lookouts instructed to sing out whenever a piece of potentially decapitating shrapnel headed our way. I fully expected the launch of a racecar to smash our stage to smithereens.

When at last the frenzy of internal combustion subsided, hours later, the fans stormed out as if to escape a trigger-happy skunk. It took only five minutes to tow the flatbed into position, but by the time we played our first note the grandstand was deserted. Apparently, each driver in the crowd had been eager to rev up his or her own vehicle, and then compete for the imaginary chrome-plated trophy that awaited the first to cross the finish line at their respective driveways.

36. The Ramblers at Thunder Road: Leo Roy, Doug Pomeroy, Eric Koeller, Kevin Healey, Jennifer Prince, Peter Williams and Rick

Peculiar Gigs

I'll wager a night's pay that never before in the history of western civilization has an ensemble played a transcription of Bach's "Jesu, Joy of Man's Desiring," and then followed it with a rendition of "Big Bad Leroy Brown." This happened while playing with the Len Ghendal Trio at the Woodstock Inn. (Woodstock, Vermont; a bastion of old-money Republicans and a long way from the south side of Chicago.)

I mention this peculiar juxtaposition to further illustrate my ability to adapt to any musical environment, no matter how disparate. Endowed with the survival skills of a chameleon, I'm as comfortable playing "Fly Me to the Moon" on a string bass at a Republican fundraiser as I am playing "Eyes of the World" on a six-string electric bass at a marijuana grower's harvest celebration. That such polar opposite musical events take place isn't surprising, but what is extraordinary is the fact that they were back-to-back gigs, on Friday and Saturday.

The tuxedo gig occurred in The Old Lantern, a cavernous wooden hall in Charlotte, Vermont, scene of countless dances, weddings, Halloween parties and, in a closely related field, political fundraisers.

The event was designed to generate cash to help finance the campaigns of Vermont's foremost Republicans, Jim Douglas for governor and Brian Dubie for lieutenant governor. The Queen City Jazz Band was the perfect choice for music; led by Mel Gold on trumpet, the band featured a crack lineup of middle-aged, silver-haired musical veterans – Roger Giroux on piano, Mike Martelo on guitar and Zip Aloi on drums. We sounded excellent, not surprising when you consider that our combined musical experience totaled almost 200 years.

Generally speaking, I like politicians about as much as Bob Marley liked them, which is to say, not at all. I've always resented their glib ability to say whatever it was they thought a particular audience wanted to hear. But nevertheless, on that evening, fresh from the barber and dressed in my new tuxedo, I, too, easily passed for a loyal member of the GOP.

The band swooped down on the hors d'oeuvres that had been laid out on long tables. We drank champagne and ate jumbo shrimp, swallowed strawberries dipped in chocolate and crackers carpeted with brie. Thus fortified, we played a set that included "Besame Mucho," "There Will Never Be Another You" (known amongst jazz musicians as "The Shepherd's Lament") and then the favorite song of political fundraising junkies everywhere, "God Bless the Child"(that's got his own.")

An open bar provided the lubrication necessary to foster a convivial atmosphere, a mood that was curtailed when it came time for the candidates to address the crowd.

Jim Douglas spoke first. A politician since his prenatal days, intent upon occupying the governor's chair, his voice was amplified through a feedback incipient Bogen PA so ancient it should've been donated to the Smithsonian long ago. Mr. Douglas promised (in gentle, well-modulated tones reminiscent of Caspar Milquetoast) to improve Vermont's business climate and to infuse local government with his own slightly myopic vision for the future. In my humble opinion, not at all the stand-up-and-cheer issues that inspire voters in Burlington, that unrepentant Socialist enclave where the Republicans get their asses kicked on a regular basis.

Then it was Brian Dubie's turn to speak. Mr. Dubie was an airline pilot and radiated sobriety and reliability, as all who fly for a living must. But although he spouted economic prophecies bursting with optimism and can-do spirit, his speech was short on specifics, as if to say, "Now, don't worry about landing this 747, folks. You leave that to me."

Neither candidate has ever felt the slightest economic pinch or twinge of hunger. Both are honest men – an admirable, albeit uncommon trait for politicians – and I commend them, but since very little of anything politicians do ever affects me personally, I've come instead to expect a certain amount of sheer entertainment from their efforts. (Like Bernie Sander's rabble-rousing Socialist bluster or the mangled syntax of little Bush.)

Alas, no such inspiring zeal from Douglas or Dubie.

After the speechifying came a memorable feast – juicy slabs of Filet Mignon flanked by scarlet lobsters drowned in molten butter. I consumed a superb dinner, although my introspective thoughts centered upon my appallingly intractable disenfranchisement. But never mind that, anyone who pays me to play jazz and then feeds me lobster, steak and strawberry shortcake has my vote. (Just kidding.)

After coffee and more potent beverages the real business of American politics began – the forging of alliances and the writing of checks.

Both candidates won election, incidentally.

37. Republican Camouflage

The very next night I played a gig at the opposite end of the socio-economic totem pole, down from its lofty apex and deep into the loam where worms wrest a living from the cold, dank soil. Blues for Breakfast had been hired to play for a private party hidden in the woods of upstate New York. A flyer for "Chickenstock" had gone out to a very select cadre. The poster featured the image of a chicken sitting on a nest of marijuana leaves, but it gave no directions; unless you knew the perpetrators, or were conducted into their midst wearing a blindfold, you'd never find it.

A classic fall day in the North Country gave way to a clear, crisp evening. An early frost had been predicted and sure enough, the temperature plummeted from a pleasant 67 degrees in the afternoon to the lower 40's by sunset. At eight o'clock the thermometer read 38 and the Pleiades shone brightly in the eastern sky (never a good omen when one is about to play music outdoors in northern New England).

Blues for Breakfast assembled its electronic furniture on a makeshift wooden platform surrounded by derelict mobile homes, broken tractors and a barn stuffed to the rafters with the recently harvested fruits of our host's agricultural activities. I wore a wool jacket, scarf and a furry Cossack hat, but there was no way to counteract the psychological refrigeration induced by the blue floodlight pointed at the band.

We opened with "Cold Rain and Snow" by the 'Dead. Someone built a bonfire to ward off frostbite, but even so, Chickenstock was the sorriest excuse for a party I've ever seen...not so much as a pretzel to eat and only one keg of some nameless, utilitarian beer. The succulent barbequed chicken I'd envisioned was nothing more than graphic allegory.

Suddenly a squad of bearded gnomes on ATV's roared out of the forest, dismounted and took up positions around the keg. Others heaped timber on the fire, prior to settling down for some serious dope smoking. The blaze spat orange sparks into the air, although wood was by no means the only substance burned in great quantities that night. The temperature continued to fall. We played in the frosty glare of the blue floodlight while the aurora flickered silently overhead.

Charlie, the leader of the band, called out for marijuana buds. A swarthy guerilla farmer ambled up, smiled and placed a fresh, leafy stalk on the electric piano.

Forget Beaujolais Nuevo. Think "New Boo."

***

And so, in the course of playing a thousand gigs I've learned that the best philosophy is to wear protective coloration, blend in and keep my mouth shut. Some gigs are more than simple studies in contrast, some redefine weirdness; like the time I played for an Arika graduation ceremony in the heart of the Northeast Kingdom. I have no idea what the seminar entailed, but a hundred and fifty people had just completed the two-day event and now sat on the floor facing a large painted canvas. "You will focus upon the blue square," intoned the guru-guy in the white suit. I sat amidst the acolytes and wondered what was going on. Ten minutes later the guru-guy with dilated pupils and a 1000-watt smile said, "Now we will all concentrate on the red circle."

I began to fidget as the crowd stared silently at the red circle. After another lengthy silence the guru-guy said, "And now we will all focus on the yellow triangle."

Finally, after another interminable wait, the white-suited sage awarded prizes. "Let's bring Frank up and congratulate him on completing his Arika training." Frank got to his feet and shuffled into the spotlight. "Tell us, Frank, how has Arika changed your life?"

"Well," he replied sheepishly. "I used to use Vaseline when I masturbated, but I don't anymore." The crowd cheered wildly.

"That's it," I said. "I'm outa' here."

***

There's nothing quite like an unexpected brawl to get the blood pumping, especially if you are a participant. Physical danger rarely threatens at a gig, but when it does, it reveals just how thin a veneer separates us all from outright savagery...or is it just me?

The last fistfight I was ever in took place in 1977 when The New Leaf band played at the Blue Bandanna, a popular ski bar at Jay Peak. Whoever heard of putting a stage up in the attic of a nightclub? Absurd but true, we were forced to wrestle our heavy equipment up a vertical wooden ladder – an unwieldy Fender Rhodes electric piano, bass cabinets, drums and the entire PA – onto a platform located high above. Once there, we retracted the ladder with a ridiculous system of ropes, pulleys and a counterweight formed by a barrel full of rocks.

We played an energetic first set, tunes by Earth, Wind and Fire, Stevie Wonder and The Average White Band. We played with ferocious energy. But unfortunately, isolated high above them in our garret, we were cut off from all visual contact with the dancers. When it came time for an intermission, we lowered the ladder by hoisting up the barrel. The musicians clambered down, one at a time. I was the last to descend and was in the process of lifting the ladder up and out of the way when a stranger screamed in my ear, "THIS BAND SUCKS!"

I'd left my earplugs in, or I would've suffered eardrum damage. But nevertheless, it was such a blatant assault that I reacted with animal fury and slammed the ladder down on the guy's head. The clout sent him sprawling, but failed to dissuade him from further aggression. He staggered to his feet, charged, and in an instant we were grappling furiously, knocking tables and chairs over and dashing people's drinks to hell. The bouncer quickly pulled us apart and tossed my assailant out the door and into a snow bank. I returned to the stage, strapped on my Fender Jazz Bass and wished I'd had it handy when the fracas erupted – I would've lambasted the guy, just like Fess Parker bashing Mexicans with 'ol Betsy atop Walt Disney's Alamo.

The incipient psychopath wandered off into the night and I never saw him again, but I later learned that he beat up a woman in the parking lot and sent her to the hospital. The State Police grabbed him, locked him up and swallowed the key.

Science Fixion

Science Fixion began as a simple acoustic duo – vibes and bass – but, like a bug-eyed alien in a monster movie from the '50's, the duo morphed into a towering seven-piece Juggernaut that left its footprints on the ceiling, in the Russian snow and on the surface of distant moons.

The expansion began when Dr. Shamms R. Mortier and I added Dave Hebert on drums and then, in a bold stroke, Peter Brown on cello. As the principal cellist for the Vermont Symphony Orchestra (and my classical bass teacher at UVM), Professor Brown was hell-bent on exceeding the limits of the classical canon. And so, he bought a pickup for his cello, an amp and a Quadraverb, a digital processor that made his instrument sound like a cedar saxophone. Professor Brown's unprecedented defection from the orchestra convinced his classical cronies that he'd taken leave of his senses. "Pete's lost his mind," they said, "but he don't seem to miss it none."

We named our quartet Northstar and played jazz standards such as "Willow Weep for Me," "Four," and "Well You Needn't," but it wasn't long before the repertoire began to expand at a rate equal to the outward expansion of the universe. Cosmologically speaking, Shamms (which rhymes with alms) has always exhibited a pronounced red shift, which, in case you've forgotten, is the systematic shift towards longer wavelengths in the spectra of light from receding galaxies.

38. Northstar; Shamms Mortier, Dave Hebert,
Peter Brown and Peter Williams

Eventually we added Lee Clark on piano, Steve Blair on guitar and Roger Berard on drums, some of the best jazz musicians to ever walk the hills of Vermont. Ken Dunbar, a talented conga player and percussionist, became the group's Seventh Son. Of Jamaican and Scottish ancestry, and a skilled woodsman, Ken looked like the dreadlock embodiment of Daniel Boone and Bob Marley.

Shamms began his intergalactic musical exploration by studying drums with the principal percussionist from the Chicago Symphony Orchestra. Then, under the profound influence of John Coltrane, Pharaoh Sanders and Rhassan Roland Kirk, he mastered the tenor and soprano saxophones... and then applied his visionary talent to the vibraharp. (The instrument of Lionel Hampton and Gary Burton, the vibraharp is a percussion instrument similar to a xylophone, but has, in addition to resonant brass ingots, an array of spinning rotors in hollow tubes suspended beneath each metal bar. Played with two, three or four mallets, the vibraharp provided the sound whenever ecstatic African natives played music on a gaping hippo's teeth in very old black and white animated cartoons.)

The KAT Mallet Controller eventually replaced Shamms' rattling old Deacon vibraharp. Superficially, the playing surface of this twenty-first century instrument resembled a vibraharp, but emitted no sound unless connected to an amplifier. Then, the KAT could reproduce the digitally sampled sound of any instrument under the sun, plus a baffling assortment that owed nothing to old Sol. As a result, we never knew what might erupt from one performance to the next... Earth-shattering tympani? A choir comprised of multiples of Shamms' own voice singing diminished chords in Klingon? Ethereal Pan pipes from Alpha Centuri? Volcanoes spewing molten sulfur on Io, Jupiter's least hospitable moon?

Absolutely.

"You know, Shamms," I said, remarking upon the group's habit of pushing the galaxies aside, "this band is science fiction."

"You're absolutely right," he replied, and immediately changed our name from Northstar to Science Fixion. Our goal had never been mere transcendence, but miraculous transformation – the essence of all science-fiction literature and film. (Shamms was, after all, the only person I've ever known who, as a kid, spent as many afternoons in the dark watching monster movies.)

Shamms was a prolific composer and wrote music that capitalized upon the strengths of each instrumentalist in the band, a little trick he'd learned from Duke Ellington. Our repertoire included music conducive to interstellar travel, the blues, swing, hard-bop, funk and a Middle Eastern dervish-stomp I nicknamed Atomic Klezmer. Science Fixion redefined eclecticism. What other band in Vermont had the temerity to play original music that fused Brazilian samba with an Appalachian reel? In one highly cinematic composition entitled "Within a Rain Cloud," we evoked (in the mind's bloodshot eye) a ceremonial Mayan procession moving slowly through the jungle…a stately pageant comprised of feathered royalty, shamans, warriors, dancers, slaves, peacocks, monkeys, jaguars and an ample supply of sacrificial virgins.

39. Shamms Mortier

Peter Brown also contributed original compositions. In "Strange, Lovely Moon," a stunning 12-tone piece, he sang the lyrics in French and in falsetto. ("Oh strange lovely moon, beneath the pale blue sky, I long to see your falling lips beneath the pale moonlight.") In "Deserted Planet," he scored the work for symphony orchestra, which we performed in concert.

Science Fixion appeared regularly at Nectar's on Sunday nights, playing to a meager crowd of obviously deranged individuals who stared as Shamms hovered in midair like an iridescent jazz hummingbird. Surrounded by an arsenal of digital vibes, saxophones, timbales and a dozen other percussion instruments, he invariably achieved escape velocity, weightlessness, and then incandescence. Did we confuse the listening public? You bet we did.

Although our concerts were well attended, Science Fixion remained an underground phenomenon, even after several live broadcasts on Vermont Public Radio. When we played for Burlington's Discover Jazz Festival, the report came back that we were "too jazzy." I suspect that one reason we attracted an ever-diminishing audience had to do with timing; we hit the local music scene just as Phish gained the momentum that allowed them to conquer the world. In the early days when Phish played at Nectar's, their music was improvisatory, accessible and danceable. Science Fixion, on the other hand, played melodies so complex no one could possibly comprehend (or whistle) them. Our harmonic structures were challenging, to say nothing of time signatures that flummoxed all dancers except Twyla Tharp. We tore the roof off as a jam band, but as Phish's reputation grew, our's shrank. (When Phish played Shamms' composition, "Never Abandon Hope," at their final concert in Coventry – the event that clogged miles of interstate median with abandoned vehicles – they never even mentioned his name.)

As graybeards two and three times the age of the kids that dominated the Phish audience, Science Fixion was unable to successfully compete in the local music arena. Then as now, the diminutive, unbearably self-congratulatory Burlington music scene relies on selling alcohol to the sexually active children known as college students.

40. Science Fixion in concert in the University of Vermont recital hall.
Shamms Mortier, Roger Berard, Peter Brown, Peter Williams,
Steve Blair, Lee Clark.

As time progressed, Shamms' compositions began to rely more heavily on his singing. In "Let the Jazz," for instance, his growling voice sounded like a mad pirate king exhorting cutlass-toting scalawags..."Let's sing, me hearties!" The second verse calls for anarchy. "Climb down from your towers and jump to the street, disrobe your psyche and stomp your feet! Knock out the streetlamps and climb a high tree, let the JAZZ shine her dark light down on Thee!"

Unfortunately, our formidable instrumental prowess could not overcome the fact that our music was too eclectic, and at times, too cosmic. (I know for a fact that the late Sun Ra loved our first CD, "Swimmin' in the Human Condition.") The album contained numerous gems, such as Steve Blair's composition, "Reflections," but each track veered wildly in musical style – from funk to be-bop to celestial – thereby eliminating any sense of continuity or unity.

My job, in addition to playing the bass, was to run alongside Shamms and nip at his flanks like some clever sheepdog trying to influence the direction of a galloping water buffalo. I came to believe that the bulk of our performances were entirely too self-indulgent. The solos were always long, but any suggestion to curtail our approach evoked only the most caustic scorn from Shamms. Science Fixion had become a dictatorship, benign perhaps, but tyrannical nonetheless. (Like being in a blues band led by Mussolini!) Finally, after years of mounting frustration, I grew fed up having my input ignored, valid opinions that might've helped the ensemble reach a wider audience. I reached the breaking point one night during a rehearsal and stormed out in a fury.

In retrospect, I regret a decision made while under the stress of a recent marriage already in a state of collapse. (Wedlock lasted less than two years and went up in flames rather like the Hindenburg.) A year after my departure, Science Fixion toured Russia, although why they did so in the dead of winter is a mystery. It would've made fine fodder for my journal, as there's nothing as bracing as a vodka-soaked scramble across the frozen tundra in trains that always departed in the blackest hour before dawn.

Eventually, Science Fixion lost cohesion, as if absorbed by the black hole lurking at the core of our galaxy; a pity because it should've endured as one of Vermont's preeminent musical powerhouses. Of all the bands I've been in, Science Fixion created the most exciting, challenging and original music. Too bad so few of the group's three albums were ever purchased. To this day, unopened boxes of shrink-wrapped cassettes and CD's linger in suspended animation awaiting the ears of musicologists as yet unborn.

Since the dematerialization of Science Fixion, the musicians have gone on to other worthy endeavors: Peter Brown atoned for his sins by selling his amp and the Quadraverb, and is now once again a respected member of the classical music community. He's still angry that we were unable to impose the slightest degree of democratic control over the band – but at least he no longer has to endure being drowned out by the larger amplifiers that flanked him onstage. Steve Blair is the head of the jazz department at Johnson State College and plays in a variety of superb ensembles. I've lost track of pianist Lee Clark (and Andy Hildebrandt, his successor), but Roger Berard still plays the drums.

"Ensembles come and ensembles go," Shamms once remarked fatalistically. True, but in my opinion a flimsy rationalization for the inability to trust the advice of one's collaborators – all accomplished musicians with a wealth of good judgment. But hey, being omniscient ain't easy!

***

For the last decade, Shamms had been hard at work in his own studio, an incredibly claustrophobic chamber I dubbed the "data-crypt." There, surrounded by computers, keyboards, MIDI controllers, synthesizers, mixers, "magic boxes" and esoteric gadgets too numerous to mention, he created stunning digital animation, electronic paintings, technical treatises, reviews of the latest in animation and music production software, and last, but not least, original music. The data-crypt had become so tightly packed that if one were to burrow behind the outermost layer of equipment, one would encounter successively more archaic forms of technology – regressing through the era of videotape, film, print and graphic design – to eventually uncover an Edison wax cylinder machine.

It breaks my heart to report that on the afternoon of May 22, in the year 2008, Shamms Mortier died. Six years ago, the doctors gave him only months to live, but now, sadly, the forces of entropy have finally caught up with him His atoms have dispersed, to once again rejoin the cosmos, from whence they came.

Shamms left behind a large, but as yet unknown number of compositions in the many notebooks he filled with music notation and on the hard drives within his astonishingly complex computer system, music that has never been heard. It is essential that this music be preserved and completed, a huge and daunting challenge – adding bass tracks and percussion to the unfinished recordings, then mixing the tracks and designing CD cover art – but one I gladly undertake. I am determined to make the fruits of Shamms' musical genius available, to inspire all who are brave enough to venture beyond the limits of what they know and understand. Such fearless exploration into the vast star fields of the galaxy has always been at the core of Shamms' creative soul.

I'll conclude this tribute to the great shaman with the opening invocation from "Celestial Mechanics," one of the many as yet unfinished albums.

Place of Lights

Come, take a trip with me, to the center of the galaxy, let us see what sights there be, in the place of lights...the place of lights.

See the stars go spinning round, hear that roaring nova sound, we are lost by what we've found, in the place of lights.

Feel the gravitation grow, electromagnetic flow, you'll forget the things you know, in the place of lights.

Giant force fields twist your mind, soon you've lost all sense of time. Space is just a nursery rhyme, in the place of lights.

Memories of eons past, tear our hearts like bits of glass. The mystery removes her mass, in the place of lights...the place of lights.

Shamms R. Mortier

Run for Cover

Nothing moved on Main Street except a frozen wind as the forlorn city of Barre squatted beneath an opaque February sky. I stood on the dark, icy sidewalk and considered my options; I could descend a few steps to Planet Rock, Vermont's only strip club, or climb an equal number of steps to Billy Bob's, a saloon with about as much charm as an abandoned mine shaft. It wasn't really a choice, as I was obliged to play in Billy Bob's with Run for Cover, a shameless Top-40 band. I heaved a deep sigh of resignation, savored one last breath of clean air and then climbed the steps, into the cloying reek of yesterday's cigarettes and tomorrow's carcinomas. Inside, the walls featured crude paintings of longhorn steer skulls and saguaro cacti. Eagles soared on the ceiling, but in my eyes they resembled buzzards seeking a meal. The stage area waited at the far end of the room, not far from a pool table where two homegrown rocket scientists conducted experiments involving trajectory, ballistics and momentum.

Ed Devarney, the leader of Run for Cover, was busy connecting wires from a PA amp to a couple of speaker cabinets so decrepit they left shards of splintered plywood on the floor after every gig. The band's repertoire was equally dilapidated. Ed had been playing guitar and singing the same tunes for thirty years – hits such as "96 Tears," "Gimme Some Lovin'" and "Gloria."

"Hello Ed," I said. "How do you like North Korea so far?"

"Button your lip, mister," he replied, his black beard wagging with every syllable.

The day's dose of Paxil was wearing off and I felt myself sinking into the quicksand. Soon, I feared, only a bowler hat would remain where I once stood.

Jason Corbierre arrived laden with drums, a cheerful guy and an excellent drummer. (Since his time playing in Run for Cover, I'm pleased to report, he's toured the world with Roomful of Blues.) While Jason assembled his kit and I tuned my bass, Greg Hansen struggled up the front steps pushing a Hammond organ strapped to a dolly. Mild-mannered businessman in Boston during the week, Greg loaded up his van and drove to Vermont every Friday after work to play gigs, sometimes through blinding snowstorms. (He, too, was a good musician, but unlike Jason, his efforts have only succeeded in catapulting him deeper into obscurity.)

Ignoring the state of my own musical dossier, I swallowed what remained of my pride, along with another little pink pill. Then I reminded myself, again, that I was playing music I loathed in order to buy food and pay the rent – a shaky arrangement to be sure – but one that gave me ample time to paint and build sculpture. (I've been an artist for as long as I've been a bassist. Remember, painting is nothing more than frozen music.)

"Good evening ladies and gentlemen," said Ed, testing his microphone. "I'd like to congratulate you all for braving the elements and venturing out to drink like fish."

"Forget the small talk, Ed!" yelled the bartender. "Play some fuckin' music"

"Hey Fred…fuck you too!" (Yes, it was that sort of place.)

We opened our first set with "Mustang Sally," but in spite of my opinion of the exhausted repertoire, our sound was as slick as a pitcher of warm maple syrup being poured over your head. Jason and I locked into a groove as Ed's durable voice infused a semblance of vigor into the song. Nearby, four frumpy K Mart cashiers sat in a wooden booth that resembled a stall – a quartet of truculent viragos with mascara-rimmed eyes that pierced like daggers. "That ain't country!" one hollered after the song's conclusion, her voice as abrasive as sandpaper.

"No, it sure as shit wasn't," Ed replied.

Thus chastened, we played a lugubrious ballad that extolled the virtues of driving along the dirt roads of life, a song about a "newfound tenderness" and other nauseating blue-collar platitudes. We waded through the same three chords at a dismal dirge-like tempo and placated our critics' outraged sense of propriety. It was going to be another long dark night of the soul.

Upon completion of the set I fled outside to gulp air. One glance at Barre's deserted downtown was all it took to persuade me to investigate the strip club downstairs. I entered and encountered a doorman wearing headphones and a wireless microphone; lacking only a battle-ax, a leather jerkin and a helmet, he reminded me of the porcine guard stationed just inside the entrance to Jabba the Hutt's palace. "I'm with the band," I informed Jabba's doorman, pointing to the ceiling. He nodded silently. Nearby, several men stared at two curvaceous, gyrating topless dancers as they gnashed Juicy Fruit gum with consummate boredom. The house DJ played what can only be described as techno-fluff as the females shimmied in the eerie sheen of ultraviolet light. Their miniscule bikini bottoms glowed bright purple, as if activated by the lust emanating from the gawking posse of men. Oblivious to the blatant ogling, the dancers thrust their pelvises and tried to appear wanton and lubricious. No longer people, the women had become purveyors of titillation (or teat-elation, as I like to think of it).

I surveyed a dimly lit room oddly devoid of cigarette smoke. Perhaps they pumped it up into Billy Bob's. All four walls bore enormous, crudely painted images of mostly dead rock stars: Elvis sneered from the left, Jim Morrison pouted on the right. Roy Orbison peered from behind perpetual sunglasses, and since I no longer trusted anyone who wore shades at night, I decided to repaint him as a scowling Ayatollah. And there, behind the bar, a visage recognizable to all, a mural devoted to the creased wreckage of Willy Nelson's face – the undisputed Big Chief of all guitar-strumming, pot-smoking millionaires.

The DJ cued up the "Barbie Song," whose lyrics triggered an entire sociology lecture in my head. ("You can brush my hair, undress me anywhere.") Then I began my imaginary discourse. "Today we will examine the definitive paean to the objectification of the female."

All the dancers were built like professional football players – solid, corn-fed tackles and guards – with one exception, a slender waif with a ponytail of blond fiber-optic filaments that wafted when she moved. Her legs were long and slender, each breast no larger than a demitasse teacup. She wore a narrow strip of satin that encircled her sylph-like waist and caressed her derriere. The little minx knew that she and she alone was the club's penultimate Barbie.

I watched the dancers run their hands across their bodies as if distributing musk from scent glands. Occasionally one reached out to touch an onlooker. Though sorely tempted, the customers were strictly forbidden to return the gesture. Should a man succeed in cupping a mound of female flesh in his hand, the ever-vigilant bouncer uttered a codeword into his microphone and within seconds, two hulking bouncers materialized through a trap door in the wall, grabbed the transgressor and dragged him away.

"What exactly are you selling here?" I asked the doorman.

"Fantasy," he replied.

"Let me get this straight. None of your customers actually gets what he most desires?"

"That's right."

What a scam, I thought; the ultimate bait-and-switch con.

A curtain of drapery illuminated by dozens of tiny white bulbs divided the room, delineating a mysterious zone suggestive of the entrance to heaven. "What goes on behind that curtain?" I inquired. But before the doorman could respond, a massive lumberjack in a red flannel shirt, jeans and muddy boots ambled up and handed him a wrinkled twenty-dollar bill. The chainsaw jockey then selected his favorite dancer and together they vanished behind the glittering curtain, watched from above by a bevy of naked hovering cherubs on the ceiling.

"They'll only be in there for the length of one song," said the doorman.

Three minutes later the woman emerged and walked briskly away, snapping her gum peevishly. The lumberjack staggered out a moment later and I caught a glimpse of his anguished, sweaty face as he lurched through the door and out into the frozen darkness.

"Did she? Did they?" I stammered.

"No!" said the doorman.

What cruelty, I thought, possibly the most perverse thing I'd ever seen. The frustrated woodsman had driven thirty miles from his greasy lair in Hardwick, paid six bucks to get in, who knows how much on booze and then another twenty for a so-called "private dance." Constrained by the "Look But Don't Touch" rule, the poor slob had subjected himself to a maddening erotic display, only to leave without the slightest release – dispatched into the night's bitter embrace, a walking sexual time bomb. "Monstrous," I said. "Simply monstrous."

By then my 20-minute break was over so I thanked Jabba's doorman and returned to Billy Bob's to play another set of moldy, moth-eaten Top-40.

***

Several hours later, after the gig, I went back downstairs to the empty strip club and stepped behind the diaphanous curtains for a peek into the sultan's boudoir. Apparently, the harem had retired for the night. All that remained was a couch that reminded me of a photograph I'd once seen of the couch in Sigmund Freud's office in Vienna. My curiosity now satiated, I slung my bass over one shoulder and departed, appalled at the thought of the tormented lumberjack and his three minutes of therapy. ("Since ven did you hoff such feah off intimacy?")

Giddy with relief at having survived another night playing tunes I never wanted to hear ever again, I hurried away. The wind had subsided and the stars shone fiercely. Fresh air revived me and I experienced a rare moment of lucidity. The next day was Saturday, a perfectly fine day except for the knowledge that another dreadful gig at Billy Bob's loomed that evening. "Enough is enough," I said and granted myself a full pardon.

gigs

I called Ed first thing the next morning and tendered my resignation. I gave him the customary two-week notice, but as there's always someone waiting in the wings, ready to take your place at a moment's notice, he said, "You can't quit, you're fired!"

Run for Cover played at Billy Bob's that night with a new bass player and it's more than likely that no one even noticed the switch.

A Jumpin' Somethin'

On the first day of November, 1999, after one final, solitary witch's Sabbath the night before, I bid good riddance to the seclusion of Panton – my supernal lakeside aerie of fifteen years – and set out for New Orleans. During those preceding years I'd not been idle, far from it; I'd earned a Bachelor's Degree from the University of Vermont (a double major in English and Psychology, although I spent most of my time in the Art department.) I'd married a manipulative shrike, a state of wedlock that ended in divorce after only a year and a half.) And I'd also earned a Master's Degree in Fine Art, devoting my attention to painting and sculpture.

I could've remained in Panton indefinitely, living cheaply and working in my studio under the watchful eyes of my goldfish, but when I realized that the senior officers on the starship Enterprise formed the majority of my exposure to humanity, I knew it was time to get out. The thought of facing another winter of isolation was intolerable. And so, I sallied forth into the Unknown, every bit as mad as Don Quixote, but without the stabilizing influence of Sancho or the luminous ideal of the Lady Dulcinea to guide me. (At the time, the knight of mournful countenance and I were both fifty years old; we both possessed gray hair, lean figures and energy sufficient to the task of attacking windmills, or, in my case, the status quo.)

After scattering tons of welded-steel sculpture to the distant corners of the state and storing a hundred large oil paintings in a friend's basement, I loaded my Toyota mini-van to the gunwales with everything I deemed essential for a six-month stint on the planet Mars – basses, amps, computer, clothes, oil paint and blank canvas. I rolled south on Eisenhower's interminable interstate, propelled as much by loneliness as by internal combustion, but I didn't travel alone – a plastic bucket bore my goldfish to a realm far beyond the scope of comprehension generated by the little dab of protoplasm they call a brain. The tedium endured by Flutter, Wow and Rumble during that 1800-mile trip was exceeded only by my own, but at least I got to look out the windows. On and on I drove. Every two hundred miles the temperature moderated enough to allow me to shed another layer of clothing, until finally, after a succession of cheap motels and grits-dispensing diners, I crossed the Louisiana state line wearing shorts and a T-shirt.

Radiant with fatigue and disorientation, I reached New Orleans on a Friday, at the height of the evening rush hour. I'd left behind a frozen landscape where nothing moved and landed on a hot urban griddle where nothing ever stopped moving – nothing, that is, except a million cars stalled bumper to bumper. I sat amidst that river of immobility and faced a city skyline gilded by the last sunlight of the day. The immense bridge spanning the Mississippi River glittered with orange lights strung out in vast sweeping arcs. Traffic began to move, gained momentum and swept me across the bridge before I could maneuver onto the correct exit. I turned around and before long pulled up in front of Chip Wilson's house on Marengo Street. The very next night I played my first gig with his band, A Jumpin' Somethin.'

***

After a good night's sleep in the spare room in Chip's spacious house, a hearty breakfast at the Bluebird Cafe and Eleanor Roosevelt's advice ringing in my head ("You *must* confront your worst fears"), I began to explore New Orleans.

"Check out the French Quarter," Chip suggested. "There are enough interesting things there to keep you amused for ten years. Just remember, if you think you're in the wrong place, you probably are."

Armed with good advice, my curiosity and a notebook, I boarded a 100-year old streetcar and rattled along St. Charles Avenue at a blistering 23 miles an hour. It may have been November but the warm air wafting through the open windows felt more like July. The streetcar line ended at Canal Street, where I disembarked. Before me loomed the mysterious 50-block square known as the Vieux Carre.

If my theory is correct – that climate equals behavior – then my worst fears were true and I'd become a taciturn Yankee curmudgeon. Although I'd escaped the cryogenic incarceration of winter in Vermont, my psyche remained blue ice to the core. Would it ever thaw? I wondered, as I walked towards the Café du Monde, a world-renowned outdoor oasis. A ravishingly beautiful Vietnamese waitress took my order and returned with a steaming mug of java and a plateful of beignets – three slabs of fried dough buried beneath an avalanche of powdered sugar. A glass of water from the notoriously carcinogenic Mississippi river accompanied the beignets – not to drink, but to help swab away the powdered sugar that invariably crop-dusts one's clothes, regardless of how careful you are.

A ceaseless torrent of humanity swirled past on the sidewalk. So many interesting faces – white, black, Asian – and not a brass monkey's backside of a chance in hell of seeing anyone I knew. Fearless urban sparrows hopped about beneath the café tables, squabbling over bits of pastry. A sax-player riffed for coins, engaged in a similar pursuit. The sidewalk itself was a stage where living statues stood perfectly still until a tourist made a small donation. The bronzed figure shifted position slightly and froze anew. But when someone deposited a greenback into the hat, the cash cowboy drew a six-shooter and drilled an imaginary hole in his patron's chest.

Nearby, the swift and turgid waters of the remarkably unphotogenic Mississippi River surged by. A sudden blast of slightly dissonant music filled the air with chords and melodies from another era, played on a steam calliope aboard the Natchez, a riverboat paddle wheeler loaded with sightseers and gamblers.

The sidewalk circus that surrounds Jackson Square beckoned as I sipped a second cup of java. I crossed Esplanade and wandered towards a battery of folding card-tables presided over by fortune-tellers, tarot card readers and fire-eaters. I hadn't expected to see a Ben and Jerry's scoop shop ladling out over-priced dollops, but there it was, looking absurdly wholesome alongside the psychic lemonade stands. The square teemed with tourists and those who prey upon them – pimps, panhandlers and persons riding unicycles while twirling flaming batons!

The rambunctious sound of live jazz beckoned and I responded like a cobra charmed by the reed flute of a turbaned fakir. I slithered through the peddlers and hawkers, ignored the purple-swathed Mystic Goddess's offer to reveal my future, sidestepped the bluegrass pickers that looked like civil war survivors and approached a 17-piece street band. Long accustomed to invisibility, I parked my carcass on a bench alongside an assortment of drummers – young kids and wrinkled old men old enough to be their grandfathers – all playing an indigenous snare drum style rarely duplicated elsewhere. The band was a regular feature in the square and featured a string bass player wrapped in a gray shroud, two guitar players, trombones, trumpets, saxophones and a large black woman who wailed on clarinet like an ecstatic banshee. A plastic pail circulated through the crowd to collect tips. I closed my eyes, basked in the warm sunlight and absorbed every glorious note. Surrounded by jazz and enveloped in the lush fragrance of strange new blossoms... slowly, imperceptibly, I began to thaw.

In the ensuing weeks I learned to navigate the city's Byzantine expanse, by car and bicycle. Assumptions gave way to verities as I adjusted to the new reality. I learned that the rest of Louisiana – a deeply conservative, bible-thumping state – does not always appreciate the smutty city that throbs on its southern border.

If you were to take a strip lined with malls, burger-joints, gin mills and souvenir shops and boil them down to a viscous mash, then add sweltering heat and humidity, a tradition of whorehouses, jazz, crime and political corruption, then what remains is Bourbon Street – a neon-lit gumbo whose ingredients include tourists, transvestites, hustlers, musicians, police, drunks and tap-dancing street urchins... an urban distillate that is the apotheosis of American culture.

***

Life settled into a rhythm: I wrote every day, rode a bike, painted, ate in a multitude of interesting restaurants and best of all, played gigs with Chip's band. Before he'd emigrated from Vermont, a few years earlier, we'd played together in several excellent groups: Swingshift, which offered classic Django and Grappelli-style Parisian swing; The Ramblers, whom you met in a previous chapter; and The Style A's, a 5-piece band that played R&B, funk and Chip's originals.

41. Chip Wilson

The music community in New Orleans quickly recognized Chip as one of their own; his talent was undeniable and resulted in free-lance work as a guitarist.

One night I visited The Red Room – a venue that forever altered my concept of a nightclub – to listen to Chip play in a 15-piece jazz orchestra, Johnny Angel and the Swinging Demons. Located on St. Charles, the Red Room looked like a giant glass cube built atop steel pillars. Higher still, an enormous steel arrowhead (reputedly built from leftover girders from the Eiffel Tower) rose into the humid night air. Truck-mounted searchlights raked the clouds with powerful blue beams. A ramp ascended from the sidewalk to the second-story entry like a bridge to the pearly gates (or perhaps to the entrance of a religious order for jazz musicians – the Seventh-Chord Adventists.)

"This is more like it," I said aloud as I entered The Red Room's plush scarlet mezzanine. "No more dingy dog kennels where live music is an afterthought." Dozens of small table-lamps gave the room a seductive crimson glow. Onstage, the Swinging Demons played a warm-up set as Johnny Angel, their leader, glided through the audience in an iridescent white tux and a pair of spats that glowed like radioactive clams. The black handkerchief protruding from his breast pocket complemented sideburns as preternaturally black as his immobilized coiffure. Johnny was a consummate schmoozer, as all bandleaders must be, and greeted his fans with masterful savoir-faire, kissing cheeks – facial and otherwise.

The Swinging Demons resembled riverboat gamblers, shady-looking characters in Zoot suits with Derringers tucked in vest pockets and an ace or two up their collective sleeves. Halfway through a rendition of "Sentimental Journey," the trombone player ended his solo with a prolonged flatulent low note. Chip laughed, took off his beret and waved it in the air to fan away the imaginary stench. After The Demon's twenty minutes of splendor, Miss Le Shay sashayed onto the stage, a stunning vision in white satin and fur. White gloved to the elbows, with sparkling sequins and a heavenly nimbus of flowing red hair, she sang a medley of the swing tunes that helped win World War II.

"If you have any requests," she purred, "Just whisper them in my ear."

The audience lapped it up.

The show's big anticlimax occurred when Johnny Angel jittered into the spotlight to sing a few songs with the band. All glitz and banter, he was a much better stage personality than a vocalist. But after Miss Le Shay's knockout performance, no one cared, except for the band.

***

A few weeks later I rode the musician's elevator up and into The Red Room's backstage area (as close to "beaming up" as this trekie is likely to get.) I looked suave in my new used tuxedo; the bullet hole over the tux's former owner's heart had been skillfully mended. A Steinway grand dominated the stage, but since A Jumpin' Somethin' had no pianist, its presence was a bad omen. The other members of our killer 7-piece ensemble arrived just in time to hear the club's manager say, "There's been a screw-up and you guys aren't playing tonight."

No one said a word. We were, after all, professionals.

The manager promised to make it up to us, and sure enough, a month later we returned to play for a spectacular post-punk fashion show; an eye-popping review in which a dozen models sauntered along a runway while wearing the latest in degenerate vogue – skimpy orange and purple swatches riddled with holes, metal studs and wispy feathers. The models pouted with all their might, each one looking more sullen than the last. All wore frazzled, post-coital hairdos. One sultry creature sported a synthetic blond ponytail that coiled around her shoulders and trailed behind on the floor like a golden anaconda. Another wasp-waisted wastrel unzipped her jeans and gave everyone a flash of chocolate-colored hipbone. The audience went ape, hooting and stomping and banging their hairy fists on the tabletops like a troop of ecstatic purple-assed mandrills.

As Chip's primary bassist, I played a variety of interesting gigs, everything from the stately antebellum parlor in the Columns Hotel, to strange outlying gin mills where slot machines stood alongside laundry machines. We played jazz at elegant diplomatic soirees where two hundred foreign dignitaries drank champagne and conversed in as many languages.

My favorite performance venue was Le Chat Noir, a club on St. Charles where we played a one-hour set on Thursdays, at midnight. The room featured the superb acoustics of a recording studio, ideal for A Jumpin' Somethin's complement of vocals, guitar, violin, clarinet, bass and drums. Our repertoire included selections from Ellington, Porter, Gershwin and Wilson. (Chip's previous CD had been selected by Offbeat Magazine as one of three finalists for their Best Traditional Jazz Album of the Year Award. Although he didn't win, the other two finalists were Branford Marsalis and Kermit Ruffin...not too bad for a white boy from Westchester County.)

The audience at Le Chat Noir consisted of slender couples dressed exclusively in black. The women all had angular cheekbones and haughty expressions, as if fresh from a triumphant tango contest. The men sported villainous pencil-thin mustaches. Together, they sat silently in the candle-lit darkness, sipping dry martinis and listening to our every note. When we played The Bamboola, a tango based upon a 400-year old melody, the dance-floor seethed.

One night, after a flawless performance, I sat tilting a Pilsner at the bar. The beautiful woman who owned the club – the Black Cat herself – sat alongside and placed her hand on my arm. She leaned in close till her lips brushed my ear and said, "I think men who play the bass have a better understanding of a woman's body."

"Yes," I replied. "Prowess with one leads to prowess with the other."

She gave me a peck on the cheek and then rejoined the gaggle of young admirers in thousand-dollar suits that quickly surrounded her in a proprietary cluster. I wandered over to join them a minute later and approached just in time to hear her say, "Oh, he's just another starving jazz musician, earning barely enough money to pay the rent."

I realized that she was describing me, and all too accurately!

Just then the door opened and in walked Tony Green, a well-known jazz guitarist who had lived in the city for many years and who was definitely not starving. Tony's career was built upon his ability to play in the style of the legendary Django Reinhardt, the original gypsy jazzman. When the Black Cat greeted him and commanded us to play, we obliged with renditions of "Nuage" and "Minor Swing."

The door opened again and in walked a bearded guy accompanied by three beautiful women. He looked familiar, but I couldn't quite remember where I'd seen him before. Then it hit me… it was Harry Shearer, the actor who portrayed Derek Small, the bass player in the spoof "This is Spinal Tap." Harry sat at the piano and began to play songs from the movie. Tony and I accompanied him in a hilarious rendition of "Big Bottom," one of 'Tap's biggest hits. Harry pounded the keys and sang, "The bigger the cushion, the better the pushin.' Big bottom, how could I leave that behind?"

Barbacoa

Midnight – high noon in the French Quarter – an impenetrable fog shrouded the narrow lanes and muffled all sound. Flickering gas-lamps illuminated a tableau as eerie as eighteenth century Edinburgh, complete with a mule-drawn carriage bearing grave robbers and their prize. The very air reeked of decay, moral and architectural, as I pushed open a door on the corner of Esplanade. A wisp of crimson smoke curled over the threshold and escaped into the gloom. Bass in hand, I stepped into the Matador Lounge, a fuliginous devil's den where candles sputtered atop grinning human skulls. As my eyes adjusted to the murk, I perceived a clientele that made your typical barbarian look like a pious spinster sipping chamomile tea in Emily Dickinson's parlor.

The circular bar enclosed a coven of emaciated wraiths pouring shots. Starved to perfection, the pale blond nymphs looked like Vampira's daughters. Not to be outdone, the men were studded and pierced – their skulls shaved to the nubs except for vaguely obscene, dangling forelocks. Like extras in a Mad Max movie, all wore black leather, amulets, chains and tattooed pythons that encircled their limbs. One muscular specimen sat at the bar with an enormous boa constrictor draped around his shoulders, a snake powerful enough to kill its owner, if not fed adequately. Everyone there smoked cigarettes continuously – including the snake – their every exhalation a noxious blue gust.

"The French Quarter," I mused. "Where every night is Halloween and deviance is the norm." I didn't belong in the Matador Lounge or the French

Quarter either, for that matter. (Neither a smoker, nor gay, nor terribly extroverted, I was the choirboy in the charnel house.)

Not another band dared to play surf music in the heart of New Orleans that night, I'll wager. None except Bill Mullins's group Barbacoa. Like me, Bill had journeyed to the Crescent City from Vermont to avoid winter's stultifying grip, and to play as many gigs as possible. Ron Ward, our drummer, was a former Vermonter, but considered himself to be fully rehabilitated. Although he wasn't as tall, Ron looked enough like the Seinfeld character Kramer to provide him employment as a double during the show's production.

Barbacoa played surf music, an energetic, Stratocaster-driven sound best described as espionage chic. (Imagine Leo Fender and Kim Philby riding surfboards, accompanied by the theme music from Goldfinger.) Bill arrived and I greeted him with the drawled "How' ya doin?" heard so often in Noir Lens. The particulars concerning our gig were sketchy so I asked, "What time are we supposed to start?"

"I dunno," said Bill.

"How long are we supposed to play?"

"Can't say. We'll see how it goes."

"How much money are we getting?"

"Not sure."

"Bill, I realize this isn't the American Legion Hall in Island Pond, so I suppose we'd better drink some Heineken, play some music for Genghis Khan's elephant handlers and have some fun. Remember, we're not here to earn a decent living or to meet our soul mates."

Suddenly Ron burst through the door with a clash of cymbals and an armload of red, sparkle-flake drums. He deposited them onstage and began to assemble them, so I wandered out into the fog, to loiter in the yellow penumbra of a gas-lantern and watch the ghostly vessels navigate the night's savage shore. I half expected to see a hunchback climb down from a church bell-tower, but instead, cadaverous devotees of Ann Rice's vampire trilogy drifted by – opium addicts and Absinthe drinkers – or so I imagined. We had time to kill before our show so I took a stroll and tried to imagine what it would be like to live in the center ring of the circus.

I passed a hole-in-the-wall antique shop that displayed a spider monkey's head in a glass case. The creature's desiccated face sneered at me with moldy fur, eyes narrowed to slits, teeth yellow and bared – the perfect anniversary gift for my ex-wife.

I returned to the Matador where confusion reigned after the manager's inexplicable decision to relocate the band from the stage to an empty, crypt-like chamber out back. Then, once we'd shifted our gear, he changed his mind, forcing us to drag the amps and drums back to the stage. Finally, at three thirty in the morning – prime time in hell's cantina – we were given the go-ahead to play.

"Surf's up!" I announced to a packed house as Ron counted off the tempo to "Delirium Tremolo," a frenzied instrumental that sounded like the Ventures whacked out on crystal meth. We sounded great but the song elicited only puzzled expressions on the tattooed faces of our listeners. "There ain't no surf in Vermont!" someone shouted.

True, but we persevered and played "Hang 'em High School," a tune with a poignant melody reminiscent of a theme from a Sergio Leone spaghetti western. Perhaps it was the memory of the film's casual brutality that did the trick, but in any event, the audience realized we were serious about surf music and began to cheer. I quickly reestablished the neurological link between my bass and the pleasure center in my brain. And once again, nothing mattered except carving out fat wedges of sound with my flat pick, thereby filling the Matador Lounge with low-frequency sound. When at last we finished lashing the crowd, at five thirty in the morning, a cool gray dawn insinuated it way through the foggy gloom. I removed my earplugs, packed up my gear and waited for my pay.

"You were awesome," said the bar-nymph as she handed Ron some limp bills.

He counted fifty bucks.

"This is insulting!" Ron shouted, his hair spiking like an electrocuted hedgehog. He raged around the room for the next ten minutes, cursing and threatening the lives of all, but no one paid the slightest attention. Finally, he cooled down and vowed to return the next day for more cash. I pocketed my sixteen dollars and change and said, "Have we learned anything yet? Club-owners here in the 'Quarter have been practicing how to screw musicians for the last hundred years."

Outside, the growing light of day forced the creatures of the night back into hiding, lest they be turned to stone. I drove back to Marengo Street and stayed up to watch a Godzilla movie on television. The sumo wrestler in the green rubber suit trashed Tokyo, Beijing, Moscow and New York. But why, I wondered, didn't he stomp the French Quarter?

Ron returned to the Matador and actually squeezed them for an additional hundred bucks; perhaps they were impressed by his fearless audacity...I certainly was. The last thing I expected was an invitation for us to play there again the following Saturday. I wasn't eager to reenter that depraved environment, but I agreed to play. Who knew when I might get another chance to observe a deviant subculture from such close range?

Later that day, after polluting my bed with Technicolor dreams, I arose, showered, dressed and then rode a streetcar to the Palace Café on Canal Street. The maitre d' directed me to a small circular table. The sound of trumpet, banjo and string bass from a "strolling" trio floated through the spacious restaurant as I waited for coffee, shrimp gumbo and a loaf of French bread. The food arrived to find me writing feverishly in my journal. But when I looked up, I discovered that the trio had surrounded my table, and before you could say, "vamp till cue," I was playing "Honeysuckle Rose" while the bass player devoured my gumbo!

We finished the song to a round of nervous applause from the other diners. I handed the instrument back to its owner and resumed my repast, but couldn't help noticing the worried looks on the faces of those seated nearby, as if at any moment they, too, might be separated from their brunch and made to play jazz.

Only in New Orleans.

The Mardi Gras

I stood on the curb of St. Charles Avenue, elbow to elbow with the entire human race, or so it seemed as we waited for the approach of Bacchus, the parade named in honor of the god of wine. Nearby, a bulwark of sofas stretched for 50 feet, base-camp for a boisterous fraternity of party animals. Dozens of speakers blared an indecipherable onslaught of rock, Cajun fiddle and funk. Behind me, crowds stood on concrete slabs tipped at strange angles by the gnarled roots of oak trees that slowly shattered the sidewalk like so many broken graham crackers.

Thousands of little platforms atop folding ladders lined the parade route, each occupied by a child or a teenage girl. Beads from last year's parades still hung from the interlocking oak limbs overhead. Darkness gradually triumphed and a ripple of excitement swept through the crowd as the flambeau carriers approached – a vanguard of black men striding swiftly, each holding aloft a rack of kerosene-fed flames. Their sweat-moistened faces reflected ancestral African fire – a splendid, fiercely exultant sight in the lurid, flickering glow. Spectators tossed coins into the street. The flambeau carriers snatched them up and strode on, quickly engulfed by the veldt.

The first band marched into view – a hundred black high school students wearing purple uniforms and toting brass instruments. The tubas wore nets over their gaping bells to prevent being clogged with beads. A whistle sounded, the signal for a squad of hefty bass-drummers to begin walloping their hollow burdens with aggressive mallet strokes. Boom! Boom! Boom! They thundered by, followed by a swarm of snare drummers that tattooed my eardrums with sharp, percussive cracks.

Next came a hundred Nubian princesses – their lithe young torsos swathed in glittering metallic purple sequins like the scales of fish. Their boots scuffed the pavement, legs thrusting and hips swiveling in a labial strut no white female can ever hope to duplicate. As if to prove my point, a marching band from an all-white private academy stepped smartly by, followed by a bevy of young women that revealed no sensuality in their gate.

A dazzling monstrosity loomed in the distance. Still hundreds of yards away, the sound of screaming increased as the float drew nearer. It was as large as a double-decker bus and pulsed with a million colored lights. Huge speakers blasted a continuous shockwave of distortion while masked dervishes stood on tiers and hurled beads in all directions, strands that flew like DNA being ejected by a spawning aquatic behemoth.

"What's the big deal about a bunch of cheap, gaudy beads?" I wondered, as the noise and frenzy began to engulf me. But when the rolling leviathan loomed before me, and the grinning maniacs filled the air with beads, I, too, waved my arms and shouted, "OVER HERE!" Their allure had nothing to do with intrinsic value, but nevertheless, I struggled to catch as many strands as possible, overcome by a tidal wave of pure Greed – as if they were real jewels and not bits of shiny plastic. The float passed by and the noise receded much the way a breaking wave travels along a curved coastline.

Next came a junior high school drill squad tromping along in red berets and khaki uniforms. They carried carbines painted white and looked like Patrice Lamumba's bodyguards. These were followed by a polished contingent of Marines, marching with a bearing and precision that put them in a class by themselves. The crowd cheered, saluted Old Glory and I, too, felt a shudder of long-repressed patriotism.

A herd of haggis-stuffed Regimental Scots Guards marched by – kilts flapping, bagpipes bleating – in sharp contrast to the Navy Band that seemed to glide smoothly along on silicon, ball bearings and Teflon. The Army's contribution to the cacophony featured a float bearing five sad sacks with guitars, under orders to play a never-ending rendition of "Louie Louie." The Trolley Band came next – a rollicking Dixieland ensemble perched atop a float. An orgy of color and sound swept by, each float more spectacular than the one before, each separated by a glittering shoal of metallic marching minnows that seemed to flounce a guarantee of eternal fecundity.

"Yes!" I shouted. "The species will be propagated!"

The next float pulsated into view, this one covered with a blinding mélange of giant Day-Glo orchids and a sweating krewe hard-pressed to fling the booty over the side fast enough. When a float paused motionless for a minute, as sometimes happened, the beads rained down in a ceaseless torrent. Sometime the dervishes onboard didn't even bother to tear open plastic bags the size of pillows before hurling their contents; if you took your eyes off them for an instant, you risked getting clouted from above by a hefty parcel.

In addition to beads, an amazing variety of highly desirable items were thrown to the crowd – rubber chickens, beer mugs, noisemakers, tambourines, stuffed animals, plastic swords, amulets, medallions, enormous fake cigars and rubber-tipped bamboo spears. Also, aluminum doubloons imprinted with the image of Bacchus. The doubloons varied in color from silver, gold, green and purple, each the size of a silver dollar. The black doubloons were impossible to catch at night and would not be picked up till the next day.

The teenage girls seated atop the folding platforms were bead magnets and caught the most. Absurdly convinced that I'd never get enough, I leapt and snagged strand after strand until I too wore a heavy, glittering garland of plastic around my neck.

The parade honoring Bacchus featured at least 25 floats and lasted for two hours. But after a short pause, another parade began. Many, such as Orpheus or Thoth, were derived from mythological or cultural traditions. Others were devoted to the rainforest, monkeys, exotic insects or the crocodiles in the Ngorogongo Crater. Every year King Kong, his wife and their impudent offspring make an appearance on a float of their own, and every year Kong's gaping jaws offer an irresistible target for beads hurled back by the insolent multitude along the way.

Although the Mardi Gras season lasts for six weeks and features more than 50 parades, the celebration builds to a mighty crescendo that reaches its peak on Fat Tuesday – the day the entire city goes kablooey! But it's one thing to observe from the relative safety of the curb and quite another to participate – to join a marching club, don an outlandish costume and mambo from one end of Magazine Street to St. Charles, all the way to Canal, and then into the most stunning vortex of sensory overload of all, the French Quarter.

A few days later I did, in fact, just that.

***

It all started when Chip and I spent time in Jimmy Ford's uptown studio working on Chip's next album. Known as "The Clinic," Jimmy's home rarely knew a quiet moment. In addition to recording equipment, the spacious old house contained an arsenal of musical instruments, sculpture, paintings,

Jimmy's children, his wife and her all-girl band, Hell's Cheerleaders. After successfully recording bass tracks, Jimmy said, "This is your first Mardi Gras. What do you think?"

"I've never seen such a volcano of hedonism," I replied.

"Wait till Fat Tuesday! Krakatau hasn't erupted yet. The rumble you hear is only the mountain clearing its throat. On Fat Tuesday the parades start at seven in the morning and go till ten at night. You seem like an adventurous guy, would you be interested in joining a marching club? As a life-long member of the Lyons Marching Club, I'm authorized to recruit new members. If you joined, you'd be in the parade instead of watching from the sidelines."

"What do I have to do?"

"Membership for a year costs a hundred bucks."

It took less than a nanosecond to reach a decision: The opportunity to participate in the largest party in the northern hemisphere was not to be missed, and one crisp C-note seemed a small price to pay. "Where do I sign?" I asked. "And what do I wear?"

"I've got a costume you can have," said Jimmy. "It's old, but I used to wear it and since we're about the same size, it should fit you. Meet me here at six o'clock in the morning, next Tuesday. We'll get ready and then drive over to the staging area in my van. I'll introduce you to the other members of the club. Then, just stick close to me and you'll be fine."

Fat Tuesday dawned with the fulfilled promise of blue skies, ample sunlight and a high temperature of 72-degrees. Millions of shattered beads glittered on the pavement as I pedaled my bicycle through the quiet, early morning streets towards Jimmy's house. Intact strands of crimson, purple, green and gold beads hung from every tree like an alien species of sphagnum moss.

"Another day in Paradise," I mused, echoing the sentiments of many.

I arrived to find Jimmy preening before a full-length mirror, draped in a flowing white cape studded with plastic rubies, worn over silk pantaloons and blouse, with a plastic scimitar at his side. A plume of iridescent peacock feathers sprouted from his chromium crown and fanned the air in his wake. "Here," said Jimmy, handing me a black bundle. "Put these on."

I complied and stood before the mirror in a somber yet elegant sable tunic covered with embroidered silver metallic leaves. Worn over black leotards, it was the appropriate attire for an errant knave from the distant realm of Vermont.

42. Mardi Gras 2000

"Time to go," said Jimmy with an ostentatious swirl of his cape. "Pin this button on and don't lose it," he said as we climbed into his van. "Without it you won't be permitted to accompany the marching club; which, incidentally, has been in existence since 1946. There are a number of interesting traditions you should know about. We'll begin the march from way uptown and make stops in all the neighborhood bars along the way. There'll be a free glass of beer waiting for us in each one."

"But it's only seven in the morning," I said.

"You don't have to drink every glass, but it's an old custom."

"What are the other traditions?"

Jimmy smiled like the cat that ate the canary and said, "Our club is relatively small and I went to school with everyone in it; some members are drug dealers and some are cops. But every year, for this one day, we enjoy complete amnesty."

A good thing too, because Jimmy's breakfast on that fattest of Tuesdays included not only a glass of beer in every low haunt we encountered along the way, but also a side order of magic mushrooms and marijuana cigarettes! And so, resplendent in cape, crown and plumes, and wearing the most flagrantly illegal grin I'd ever seen, Jimmy sauntered down the center of the sunny street in a regal, hallucinatory amble that on any other day would've resulted in his immediate arrest.

"Have a hit of this," exhorted a fellow club member, thrusting a mysterious but highly potent elixir in a blue flask into my hand. Determined to pace myself and survive, but also aware that the definition of moderation does not say "none at all," I imbibed sparingly. (All that day I practiced sleight of hand to feign consumption before passing along a dizzying assortment of scurrilous substances.)

The Lyons Marching Club rendezvoused with its musical accompaniment, a 6-piece brass band on a small flatbed trailer towed behind a pickup. (I never knew that such fluid and funky bass lines could be played on a tuba.) Mambo rhythms and second-line Dixieland jazz propelled us towards Magazine Street, our route lined with steadily growing numbers.

Our marching contingent began with a police car that rolled along at our pace, so we set our beer mugs on the cruiser's rear hood, a practice tolerated only on Fat Tuesday. Fortunately, the pickup truck that towed the band also bore a simple wooden closet where a large barrel waited to collect all those gallons of used beer.

An unforgettable day ensued – the blue sunlit heavens shared by puffs of cumulus clouds and the Fuji blimp, the source of a brief shower of little foil packets. "It's raining condoms," I marveled as I retrieved one from the pavement, thus demonstrating the meaning of optimism.

"Jimmy, what's with the canes?" I asked, pointing to the carnation-covered walking sticks carried by the majority of our delegation.

"You can borrow mine," he replied enigmatically, "after I demonstrate its proper use." Jimmy swept to a halt before a beautiful young woman standing nearby. He twirled his cape, bowed gallantly and handed her a carnation. She accepted it and gave him a long, succulent kiss.

"One carnation, one kiss," he said, wiping the scarlet smear from his lips. "The hard part is choosing each recipient."

Thus instructed, I too bestowed carnations. The first went to a tawny creature dressed in a safari outfit. She accepted a carnation and we enjoyed a deep, passionate kiss.

"Leave everything and run away with me," I murmured in her ear.

"Yes! Yes!" she cried breathlessly, but it was too late and I had to dash away to catch up with my compatriots. What an amazing custom, I marveled – a display of lust, but with little or no danger to either participant. I regretted not having cards with my email address handy.

When we reached St. Charles the swarm of humanity lining our route increased until the boundary between normal spectators and a million costumed zanies evaporated entirely. And so, for the next ten hours, every time my eyes came to rest I witnessed an astonishing sight: I observed Pashas, sultans and corpulent, turbaned eminences from near and far; Asian beauties with inscrutable vulpine faces dyed fluorescent blue; platoons of conga drummers in gorilla suits transmitting telegraphic jungle messages; silver Mylar aliens with ping-pong ball eyes on stalks; a cigar-smoking Che Guevara look-alike that handed out "Che" medallions; gorgeous birds of paradise in feathered flocks and a surprising number of renegade nuns turned harlot!

A maniac on roller-blades carried a sign that said, "ASK ME ABOUT CUNNILINGUS" on one side and "ASK ME ABOUT SODOMY" on the other.

I noticed Satan eyeing the crowd appreciatively. It wasn't some stumblebum wannabe assistant painted red, but clearly, the archfiend himself. He wore a magnificent crimson tuxedo – his vermilion skin creased with wrinkles born of time and ungodly experience, horns clearly visible and a long shiny tail like a rat's.

"Greetings, your eminence," I said, as politely as possible.

Satan smiled and nodded, bestowing dreadful status on us all.

Another lunatic caught my eye: Wearing only a grass skirt and a coat of gold paint on his bald pate, he danced an obscene hula atop a besieged minivan from Iowa, then jumped through its open sunroof and scared the old ladies inside half to death.

In such delirious anarchy, the potential for danger lurks vigilant and unseen.

One member of our little marching club got so whacked out on hallucinogens and alcohol and God only knows what, he stumbled and sprawled onto the pavement. No one noticed when a wheel on our trailer rolled over and broke both his ankles. The crazy fool never said a word. Instead, he got up and marched on. Someone finally noticed his swollen, purple ankles and rushed him to the emergency room. He spent the next two weeks in traction; but wait, it gets worse. After his release, the idiot returned to New York with casts on both legs – on crutches – then ignored his doctor's advice and came damned close to having both feet amputated!

Minus one, we moved on, ever deeper into boundless estuaries teeming with exotic wildlife. But after so many hours of sensory overload, my brain's ability to register what my eyes perceived began to diminish, as if the computer in my head needed a lot more RAM. The Lyons Marching Club was miniscule in comparison to the various krewes that comprised the contingents now merging. Preceded by a dozen black stretch Mercedes filled with black VIP's seated behind tinted glass, we intersected and then joined the massive tributary formed by Rex and Zulu – two of the oldest and largest krewes in the Mardi Gras.

Now completely engulfed by countless hysterically screaming onlookers, there was no escape. Under such conditions, as in the Saint Vitas Dance of life itself, one can only hope to summon sufficient energy to keep dancing. The mad, cacophonous tumult gathered momentum as we neared the end of St. Charles. We crossed Canal street and entered the indescribably dense littoral of humanity jamming the French Quarter, where everyone was high as a kite on whatever they could get their hands on (LSD being the pharmaceutical of choice). No longer content to skulk in their wretched hovels beyond the city walls, the rampaging mob had stormed the castle, and was, at that very moment, wearing the emperor's pajamas and smashing his best china.

I glanced up at the second-floor windows on either side, where every rectangle framed scantily clad women dancing with giddy abandon.

Once in the Quarter, our troupe of marchers dispersed like platelets in the bloodstream. I staggered into a bar, found a stool and quaffed a Guinness, while outside, the madness raged with undiminished ferocity. It had been quite a day. My feet hurt from doing the mambo since early morning and the muscles in my face were exhausted from continuous laughter. I tried to form a visual analog equal to the task of describing the experience: The most accurate has me seated comfortably beneath the Space Shuttle's booster rockets at the moment of lift-off. I sit there, quite invulnerable and sip a cup of Earl Grey amidst the white-hot, vaporizing blast!

Even now, any thought of Fat Tuesday – the most extroverted day of my life – evokes a chortle and a daft smile. But what I'd really like to know is, how the hell did I manage to reach the age of 50 before experiencing the Mardi Gras?

***

Ash Wednesday.

The city staggered to its feet and even the dogs were hung-over. A pall of post-inebriation torpor enveloped a city as silent as on Christmas morning. Countless Advils washed down the gullets of a great many repentant pelicans – a bird featured on the Louisiana state flag. Fairing better than most, I ate breakfast in the Bluebird Café and then decided it was the perfect time for a contemplative stroll through Lafayette Cemetery, city of the dead.

The Orleans parish cemetery sprawled amidst the Garden District – a walled expanse that does not clasp its dead in the traditional embrace 6-feet under. Instead, hundreds of mausoleums huddle cheek by jowl, built in response to the flooding guaranteed by the city's position below sea level. The cemetery tour-guide recounted incidents from the bad old days prior to the building of the mausoleums, an era when torrents unearthed corpses and floated them down the avenue in a ghoulish parody of Tom Sawyer's rafting excursion on the Mississippi.

The crypts exhibited varying degrees of decay. One would think a stone vault capable of enduring the slow but indomitable tread of Time, but this is not the case. Many are crumbling and in need of repair; all are covered with epiphytes, ferns and lichen. I wandered from tomb to tomb, read the names carved into the stone and then sat on a bench to ponder the meaning of life.

We try – with whatever resources available – to insulate ourselves from the ultimate certainty of death. But, as the disintegrating mausoleums so clearly attest, nothing lasts forever. When solid rock dissolves like a sugar cube in hot tea, what can hold mere flesh together? And so, we dart and flit, mate and die, with only the frayed cloak of habit separating us from the silent, dark, infinitely patient confines of the waiting sarcophagi.

Carpe Diem, dude.

Blues for Breakfast

I completed six months in New Orleans as planned, then aimed my Toyota van north on Interstate 10 and drove across the 20-mile causeway accompanied by feelings of relief and regret. Relief at having survived for half a year on Mars, regret at leaving such a vibrant musical environment. I could've stayed the summer, enduring five months of temperatures in the mid-nineties, each day bolstered by relentless, crushing humidity – but I knew the heat would choke off the seasonal tourist influx so essential for supporting live music.

All in all, it had been a very educational experience. I learned that I could go to any city in the world where jazz flourished and find work as a bassist, but this awareness was tempered by the realization that my concomitant position on the bottom rung of the hierarchical ladder was insufficient. I'd met bassists who had lived in New Orleans all their lives, excellent musicians known by all, and consequently, the people called first. Although I worked often, I earned just enough money to pay the rent and eat – an acceptable arrangement while in my twenties, thirties and forties – but now, having whacked my forehead on the doorway to middle-age yet again, the disparity between surviving and thriving rankled ever more deeply.

I returned to Vermont but my goldfish stayed in New Orleans. I'd met a woman who owned a house on Magazine Street and her backyard featured a fishpond with a waterfall and a dozen goldfish, each about the same size as my fish. When she suggested I add mine to her population, it struck me as a fitting reward for Flutter, Wow and Rumble, my faithful Piscean buddies. (The city's reputation as being dangerous is true for people and goldfish. My

268

fish were doomed. I've subsequently learned of the unannounced mosquito-control spray that killed them all. Had they not succumbed to poison, hurricane Katrina would've destroyed them.)

The long, uneventful drive north brought me back to Burlington, Vermont – not the heart of the Green Mountains, but the spleen. Burlington is a small, college town that generates big city pretensions, a place where playing in a band is a hobby as widespread as owning a dog, but where the prospects for a professional musician are slim. Given these limitations, I rejoined a band I'd been in a few years before. (Given the choice of playing live music onstage or sitting at home, I'll opt for playing every time, regardless of a band's problems.)

Blues for Breakfast had been around for a long time, sometimes as an electric blues band, sometimes as a Grateful Dead cover band. Either way, the group appealed to a very narrow demographic, the "wake and bake" crowd – young people who began each day by smoking the most powerful marijuana ever grown. Charlie Frazier was the band's leader, a tough-as-nails drill sergeant who barked needless orders to his sidemen in order to make absolutely clear to everyone within earshot that he and he alone was in command. Although The Grateful Dead were his heroes, Charlie demonstrated a bizarre schism between the infinite flexibility of their ideology and his own pathetic need for control. To say his personality was abrasive is an understatement. Charlie was better suited to be a guard at Danemora State Prison. This unfortunate propensity resulted in a revolving-door line-up of players that grew weary of his bullshit and quit, or were fired for defying one of his absurd edicts. I managed to accomplish both.

Although there were exceptions, Blues for Breakfast generally played only the most appalling venues, like the Monopole, in Plattsburg, a century-old brick structure where throngs of college kids smoked bongs and got "wicked hammered." We played regularly at Nectar's, a considerable improvement, before the new owners took over and eliminated all traces of the club's former ambiance. (Today it is indistinguishable from any college-bar in the country.)

There was one exceptional gig, a spectacular Sunday afternoon in July – a day of warmth, sunlight, deep cerulean skies and cumulus clouds that billowed like mashed-potato mountains. Blues for Breakfast had agreed to participate in an outdoor concert intended to generate cash for flood-stricken farmers in northern Vermont. "Floodstock" took place in an immense open pasture in Highgate, Vermont; the exact spot where, only a year before, 65,000 fans had each forked over $37.50 to hear the Grateful Dead.

Considerable planning and effort had gone into organizing the benefit. A blitz of newspaper and radio ads appeared; Red Cross personnel waited in tents, ready to administer sandwiches, coffee and doughnuts; a platoon of State Police stood by to direct a massive influx of vehicles; a National Guard helicopter sat poised to evacuate anyone in need of emergency medical treatment and a security team with walkie-talkies patrolled the perimeter. A magnificent altruistic gesture, everything had been donated for free – the bands, the equipment, the sound technicians, the cops and the National Guard.

As I said, it was a perfect day, but only one problem…no audience!

Where 65,000 fans had trampled the grass a year before, fewer than 65 now dotted the vast empty field. Undaunted, a dozen bands awaited their turn to play through a sound system impressive by local standards, but miniature in comparison to the five-story behemoth that had been erected to honor the Dead.

Blues for Breakfast went on and played an energetic set. And as the last note of the last song echoed through the surrounding hills, Charlie brayed, "Come on, let's have a big hand and thank everyone for coming out to support such a good cause!"

A solitary, distant figure yelled "Yeah!" as his bandanna-wearing golden retriever chased a Frisbee across a hundred acres of green emptiness.

Not every performance by Blues for Breakfast was so poorly attended. "Pondstock" began as a private party deep in the woods of northern New York State, but the event quadrupled in size every year, making it necessary to sell tickets. Named after a shimmering watery ellipse located not far from the stage, Pondstock offered three days of music, sex and drugs and best of all, not a cop in sight for miles.

Like pilgrims on a Haj, two thousand people of varying ages descended from all points of the compass. Many arrived days before the first note was played, then swarmed through the woods before hunkering down in tents, teepees and wigwams. A transient village sprouted as swiftly as mushrooms after a summer rain – an outlaw outpost complete with paths connecting tattoo parlors, tie-dyed T-shirt shops, bong peddlers, crystal hawkers, tofu vendors, drug dealers and a squad of so-called "officials" that sped around on ATV's wearing T-shirts that identified them as "The Pussy Posse."

I crossed Lake Champlain on a ferry and then followed the directions on a hand-drawn map to a nameless dirt road. A checkpoint suddenly appeared like some rustic tollbooth on the edge of Sherwood Forest. I stopped, showed the scruffy sentinel my plastic-laminated VIP stage-pass and said, "I play bass with Blues for Breakfast."

"You're cool," said the sentry with a malnourished goatee and an illegal smile. "Follow this road another half mile and take the first right. There'll be somebody there to open the gate for you. Keep going till you see the band parking area alongside the stage."

I thanked him and drove through a pine forest where bleary-eyed teenagers wandered aimlessly or stood motionless, apparently in the thrall of a mysterious drug known simply as "K." I continued on, past a field clogged with parked cars, VW buses and minivans. Nearby, a large, hand-painted sign said, "NO EXIT TILL SUNDAY."

I parked and surveyed the scene. A stage had been built atop lofty steel scaffolds and behind it loitered a throng of would-be guitar heroes that clattered the necks of their electric guitars like young narwhals dueling with their tusks. A bevy of groupies and lesser luminaries hovered in attendance nearby. Clouds of marijuana smoke mingled with the dust rising from hundreds of shuffling feet as the audience waited for the next group to play. The crowd pursued a common goal, get as high as possible and enjoy a musical onslaught provided by a continuous, day and night rotation from 30 different bands.

I entered the musicians' hospitality tent and met Ezra, Pondstock's beleaguered audio engineer. He was only halfway through the second of three days, but he was already burned out. The next band went on and the volume emanating from two gigantic stacks of speakers made talking impossible. Ezra and I exchanged gestures of commiseration while the vocalist stomped around the stage screaming, "Die, die, die! Piss your life goodbye!"

A peculiar distinction divided the crowd into two disjunctive factions: Smiling proto-hippies in colorful tie-dye, on one hand, and pale Goth-punks dressed entirely in black, on the other. Each subsequent band reflected the predilection of the two opposing blocs: When a hippie jam-band started playing, the metal-heads slunk away into the woods like some giant retreating slime mold. When a metal thrash-band filled the air with guitar-distortion, the proto-hippies retreated to their hooches to eat granola and listen to Phish through headphones.

At eight o'clock – prime time in Bedlam – a delirious carnival atmosphere prevailed, as if J.R.R. Tolkien and Timothy Leary had joined forces with Dracula to throw a party for the combined residents of the Shire, Millbrook and Transylvania.

A magnificent summer evening was in progress as Blues for Breakfast took the stage. Gentle warm breezes wafted dust and dope smoke heavenward. A crescent moon sliced through a cloud like a dorsal fin. I climbed atop the apex of a pyramid, to stand on a riser between two sets of drums, 20 feet above a sea of smiling, expectant faces. My custom-made 6-string electric bass (the Belchfire 6000 Thunderpaddle) was plugged into 10,000 watts of amplification, enough power to double the barometric pressure every time I hit a low B.

Charlie walked onstage wearing a shirt made from an American flag and looked like a stoned-out Uncle Sam; a leather bandoleer stuffed with blues harps crossed his chest like chrome-plated machine gun bullets. He was exhausted and especially irritable after having micro-managed a thousand details that shouldn't have concerned him. Nevertheless, Charlie was determined to hit the audience over the head with overwhelming force, and so, in addition to our regular personnel, he'd hired a second drummer, an extra keyboard player and an extra guitarist revered for his ability to play fluid guitar-lines reminiscent of Jerry Garcia's. Our guitar-ringer was still fussing with his sound system – three refrigerator-sized cabinets filled with vintage Macintosh power amps and JBL speakers (just like Garcia's) – when Charlie hollered, "Are you fuckin' ready yet, Eric? Because we're starting now, whether you're ready or not!"

The crowd cheered as we ripped into "Bertha," a classic Dead tune. A shock wave emanated from the massive sound system, a sonic boom that expanded outwards at 600 miles an hour, traversed Lake Champlain, the entire state of Vermont and was clearly audible in New Hampshire. Eric's amp suddenly emitted a cataclysmic burst of noise that threatened to ruin our opening number. Charlie skewered him with an ugly scowl and bellowed, "Fix that fuckin' amplifier!" But, perhaps in hopes of earning a passing grade on the Acid Test, Eric had swallowed a hit of "K," the mystery drug, and was frozen in a confused delirium, as immobile as a bug pinned to an entomologist's board. The awful noise continued until Ezra scrambled onstage and pulled the plug on Eric's amp. For the rest of the performance the bumfuzzled schmuck stood rooted to the spot with a sad smile on his face, his guitar hanging untouched and the words "NO SALE" lighting up his eyes like an old-fashioned cash register.

Once more on track, though minus one guitar, we played with ferocious primal energy. Darkness smothered a crowd that merged into a hydra-headed, pulsating organism. Dozens of par-lamps bathed the stage in a vivid wash of orange and purple. A laser projected scintillating patterns on the foliage above and behind us as Roman candles spat flaming orbs into the velvet sky. Bonfires dotted the field as far as the eye could see and I felt like a breach-clouted native beating on a hollow log while the jungle mated at my feet! At any moment I expected to see Montagnard tribesmen with machetes dancing ceremoniously towards an anointed cow, moments before hacking the beast in two and roasting it over a bonfire.

"If only Abraham Maslow could see me now," I exulted, as self-actualized as a salmon that has attained the headwaters of its origin and now has only to spawn, roll belly up and expire!

43. Playing the Thunderpaddle at Pondstock.

Gigs from Hell

I'm not sure why, but Blues for Breakfast endured more than its fair share of gigs from hell. And as any divinity student fluent in Italian can attest, Dante's "Divine Comedy" offers the reader a tour of the numerous infernal bardos that awaited the souls of impious Florentines. Each bardo inflicted punishment appropriate for the caliber of offense – from small-bore ethical indiscretions to the heavy artillery of unforgivable moral transgression. And so it was in Charlie's band, where noisome hellholes inflicted retribution fiendishly appropriate for a musical miscreant like me. Since Charlie's sins equaled my own, albeit of a different nature, our close proximity was simply an efficient way to torment two for the price of one.

The Christmas party in the discotheque in the Plattsburg mall began innocently; the mirrored walls, chromium décor and spinning disco-lights gave no hint as to how fast the holiday spirit could turn ugly. Kurt, the president of Hamfist Industries, shelled out a wad of cash to hire Blues for Breakfast to play for the company's annual holiday party, but his employees were subdued on that first night of winter. Unaccustomed to relating to one another in a social context, the secretaries, salesmen and office boys drank heavily in hopes of alleviating their awkwardness.

The band packed away an excellent dinner – gargantuan helpings of roast beef, mashed potatoes, salad and cheesecake – then heaved a collective sigh of bovine contentment before succumbing to a digestive torpor numerous cups of coffee did little to alleviate. Kurt got to his feet and raised a glass to deliver a toast. "It's been great working with everyone this last year," he said.

"I'm sure we'll move forward as a team into a prosperous future. So have fun but don't be late for work tomorrow, like last year, ha-ha."

Although the discotheque had been closed to accommodate the private party, the amusement arcade just beyond its door was going full blast. Fifty arcade machines whirred, beeped and buzzed as a growing pack of bored teenagers squandered their money in hopes of winning a lava lamp. Every few minutes the malevolent sounding synthesized voice of a machine known as The Sniper said, "A sniper must be unemotional. You have been chosen!" The device's realistic, high-powered hunting rifle gleamed with malice. I wouldn't have been surprised to hear the machine say, "Fed up with your parents? Blow them away, now!"

Promptly at nine, the members of Blues for Breakfast rose heavily from the table and picked up their instruments. Our first song of the evening was the perennial Christmas classic by Bob Dylan, "Tangled Up in Blue." We played a listless set to an indifferent crowd, even though Kurt and his wife blazed a trail to the dance floor for their only moment of glory. But then, our host succumbed to an inexplicable spasm of benevolence and threw open the doors to the arcade crowd. And since no good deed ever goes unpunished, in rushed a throng of high school drop-outs, aspiring car thieves, skinny punkettes and the pale disciples of Goth, each convinced of his or her preeminence on the coolness scale and all in denial of the fact that they not only inhabited a dreadful cultural backwater, but were, in fact, a product of that environment.

Borne on the incoming tide like a floating turd, the house DJ scrambled into his booth and inundated us with nerve-wracking rap music at twice the volume of our band. The dance floor immediately filled with twitching, jerking bodies, while those seated nearby looked on with faces blanched by boredom. (Rap music may be defensible from an anthropological or socio-cultural perspective, but I've always thought the letter C should be added to the term.)

Just a reminder: Music is comprised of three elements – melody, harmony and rhythm – and rap employs only the latter.

When it came time for the band to play again, a Goth-chick walked up to me and said, "Are you sure you want to do this?"

I explained that we didn't have a choice; we'd been hired to play for the Christmas party and that's exactly what we were going to do. We opened our second set with "Boogie On Reggae Woman," cleverly matching the canned music's tempo. The DJ gradually reduced his volume to the point where we alone supplied the beat, but as soon as the dancers realized they were gyrating to live music, they scattered faster than cockroaches at a square dance. Kurt immediately leapt onto the empty dance floor and began to do the Twist.

"Should we stop playing?" I asked.

"Hell no!" he replied. "It's *my* Christmas party, fer' chrissakes. Keep playing! I want you to keep the dance floor empty for as long as possible."

Our role as musicians suddenly reversed, we played "Soul Man," just like the Blues Brothers in Bob's Country Bunker. I wanted to play "Rawhide," but the irony would not have registered. Halfway through "Born Under a Bad Sign," the teenagers started booing and yelling, "You suck, you pathetic old dinosaurs! Get off the stage! Go home!"

"Who do these ungrateful whelps think they are?" I asked. "Crashing a private party and then complaining about the music!"

Kurt did nothing to intervene. The verbal abuse got so bad that the other musicians left the stage. I stood in the glare of a spotlight, faced the hostile crowd and repeated a mantra, making sure every belligerent yahoo in the audience could read my lips as I intoned, "Fuck you...Fuck you...Fuck you." Over and over again.

***

In spite of all assertions to the contrary, Hell does occasionally freeze over. One February afternoon Blues for Breakfast set out for a gig under a cloud-wracked sky. Our destination lay a hundred miles to the west, a roadhouse called the Hoot Owl, located in deepest darkest New York State. "Don't worry about the weather forecast," said Charlie from behind the wheel of his disreputable-looking Chevy van. "Those bozos are always wrong."

The blizzard began with an almost imperceptible haze of very small but very determined snowflakes. I sat and stared at the road ahead, even though my view was obstructed by a diorama of New Age trinkets atop of the dashboard – a welter of pinecones, feathers, shells, roach clips, a bottle-opener, a rubber spider and a crystal amulet that dangled from the rearview mirror on a silver chain. Visibility shrank to 50 feet as countless tiny flakes sheared through the air. With little to see out the window, I stared at the stickers plastered all over the dashboard. The lightning bolt inside a skull was familiar to Deadheads the world over, but the iconography of a rodent smoking a joint was recognizable only to the hardest of hard-core Blues for Breakfast fans.

44. Onstage at Nectar's

The license plate bolted to the van's front fender exhorted all to "ARRIVE STONED." Charlie steered with one hand and lit a pipe with the other. "I love playing gigs," he said. "Where else can you get paid to smoke herb, blow harp and sing the blues?" Then he sang a lyric from a Grateful Dead song, "I may be going to hell in a bucket, but at least I'm enjoyin' the ride."

"Unhand that pipe," said Woody, our drummer.

"You're not getting any," said Charlie.

"Oh yeah? Why not?"

"Because you fuckin' sucked on drums last night, that's why."

"Charlie, you're so uptight you could ruin a wet dream."

"I am *not* fuckin' uptight!"

"Maybe if you got laid more than once every five years you wouldn't be all groovy good vibes one minute and a total asshole the next."

"Watch your speed, Charlie," I said, "You don't want to get pulled over by some trooper fresh from the academy, especially with that license plate informing them that something illegal is going on in this van."

"Don't worry," he said. "If they haven't caught me by now, they're not going to."

Charlie inhaled another lungful, further clogging the already clogged synaptic junctions in his brain. He was a genuine rock 'n roll barbarian; a beard wreathed his narrow face and sunglasses shielded patriotically bloodshot eyes – red blood vessels, white sclera and blue irises. Of Scottish ancestry, Charlie would not have looked out of place in Mel Gibson's cinematic army, face painted blue, wielding a broadsword in the film "Brave Heart."

When at last we slewed into the Hoot Owl's empty parking lot, the snow fell at the rate of an inch an hour, quickly adding to the five inches already on the ground. The cavernous stone building had once been a functioning train station, but now loomed as cold and dark as a dungeon where hooded inquisitors flayed heretics.

"Think of this gig as a paid rehearsal," said Charlie when he realized that no one was about to venture out into a blizzard to hear us play. The wind tore at the eaves as we unloaded and then assembled our electronic gear in the gloomy hall.

Whenever Blues for Breakfast played an empty house, its members went to great lengths to counteract the morbid stagnation and to create the illusion of forward momentum. In other words, we guzzled beer and packed our alveoli with the molecular residue created whenever marijuana buds are burned (a process that destroys the delicate, cone-shaped structures visible only under an electron microscope.) And as the green turban of intoxication wrapped around our heads, the band became more plant than animal.

For the next four hours we played to an empty building and the bartender, deafening one another with endless guitar solos, relentless harmonica clichés and consistently atrocious attempts at vocal harmony. By midnight, whiteout conditions and two feet of unplowed snow made any thought of driving impossible, but it didn't matter; we'd been promised shelter in one of the two apartments located above the station. There was only one way to reach our quarters, a climb up a treacherous metal fire escape that ascended an outside wall.

Our accommodations made the cheesiest Motel 6 in Orlando look like the Hyatt Continental in comparison – a barren, unheated room illuminated by a naked light bulb dangling from the ceiling. The loud party in the adjacent apartment exhibited as little a chance of ending as the blizzard. The wall that separated us was thin and did little to minimize the sound of Jimi Hendrix singing, "Manic depression is a frustrated mess!" at full volume. We arranged our sleeping bags on the floor, slumped against the wall and stared through windows black and vacant. After enduring the noise for forty-five minutes, Charlie rose to his feet and grasped the heavy, industrial-size adjustable wrench he kept handy at all times. He padded into the hall in his long johns and paused to listen at the door to the other apartment.

"TURN THAT FUCKIN' THING DOWN!" he shouted, bludgeoning the door repeatedly with the wrench. No response, so he hammered some more, imparting deep indentations in the wood. The door finally opened slightly and one red eye peered through the crack.

"It's after three and we're trying to sleep," said Charlie. "Would 'ya please turn the fuckin' music down?" The eye blinked once and the door swung shut. A minute later the sound of Jimi's guitar feedback diminished slightly. We breathed a sigh of relief. But five minutes later the noise went back up again, louder than before.

"I'm gonna' kill those fuckers," muttered Charlie as he lurched into the hall with the wrench held aloft like a tomahawk.

"MUSIC, SWEET MUSIC," shrieked Jimi.

Suddenly, I heard a loud "SSSCREEEEEEK" as the stereo's needle skated across the vinyl disk. And then a tremendous crash, followed by abrupt silence – a quiet enhanced by the faint tick of sleet hitting the windows. Apparently, the last reveler standing had collapsed onto the record player and squelched it as surely as if a hippo had stepped on it. Charlie returned with a smile on his face and for all I knew, he'd just dented someone's cranium with the wrench.

"Good work, Charles," I said.

The ensuing glacial silence was broken only by the hiss of blood circulating through my eardrums. Someone switched off the light and I drifted off. My heart rate slowed as sleep overcame all higher brain functions. And then it happened…

The rumble began softly, a deep resonance from below the auditory range, a sound that grew steadily in volume. I opened my eyes as the vibration filtered up through the floor and into my bones. The windows began to rattle.

The ominous rumble grew so loud that all five of us leapt up, barked our shins on crates and bumped into one another in the shuddering darkness.

"What the fuck?" shouted Charlie.

"It's the end of the world," I hollered as the entire building trembled. The black rectangles formed by the windows began to glow as a glaring Cyclopean eye cast a strengthening beam of light. The noise grew deafening. And when the thundering diesel engine loomed only inches away – hundreds of tons of hurtling steel – the engineer unleashed a stunning air horn blast. "BWWWWAAAAAAAAAAAAGH!"

My vision blurred and my teeth threatened to vibrate loose as the freight train thundered by for five long minutes. We capered through the darkness, laughing like drunken madmen. The empty station may have been dormant, but the rails were not.

***

Why, then, did I twice subject myself to a band led by an abrasive miscreant endowed with a vocal range of half an octave and the leadership skills of a brown-shirted fascist? The answer is simple: I had a severe case of what the psychobabblers call "habituation to intense experiences," a term first applied to grunts returning from the Vietnam War, only to find normal daily life intolerably dull. For me, after so many decades playing in bands, I'd become habituated to the live-ammo excitement of performing for people determined to dance their blues away.

As I mentioned before, I hold the dubious honor of quitting Blues for Breakfast, as well as getting sacked. The latter occurred after we played a class-reunion gig in a historic old hotel in Smuggler's Notch. The evening commenced smoothly; our gear was set up an hour early and a splendid buffet awaited us. "I'm going to check out the food," I said.

Charlie spun around and yelled, "WE EAT TOGETHER!"

"You don't tell me when to eat," I replied. "I'm an adult."

"I tell you if you come to the next gig or not," he responded.

"True, but is that really the issue here?" I stormed out, furious at being treated like some flunky hired to wash the windows. I cooled off outside and returned.

The band played as scheduled, but the next day Charlie left a message on my telephone answering machine, "It's unanimous," said the recorded voice. "You're fired!"

Moira Hill

My mother succumbed to bone marrow cancer at the tragic age of twenty-seven. I was only two at the time of her death, too young to be aware of the pain and morphine that accompanied her decline. Presumably, during those first two years she imparted nurturing sufficient to prevent me from becoming a psychopath (although such an assertion is debatable). In all the years since then I've never been able to conjure up a single memory of her, and until recently, not even the fleeting resonance of a dream.

In the dream a woman's face hovers in my mind's eye, a shifting, amorphous countenance I know to be Moira. The dream quickly faded and I understood – at the deepest core of my subconscious – the image was not her face, but a composite meant to signify her. Other than visualization so tenuous as to make a veil of mist as substantial as a brick wall, my only links to her existence are genetic and photographic.

As a result of the abysmally poor communication between my father and me, I know nothing of Moira's life, her personality or her ancestry. Instead, I have a number of photographs, one of which captured the image of a serenely beautiful young woman with long dark hair, averted eyes and the insinuation of a smile worthy of Leonardo's brush.

And always, unanswerable questions: What basic behavioral traits did I fail to acquire as a result of her absence? Would I have been better able to make better connections with people, to say nothing of eye contact? How would my life have been different had she lived?

***

One lonely Christmas day not long ago I spent the afternoon poring over an ancient photo album filled with the ghosts of relatives and strangers long gone. A small snapshot caught my eye and I wondered, who is this young girl? I'd noticed the photo before but had paid little attention. This time, however, I studied the image closely with the help of a powerful magnifying glass. The child stood in a garden, dressed in a fancy Edwardian gown, clasping a bouquet in one hand and smiling demurely. A circlet of flowers graced her brow.

An idea occurred to me; I compared the shape of the child's eyebrows and nose to photos taken of my mother as an adult. Sure enough, this could only be my mother as a child. Then I compared the shape of her hands, specifically, the negative space between thumb and forefinger, and realized they were precisely the shape of my own. My suspicions were confirmed when I pried the snapshot away from the page and read the faded inscription that said, "Age 6 - 1930."

45. Moira Hill, age 6.

Ever since that day I've kept numerous enlarged photographs up where I can see them every day, as a way to convince myself that my birth was not the result of a mad scientist's experiment gone terribly awry. Among these images is an oil painting created by Roger Jasaitis. In it, Moira shares the frame with a bouquet of flowers in a vase. The canvas hung in a gallery in Brattleboro, where it caught the eye of Luis Tijerina, a columnist who reviewed the exhibit for the local paper. "I saw a painting of a woman and fell in love," he wrote. "She had a magical quality, as if she might live forever."

How poignant, for in spite of her brief lifespan the painting had taken on a life of its own.

Another mysterious photo in the tattered old album drew my attention. Taken in the late fifties, an attractive woman with dark hair stands alongside a brick wall at a golf course, presumably somewhere in the British Isles. I studied her face with the magnifying lens; the resemblance was unmistakable and I concluded that the woman could only be my mother's sister. I recalled that as a child, I'd written letters to a pair of aunts and uncles who lived in England. My letters always began, "Dear Auntie Valerie and Uncle John" or "Dear Auntie Sheila and Uncle Ron." But by the time I hit adolescence the tenuous connection no longer existed.

Could any still be alive, I wondered? I scoured my father's ancient address book and sent out queries to every address listed. Six weeks later and all had been returned with "Addressee Unknown" stamped on each envelope in the red ink of utter finality.

The more I pondered this appalling gap concerning my mother's life, the more it haunted me. She was born in Belfast in 1924, her maiden name was Hill and she died in Hackensack in 1951 – the sum extent of my knowledge. Using the internet, I acquired a copy of the page from the Belfast phone directory that listed the name Hill preceded by the initials V, J, S or R – for Valerie, John, Sheila and Ron – a total of fifty possibilities. Since the computer had not yet become as ubiquitous in Belfast as it is in Burlington Vermont, and the cost of trans-Atlantic calls is high, I decided that my best chance for finding them necessitated a trip to Belfast.

***

Six months later, after a grueling 24 hours of continuous motion in ever-slower conveyances – jet, train, bus, taxi, mare's shank – I arrived in the grim industrial city of my mother's birth. (And, incidentally, where the Titanic was built.)

The gray, mid-April sky scowled and an incessant wind whipped flecks of sleet as I trudged the city's sidewalks. Too fatigued to look any further, I plunked down nine pounds at the Belfast Youth Hostel for a bunk with clean sheets and a glimpse through a third-story window at the surrounding hills. After a sound sleep and a hearty breakfast, I poured a king's ransom in unfamiliar coinage into a payphone and dialed every number on my list from the phone directory. Again and again I introduced myself and rattled off a query; "Did you, by any chance, have a sister named Moira?" It was not my day to win at Bingo, alas, although I experienced an increase in heart rate when a Mrs. S. Hill gave me the unlisted number for a Mr. Ron Hill. I dialed the number; Mr. Ron Hill listened politely but soon dashed any hope of a match.

The next logical step was a visit to Belfast's imposing City Hall, where an indomitable bronze infantryman holding an Enfield rifle perpetually guards the entrance, silently reminding all who pass of the lingering might of the British Empire. The lady behind the counter at the Office of Birth, Marriage and Death listened to my inquiry and then asked, "What denomination?"

I had no clue. My mother might've worshipped a golden calf for all I knew. The question demonstrated the persistent schism in Irish society between the Catholic and Protestant faiths – neither of which had influenced my belief system (or lack of) to any degree. The city employee found nothing in her files but suggested that I "nip 'round to the Belfast Heritage Society."

Before I left City Hall I bought a bone china teacup emblazoned with Belfast's official coat of arms – a wolf standing on hind legs facing an unusually fierce sea horse, rampant above a vaguely sinister phrase in Latin – Pro Tanto Quid Retrobuamos, which translates into "After All This, What More."

Out on the bustling street again, I boarded a bus for the jaunt across town. I circled numerous roundabouts and passed through tough working-class neighborhoods where brick walls bore huge paintings of defiant masked IRA militants holding AR-15's. When I stepped off the bus and gazed at the sky, I noticed a military helicopter hovering high above, probably observing me at that very moment through powerful optics. Closer to the ground, numerous closed-circuit surveillance cameras pointed this way and that from every cornice. I located the Heritage Society's door but it was locked. A note informed me the office would be open the following day, and for the rest of the week. I returned via bus to Belfast's Center City in search of the fish and chips the Irish love as much as Americans love burgers.

The circular esplanade at the heart of Center City teemed with unsmiling urbanites, as well as flocks of little old ladies – frail, diminutive creatures that tottered around like aged budgies towing two-wheeled carts in some dreadful penny-circus. I scrutinized the young women, seeking the "dark Irish" and perhaps a glimpse of one that resembled Moira. Now and then I noticed an eyebrow arched just so, but mostly it was the under-twenty set – all smoking cigarettes and talking continually on cell phones – plus a bevy of dour harridans with heavy-lidded, crocodilian eyes.

After the best fish and chips I've ever tasted (in the tiniest hole-in-the-wall shop imaginable), I wandered in search of the enduring landmarks that my mother had once seen as clearly as those now before me. Conversely, every pub and coffeehouse I entered was dominated by vacuous American pop-music or MTV on a wide-screen. Amidst the corporate hegemony, a sneaking suspicion arose in my mind, the notion that Northern Ireland would probably welcome the chance to become America's fifty-first state.

Mid April and the tourist season had yet to begin; I encountered only one example of indigenous music – a lone, deranged penny-whistler seated in the gutter, tootling furiously in hopes of earning a coin (which I was too damn cheap to give him). I hurried away and wondered why the sight repelled me. Did I see a hideous reflection of myself at some point in the future? I realized too late that I should've bought the poor blighter a meal and quenched his thirst.

As if in penance for my stinginess, I dined that evening in somber isolation in a dismal Italian restaurant. The food was bland, and to make matters worse, I had nothing to read. I sat facing an awful Arcadian mural that had been applied with a sponge and viridian straight from the tube. Halfway through my lasagna I realized I was eating dinner with the ghost of my ancestors!

Now, I have never before lapsed into superstition, nor have I embraced the dogma promulgated by either of the two great sparring Goliaths of western religion, but too many unquiet souls were now stirring. I couldn't see them but I felt them near – an incorporeal mob of mumbling Gaelic spirits pressing in – gradually overwhelming my tenuous grasp of reality. By the time I'd finished my meal, the murmuring voices in my head had overwhelmed the real ones all around. What to do, I wondered?

"I know just the thing," I announced to the ethereal throng. "A visit to a pub."

A pint of Guinness in the Empire Pub in the heart of Belfast is just as expensive as it is anywhere else in the world, I soon discovered. I quaffed the thick, brown liquid and decided to no longer think of Ireland as The Emerald Isle but instead, The Umber Isle. After a second pint I hit upon The United Republic of Guinness. After all, what other indigenous commodity could conceivably unite such a divided country?

It had been a long day and I was profoundly jet lagged as I hiked back to the Youth Hostel. I trudged the stairs and retired to my humble bunk, unaware that the sound sleep I'd experienced the night before had been the exception rather than the rule. I slumbered till two in the morning, at which time the door burst open and three large, drunken Russians crashed headlong into the room. They dropped their suitcases and stumbled about in the darkness until I suggested they switch on the light. For the next half hour they jabbered in Russian and lumbered about the tiny room like bears preparing for hibernation – brushing their teeth, gargling, spitting – before hauling their heavy ursine asses into the bunks and finally switching off the light.

Within minutes, I heard the first wheeze before the storm. First one, then a second and then all three began to snore – great stertorous gasps reminiscent of a woolly-mammoth smothering in a tar pit. Every few minutes the fibrillating lump in the bunk above me shifted his weight and shook the entire bed. Soon all three Ruskies were snoring like tuba-players practicing the one note each had mastered. And when their snorking achieved momentary synchronicity, they played a triad of astonishing volume and dissonance. Yes, the Soviet Olympic Snoring Team had arrived. I lay awake and considered smothering each defector with a pillow, then vowed to never again endure a youth hostel anywhere on the planet. (What more, indeed!)

At the first gray light of day I arose, donned my clothes and backpack and hit the streets, determined to find breakfast and better lodgings. After numerous fiascos involving pricey hotels and grubby little rooms that made a typical college dorm look like the Presidential Suite, I inquired at the deserted Helga Lodge. "Yes, I think we can squeeze you in," said the clerk after scrutinizing his blank ledger. "Here's your key. Breakfast is served in the dining room between eight and ten."

Once more assured of a place to sleep, I set off for the Belfast Heritage Society and again found it locked up tight, as it would remain the entire week. From there I visited the General Register Office where an official said they would be delighted to see me in a fortnight (the day after my scheduled departure). Next I paid a visit to the Linen Hall Library, reputed to contain vast archives, only to learn that Belfast's formidable bureaucratic machinery is geared towards transactions concerning the dead and has great difficulty with the living. Although their voluminous records seemed entirely capable of tracing the ownership of a clod of earth the size of a brick all the way back to the Bronze Age, they could not assist in my search for living relations.

46. Moira Hill

All that week I scoured the city, hiked its length and breadth from morning till night, walked through residential neighborhoods and past the charred ruins of buildings shattered by sectarian explosions. I inspected the only art gallery the city had to offer – a miserable assortment of tepid watercolors – and realized that starvation awaited an artist in Belfast as surely as in Vermont. Next I visited the college museum, the botanical gardens and a café, where I overheard strange new slang and wisely avoided a gobsmack! Also known as a smack in the face.

Back in the Helga Lodge that night, after a visit to an ear-splitting nightclub, I discovered a television quiz show from England in which the host flashed a photo on the screen and asked his contestants, "Is he gay or is he Euro-trash?" I found a channel devoted to an endless snooker tournament in which two grim, weasel-faced opponents sank ball after ball. I read an article in a Belfast newspaper that spoke with unbridled stridency of "a world spinning rapidly out of control and out of favor with anyone in possession of any semblance of decency or manners."

I spent a chilly afternoon wandering through an immense graveyard, accompanied by my tenacious cloud of ancestral ectoplasm. The graveyard was a huge rolling expanse where time and creeping vegetation had overwhelmed many of the headstones. The most ancient quadrant exhaled enough fuliginous atmosphere to satisfy Bela Lugosi; and certainly, under a full moon, I would not have hesitated for an instant before driving a wooden stake into the heart of anyone who dared approach. I searched in vain for a headstone inscribed with the name Hill. But in all those hundreds of acres I found no trace of the name. I was so desperate for evidence confirming the existence of my mother's ancestors that any Hill would do. But apparently, I'd stumbled into a cemetery of the wrong denomination. In Belfast, the dead are as segregated as the living.

The city wrapped me in its magical cloak of misery and I endured a cold, lonely week. The very air itself seemed to be saturated with premeditated violence and I found it impossible to strike up a conversation with a single living soul. I'd become as incorporeal as the object of my quest, and in spite of my efforts, I hadn't learned one iota about my antecedents. My only solace was the notion that at some point my steps had to have taken me close to the scene of my mother's childhood.

On my last morning in Belfast I entered the Helga Lodge's dining room for a bowl of Wheatabix, a hard-boiled egg and a cup of tea. I'd hoped to encounter a flock of convivial guests chattering like magpies, but instead, I found the room empty except for two ancient albatrosses (apparently as deaf as planks) who sat hacking away at sausages, eggs and fried tomatoes while communicating in sign language! I nodded a greeting and ate my breakfast, the silence broken only by the rasp of a butter-knife on cold toast. I returned to my room one last time and switched on the telly. The news came on and I learned that my train to Dublin had been cancelled due to "concern over security" – a code phrase to indicate a bomb threat. The best the weather-girl could offer on her 5-day forecast was "A hope for high pressure." The bad news continued: During the night some bloke bearing a 400-year old grudge had driven an iron stake through the skull of someone with a different religion, not simply to kill him, but to deny his mourners the option of an open casket. The television news concluded with the announcement, "A hand-grenade lobbed over a wall into a police yard damaged only bricks."

"Ye gods," I muttered. "The 'troubles' haven't ended. The 'Big Enders' are still at war with the 'Little Enders.'"

I'd gone to Belfast with a wisp of hope, but left with not so much as a goose egg, nary a scrap of information about my maternal forbearers. I realized that the only clues to Moira's nature lay in those aspects of my own genetic make-up that were not imparted by my father. Do I seek the Jungian anima or is this simply a game of post-mortem chess with Arnold? Either way, not much terra firma on which to tread.

Once more in my bachelor apartment in Vermont, I see the images of Moira every day. Only now, I'm not alone. The ghosts that embraced me in the sepulchral gloom of Belfast accompanied me across the Atlantic. I don't suppose I'll ever be able to shake them off, but I'm sure they regard me with only the deepest proprietary fondness.

Surfing on Alpha Waves

One of the great secrets about playing an instrument professionally is the gratification it generates, not in the listener but in the player. (I'm certain that if the audience knew how much fun we're having, any thought of paying us would vanish.)

Yes, playing a bass guitar through 800-watts bi-amped into a stack of 15-inch woofers is an incredibly sensual experience. There's nothing like the electro-magnetic high derived from quaking the air around you with absolute precision. (Authenticity is paramount. Pay no attention to the self-congratulatory baboons electronically sampling and rearranging the notes produced by real musicians; any chimp can learn to manipulate a computer).

Best of all, playing a musical instrument harms no one, perhaps the most persuasive rationale for a life devoted to music – unlike the production of Vulcan cannons, for instance. Not only that, how many people get to hear drums every day? Not recordings transmitted via ipod, or a djembe tapped by a weekend hobbyist, but a full set played by an expert – ride cymbals sizzling and floor-toms pounding! Bass players experience this primal thunder on a regular basis, a pleasure not often shared by the gray-flannel dwarves riding the Erie Lackawanna in and out of Manhattan every day with their noses buried in the *Wall Street Journal*.

Any attempt to comprehend this enjoyment requires a visit to a university psychology lab, where white rats press levers to self-administer tiny jolts of electricity via the electrodes implanted in the pleasure centers of their brains. By using a method known as "behavior modification through reward for successive approximation," a rat can be trained to do strange things. I know, because as a psyche major at UVM, I taught my whiskered accomplice (named Bumby) to sit on a golf ball on command. The little buggers will dance through fire if necessary to attain one more joy-buzzer handshake deep in the lateral hypothalamus.

The process is more complex however, in humans. Although I do not as yet have electrodes in my brain, I understand the motivation vital to attaining a fresh, prodigious surge of rat-brain style ecstasy. Scientists have determined that the use of recreational drugs alters the chemistry of that palpitating sponge known as the human brain. Discontinue consumption and the adverse consequences of withdrawal result. (The same holds true for coffee; cut out your daily intake and a weeklong headache will ensue.)

I have a theory, difficult to prove, but a dandy topic for a doctoral thesis: I suspect that the same mechanism that produces chemical changes (and dependence) in the brains of rats, coffee drinkers and recreational drug users is also at work in the brains of jazz musicians. I've singled out jazzbos because of their highly developed skills as improvisers. Classical musicians, in general, have never had to rely upon sheer invention from one measure to the next – their notes are indelibly printed, thereby eliminating the need to pluck them from thin air.

Dubbed "spontaneous composition," the jazz musician's ability to improvise requires decades of practice before he or she attains a level of fluency that, among the best, exceeds that of spoken language. In addition to a well-developed language center, a jazz brain includes a specific zone where musical ideas originate (to say nothing of the murky regions where the subconscious stomps its feet).

The question arises: When a jazz musician is forced to discontinue playing, or does so by choice, does that person undergo a brain chemistry alteration similar to withdrawal? I think so. But, as I am unwilling to curtail my own practice regimen for the sake of subjective observation, the question must go unanswered.

Yet, as all serious musicians can attest, the 10,000 hours of practice required to excel on an instrument indicates more than simple obsession. Daily practice maintains the fluid motor-pathway between brain and hands – that seemingly effortless translation of idea into sound that "normal" people will never experience or comprehend. For me, adequate practice sustains the electro-chemical balance in the brain and minimizes the risk of a derailment occurring somewhere between inspiration and where the fingers meet the strings.

Be that as it may, I've discovered a novel way to make the hours devoted to practicing a lot more interesting. First, procure an electronic gizmo known as a surf-generator. Designed to produce a gradual sweep of white noise that convincingly mimics the sound of waves breaking on the shore, the device is marketed as an aid in stress reduction. The idea is to run a metronome and a surf-generator at the same time. Instead of playing scales, modes and arpeggios to the steady tick... tick... tick of the metronome, I practice with both gadgets running simultaneously.

Theoretically, the fixed beat of the metronome creates theta waves in the brain, while the soothing wash of white noise from the surf-generator induces alpha rhythms. Ideas thus fostered exhibit the meditative serenity of alpha, and the open, cosmic space inspired by theta.

Epilogue

In my career as a bassist I've endured a daunting number of smoke-filled nightclubs, never dreaming the day would come when cigarettes would be banned in public places (at least in Vermont). I've played for shifty-eyed club owners that double-booked me, cancelled gigs at the last moment and refused to pay the agreed-upon figure. On the other hand, I've played for Nectar Rorris, who fed me turkey, fries and gravy and treated all musicians with respect.

I've played for people who danced as if there were no tomorrow, which, unfortunately, proved to be the case one night in the mid-seventies, the night the last two couples on the dance floor at the Blue Tooth departed in a vehicle and promptly collided head-on with a truck.

I've played gigs that made a job on an assembly line look appealing in comparison, while at other times the stage became a launch pad for transcendent ecstasy.

During the drive home in the wee hours of the morning, I've swerved to avoid hitting deer, moose, raccoons and skunks, in addition to outmaneuvering a gauntlet of drunks behind the wheel. I've observed lightning strikes, comets, bolides, the aurora, moonset and sunrise.

Does this sound like the sort of lifestyle you'd be interested in?

If you are young and lack guidance – let's assume that you have not yet regained your wits and entered the family business – then the spurious rewards offered by a life of professional music are adequate. But as time staggers downstream and you mature, cracks in the façade appear like so many crow's feet around your tired, bloodshot eyes.

If you persist in your quest to become a professional musician, a few suggestions are in order: First of all, a tolerant attitude is essential. Do not harbor any expectations prior to a gig. Play it with the full awareness that you're only doing it for fun, regardless of your dependence upon the money for food or rent.

Keep in mind the fact that you are probably not essential to your band's success or even its continued existence. There's always someone else who not only plays better than you ever will, but who will drop everything at a moment's notice to take your place.

As a last resort, strike a bargain with the devil – your soul in exchange for a Grammy or the adulation of a million teenagers eager to buy your latest recording the minute it's released. (If this option appeals to you, good luck. The market is already glutted with souls.)

Bearing all this in mind, perhaps it might be better had you not been endowed with the intellectual wattage required to conceive of and then pursue the life of music you've chosen. And remember, it is, after all, a choice.

Why then would anyone devote themselves to music, the most ephemeral of the arts? An activity that produces nothing more tangible than repeated impacts upon the tympanic membrane, a sensory experience so evanescent that its meaning defies description – a commodity so fleeting it evaporates the instant the performance (or recording) ends. The answer is simple – playing music feels good; a fact that can never be fully understood without first undergoing the many years of toil necessary to attain the level at which the instrument becomes a part of your being, not a clumsy adversary, but an extension of your own exquisitely tuned nervous system. The reward for attaining this goal is the precise articulation of your heart and soul, conveyed with fluidity that surpasses the spoken word.

In an old joke best understood by musicians, the sound of distant drums accompanies a safari as it wends through the African veldt. The big bwanna in the pith helmet nervously asks his bearer, "What happens when the drums stop?" The bearer solemnly replies, "Bass solo."

As I prepare for my next bass solo, the question arises: How could a reasonably intelligent individual persist in playing an instrument for four decades without ever experiencing ensemble longevity, the slightest rumor of recognition or monetary compensation beyond the poverty level?

I'm just plain stubborn, I 'spose.

Having achieved this state of profoundly flexible invisibility, who can say what musical adventures still await me? I possess energy sufficient for arduous expeditions into unknown musical terrain, as well as leisurely strolls across the putting green of a country-club soiree. I'll continue to seek other accomplished musicians in hopes of playing gigs and enlarging my sonic scrapbook with new recordings. I'll add chapters to my music journal with the help of a word processor specially equipped with features inspired by a food processor – buttons marked "blend, whip, crush" and my favorite, "liquefy."

I could go on and on. This collection of essays is, after all, only Volume One. Since my time playing in the last band herein, I've played in ten additional bands. Some of these rarely made it to the stage – like Dreamland, Past the Point, The Summit Jazz Band and The Manhattan Project. While others (like Deja Nous, The Dixie Six and The Onion River Jazz Band) help me pay the rent. In addition, I play in an ensemble that accompanies a talented group of vocalists who perform with Café Noir Productions under the musical direction of Piero Bonamico, here in the Waitsfield valley of Vermont, home of the Sugarbush Resort (and Mad River Glen).

To conclude: I'll continue to practice scales, arpeggios and modes on the string bass and on the 6-string electric bass. I'm always looking to play more gigs. So with that in mind, if you hear of someone looking for a good bass player, please mention my name. And thanks.

LaVergne, TN USA
26 November 2009
165370LV00001B/3/P